The Gang and Beyond

Interpreting Violent Street Worlds

Simon Hallsworth

Professor of Sociology and Head of School of Applied Social Sciences,
University Campus Suffolk

palgrave
macmillan

Simon Hallsworth © 2013

All rights reserved. No reproduction, copy or transmission of
this publication may be made without written permission.

No portion of this publication may be reproduced, copied or transmitted
save with written permission or in accordance with the provisions of
the Copyright, Designs and Patents Act 1988, or under the terms of any
licence permitting limited copying issued by the Copyright Licensing
Agency, Saffron House, 6-10 Kirby Street, London EC1N 8TS.

Any person who does any unauthorized act in relation to this
publication may be liable to criminal prosecution and civil claims
for damages.

The author has asserted his right to be identified as the author of this
work in accordance with the Copyright, Designs and Patents Act 1988.

First published 2013 by
PALGRAVE MACMILLAN

Palgrave Macmillan in the UK is an imprint of Macmillan Publishers
Limited, registered in England, company number 785998, of
Houndmills, Basingstoke, Hampshire RG21 6XS.

Palgrave Macmillan in the US is a division of St Martin's Press LLC,
175 Fifth Avenue, New York, NY 10010.

Palgrave Macmillan is the global academic imprint of the above
companies and has companies and representatives throughout
the world.

Palgrave® and Macmillan® are registered trademarks in the
United States, the United Kingdom, Europe and other countries

ISBN: 978-1-137-35808-0 hardback
ISBN: 978-1-137-35809-7 paperback

This book is printed on paper suitable for recycling and made
from fully managed and sustained forest sources. Logging, pulping
and manufacturing processes are expected to conform to the
environmental regulations of the country of origin.

A catalogue record for this book is available from the British Library.

A catalog record for this book is available from the Library of Congress.

10 9 8 7 6 5 4 3 2 1
22 21 20 19 18 17 16 15 14 13

Printed and bound in Great Britain by
CPI Antony Rowe, Chippenham and Eastbourne

Contents

Acknowledgements

For those who are familiar with my work, it is will become clear that in the chapters that follow I present some arguments that have already seen the light of day in various journals. Chapter 1, for example, draws on a chapter in a report produced for London Councils which I co-wrote with Kim Duffy. I have no hesitation at all in recognising and acknowledging her contribution as a fellow author here. But I also owe a huge debt to many other friends and colleagues who have inspired me and continue to inspire my thought and thinking. Tara Young has been my long-term (I often suspect, long-suffering) partner in criminological endeavour and to her I owe a huge debt of gratitude. None of what I have written here would have been remotely possible without her. Sveta Stephenson, John Lea, Mike McGuire, David Brotherton, Jeff Ferrell and Jock Young have also been inspirational. Finally, a huge thank you to Maria Kaspersson for her patience and kindness.

If I sign my name as author here, it is only because I feel obliged to take responsibility for the orchestration of the ideas presented here. In saying this, I am also mindful of Deleuze who reminds us that none of us are one, but several. I honestly do not know where my ideas start, Tara's end and Sveta's begin. I honestly cannot claim ownership for any of the ideas developed here. This book, then, is the result of a collaborative venture and one that has evolved over many years, deep into the night, in many bars and restaurants. I therefore have no hesitation in dedicating these *fleurs du mal* to these, my dear friends and colleagues.

Introduction

Welcome to Gangland UK

We are in England, it's August 2011 and London is burning. The police have managed to shoot dead yet another black male in dubious circumstances and across the city thousands of people have taken to the streets. The resulting disorder unfolds for a further four days as the riots reach out beyond London and take hold in metropolitan cities across the country. It would be the worst outbreak of urban disorder England had witnessed in three decades. Someone or something had to be blamed and it was not going to be the police or government policy. Within three days of the riots the Prime Minister, David Cameron (reluctantly pulled back from his Tuscan retreat), convened a press conference at Downing Street and identified 'gangs' as the criminal masterminds responsible for organising the riots and 'gang culture' the background cause. Put together, these were responsible for what he went on to identify as a 'major criminal disease that has infected streets and estates across the country'.

At the heart of all the violence sits the issue of the street gangs. Territorial, hierarchical and incredibly violent, they are mostly composed of young boys, mainly from dysfunctional homes. They earn money through crime, particularly drugs and are bound together by an imposed loyalty to an authoritarian gang leader. (Cameron 2011)

The media (and just about everyone else) had no trouble at all in taking up this, the gangland UK thesis (Hallsworth and Brotherton 2011). Even when compelling evidence began to emerge that gangs were not responsible for the riots and even when faced with what might appear a stark disconfirmation of the 'gangs caused the riots' thesis; the government's first policy response in the wake of them was to convene an international conference on gangs and, for good measure, invite the

1

American architect of zero-tolerance policing, Bill Bratton, to provide policy advice on how to suppress them.

By 2011, culpability for organising riots was not the only crime being blamed on the urban street gang. Since their dramatic rediscovery in the opening decade of the twenty-first century, gangs have established themselves as, quite literally, the UK's premier public enemy number one. In this guise they have been held responsible for what has been defined as a new and ominous 'gun and knife culture'. And 'gang culture', as the media like to term it, appears to be spreading. According to Ofsted school inspectors, gang culture is now rampant on the playing fields of English schools (Ofsted 2005). Fundamentalist Islamic gangs, meanwhile, are now apparently well established in British prisons where they are forcing other prisoners to convert to Islam (Beckford 2012); while, according to a self-styled 'watershed' report by ROTA (Race on the Agenda), gangsters are now deliberately targeting privileged grammar-school girls in sweet suburbia (Firmin 2010).

Large corporate gangs, it is alleged, have seized control of the illegal drugs trade and are responsible for a spate of fatal shootings that have seen scores of young men die at each other's hands (Clements and Roberts 2007). Nor are gangs today armed only with knives and guns. According to the Mayor of London's Office and the RSPCA, gangs are now using dogs such as pit bull terriers as their 'weapon of choice' (Monks 2009; RSPCA 2010; Harding 2012). Nor would it appear that 'weapon dogs' are their only preferred weapon because they appear to have many. According to ROTA, gangs are now using rape 'as their new weapon of choice' against girlfriends and mothers (Firmin 2010). Indeed, such is the scale of the threat now posed to British society by the urban street gang that government minister Iain Duncan Smith has identified them as responsible for 'breaking Britain' by literally destroying the very communities of which they are a part. 'Gangs', he argued, 'are at the very epicentre of the problems we face.' They are 'both the result of all this social breakdown, they are also the drivers of it' (Wintour 2011).

Whereas, at least until recently, gangsters were predominantly male, this is now apparently changing. Girl gangs are apparently on the move and are organising as we speak (Sikes 1997; Bracchi 2008; Lee 2008). And gangsters are also getting younger by the day, with members apparently no older than the age of three. These, the 'tinies' as they are known, are apparently armed with weapons and can be found distributed across estates in the UK (Clements and Roberts 2007).

Nor are gangs today simply facsimiles of groups that have always been around. On the contrary, it is claimed, they are very different. They are apparently far larger, and have evolved elaborate corporate structures with complex divisions of labour. In some estates, it would appear that the gangs have become so powerful that they exercise total control over social life in the territory they claim (Toy 2008; Antrobus 2009). Whereas, in the old days, groups would spontaneously form, now they 'recruit' and 'groom' would-be members, many of whom are forcibly coerced into gang membership, at least according to British academic John Pitts (Pitts 2007).

In response to the arrival into the UK of a problem everyone once believed, at least until recently, was all American, the British state has, quite literally, declared an all-out war against the gang. And the institutional response to its discovery, as we shall now see, has had a dramatic impact on a wide range of institutions and social arrangements. But to chart these we need to step back a bit, back in fact to the years immediately preceding 2005 when the urban street gang was first discovered, to make sense of them.

My Goodness, How Things Have Changed ...

Up to the beginning of the twenty-first century, England constituted a society that had no established gang experts and there were few practitioners offering bespoke models of gang intervention to would-be gangsters. The police had no dedicated gang suppression units and the government did not deem it necessary to derogate to the agencies of law enforcement exceptional powers to suppress them. Nor did the mass media spend that much time discussing gangs despite its salacious interest in group offending and youth crime. The criminological research community, after displaying some interest in American gang theory in the late 1950s and 1960s, had moved by the 1960s to study instead the wave of flamboyant subcultures that had surfaced in postwar Britain, having failed to establish that gangs were a tangible presence on the streets of British cities when they tried to find them (Downes 1966; Hall and Jefferson 1976). The gang, at least as far as the British were concerned, was a uniquely American problem and one they had no need to worry about. There were, of course, gangs in cities like Glasgow and Sheffield but by and large these were rare occurrences (Patrick 1973; Bean 1981). The same story can largely be told for other European societies; they might well have had some problems with groups of troubled kids but this did not constitute or imply a 'gang' problem - or so they thought.

How things have changed. What was once considered a uniquely American problem appears to have migrated across the Atlantic where it has taken deep roots, not only in the UK but in many other European societies that previously did not experience themselves as having a 'gang problem'. Where, until recently, the UK had no recognised gang experts, today the UK has amassed an army of them; indeed, so many that the British Home Office, in the wake of the riots, recently recruited 100 'gang experts' to become part of what it grandly terms it's 'gang expert forum' (Home Office 2011). This forum brings together academic 'experts' along with policemen and practitioner 'experts'; a number of whom claim to have once belonged to various criminal gangs. These meet regularly to debate gang issues and offer advice to a burgeoning army of practitioners now offering an increasing array of bespoke programmes and initiatives to suppress gangs across most British cities.

Where previously there were no gang-specific policies and no gang-dedicated policy-makers specialising in gang policy, this has also changed. Today every statutory enforcement agency has dedicated policy advisers working on gang issues in organisations that now come replete with dedicated gang-busting units. This growing constituency of gang 'experts' produces an ever-burgeoning literature on the developing gang problem as they imagine it. They also identify the policies, tactics and strategies that law enforcement agencies and practitioners are now expected to apply to suppress them. These provide the policy blueprints for what is now a burgeoning anti-gang industry.

Nor has the government been lax in its response to a problem now conceived as a serious developing threat. It too has established policy groups with a brief to confront gangs and recently established a national 'task force' mandated with a wonderfully unrealistic ambition of 'ending gang and serious youth violence'. Where, until recently, there was no gang-specific legislation, this too has changed as the British government has begun to initiate an array of legislative responses as part of its fight against and 'war' with gangs – many, it could be noted, imported wholesale off the shelf from the US, a country with a well established gang-suppression industry. These range from powers to create dispersal zones designed to prevent gangs from gathering (and which give police the power to disperse them if they do (Home Office 2008)); to an array of coercive sanctions designed to suppress them such as 'gang ASBOs' (anti-social behaviour orders), which allow enforcement agencies to place an extraordinary series of restraints on gang members (Home

Office 2010). These include but are not limited to specifying where they can go, what they can wear and who they can and cannot associate with. New legislation has meanwhile been passed which allows the police to make being a gang member an aggravated offence in its own right. On the basis of a 'collective responsibility' clause, gang members can now find themselves imprisoned, often for long periods of time, even if they have not committed an offence.

The mass media meanwhile has had a field day discovering gangs everywhere and promiscuously applying the gang label to describe just about every group occasioning some form of nuisance to someone. In its new guise as a folk-devil incarnate, the gang has provoked banner headlines, many following fatal shootings invariably identified as gang-related even when many, on subsequent inspection, are not. Not only has gang violence generated sensational coverage, the gang has provided the staple diet upon which an army of columnists and other right-thinking people have fed. Such commentary, it could be noted, not only reflects upon what the gang is doing today, but also reflects on what the presence of gangs says about the moral state of British society today. Invariably but not surprisingly the findings are grim. Yes, the gang is responsible for 'breaking Britain'. Filmmakers have also entered the fray by making a number of documentaries about gangs. Few, it could be noted, are very good; most striving for effect by taking the time-honoured journalistic device of dropping fearless journalists into rundown estates represented as war zones (cue shots of empty playgrounds, places where children would once happily play but today are empty because of the gangs). Suitably attired ghetto youth, hanging menacingly around dark streets, are then asked to confirm the gang picture, which they invariably do (Hallsworth and Young 2008).

So powerful is the hold of the gang on the public imaginary it has now become the subject around which fictional movies are now being made. One such film, *Shank*, follows the antics of a group of black ghetto youth in a suitably post-apocalyptic England. They even have a pit bull terrier which they touchingly keep on a muzzle. Like many gangster-style movies this one is ultimately about the stupidity of black people who, apparently, have nothing better to do than kill each other. A follow-up film, *Skets*, explored the new phenomenon of girl gangs, which are also apparently on the rise.

The academic fraternity, meanwhile, have also responded by paying a lot more interest to gangs than had previously been the case. Of particular significance here was the arrival into Europe of the Eurogang Network, a loose confederation of gang researchers dominated and led by a group of professional American academics under the leadership of Malcolm Klein (Klein 2001). Committed to a positivistic and numbers-driven species of criminology, the group is dedicated to discovering the truth about European gangs and by so doing demonstrating to Europeans that we have been in denial of our gang problem. In the wake of the gang's sensational (re)discovery, the study of gangs has mushroomed in UK universities and growing numbers of people, including doctoral students, are now conducting research into the developing field of gang studies.

Themes

In this book I want to use Britain's sensational rediscovery of the urban street gang as a case study for thinking about what I will generically label 'violent street worlds' and the way in which we interpret them. And I want to do this both because, for reasons that will become clear, I have a number of problems with what we might generically term the 'gangland UK' thesis, and because I think there are different ways of looking at and interpreting violent street worlds without reducing their complexity back to corporatised gangs read as the harbinger of twenty-first-century mayhem as we know it.

To develop these themes the book is divided into three parts. In the first part, which is comprised of Chapters 1 and 2, I subject the gangland UK thesis to critical scrutiny, asking is Britain really being overrun by a plenitude of armed corporate gangs and are these gangs quite as novel that they are made out to be? In the second part (Chapters 3 and 4) the focus of my analysis turns to considering why the urban street gang has come to be positioned as public enemy number one, even though most of the claims made about it do not stack up when subjected to critical scrutiny. In the third part (Chapters 5, 6 and 7) I return to consider the nature of informal street organisations and the wider ecology of the street worlds of which they are a part. This part concludes by examining what, if anything, has changed in the ecology of urban violence in the postwar period. In what follows I will develop further the themes explored in each part.

Part One

In Chapter 1, I critically review the claims that have been made about gangs today and consider the status of the evidence that has been produced to substantiate the gangland UK thesis, including claims such as those that have been made blaming gangs for orchestrating riots, shooting people, controlling the illegal drugs trade, abusing women and using 'weapon dogs'. By subjugating these claims to critical analysis, I will show that these conjectures simply do not stand up when subjected to critical interrogation. There is, I will suggest, always an excess to the crime and violence blamed on gangs which is simply not gang related. Not only are many of the crimes currently blamed on gangs not gang-related, they can be explained, I will argue, in ways that do not require invoking gangs or 'gangness' as a key explanatory factor.

Taking this critique further, in Chapter 2 I take issue with another claim often made about gangs today, namely that they represent a phenomenon that is in some sense entirely new insofar as we have not witnessed its like before. In contesting what can be considered the 'gang as the new face of youth crime' thesis, my aim here is not just to refute it, but to approach the issue of contesting it by reference to a methodology that has not commanded much attention in criminology. Rather than contest the claim by looking at the historical record, as Pearson does (Pearson 1983; Pearson 2011), in order to establish that contemporary fears about folk devils (such as gangs today) were also present in our immediate past, I develop instead an auto-ethnography. By drawing directly on my own experiences of growing up between the 1960s and the 1980s, I will show that groups that bear all the hallmarks of what today would be termed 'gangs' have been a longstanding part of the street furniture in most working-class areas. In developing an auto-ethnographic account my aim is also to suggest that criminology has much to gain by engaging with a method which, while popular elsewhere in the social sciences and humanities, has not, with some notable exceptions, had much of an impact in criminology.

Part Two

This book, however, is not simply an exercise in the gentle art of demolition criminology, however enjoyable the exercise is. If the first two chapters throw doubt on the validity of the gangland UK thesis, it leaves unanswered the question of explaining why, given gangs are not quite the architects of twenty-first-century mayhem, everyone is doing so much gang talking. In Chapter 3 I consider the proposition that, in part, an explanation for this can be found by examining the structure of gang talk itself. This requires not only discourse analysis but also an excursion into hermeneutics, the interpretation of interpretations. Gang talk, I suggest, needs to be understood as a discourse that does not trade in what, following Lefebvre, I will term *street representations* or *street practices* but *representations of the street*: a representation typically made by those who are not part of the street world their gang talk describes and who have, as such, a distance from this world. The gang talk they produce, I will argue, can best be understood as a discourse about the street that floats wholly free of the street world it claims to describe. It is, however, a discourse that has a structure and this can be studied in terms of what Wittgenstein termed a language game. That is, as a discourse that has its own (primitive) language and rules that govern its composition. To play the game, gang-talkers abide by common rules they intuitively grasp. To be heard, the gang talk they produce has to resonate with the rules of the game. If it does not, they will not be heard. As we shall also note, gang talk does not proceed by way of refutation but by continual iteration and confirmation of a series of tropes around which it is organised.

In Chapter 4 I examine less the discourse that has surfaced around gangs but study instead the constituencies that produce it. This chapter takes me towards an engagement with two interrelated phenomena. To explain the disproportionate and exceptional coverage the gang has received we need in the first instance to engage with moral panic theory (Hall and Jefferson 1976; Goode and Ben-Yehuda 1994; Critcher 2003) and we need to do this because the reporting that has followed the gang since its discovery in the twenty-first century has all the hallmarks of a full-blown moral panic. The chapter begins by examining the circumstances that led to the gang being discovered as the new face of youth crime. It then traces how gangland realities became lost in a deviance-amplification spiral, where only versions of gang talk would prevail. This is a journey I trace as one characterised by the movement from reality into a collectively induced fantasy. The chapter then charts what I take to be the second characteristic feature of a full-blown moral panic, namely a social response to the alleged problems posed by gangs shaped by gang-talking fantasies. The response of the British state to the August 2011 riots is wonderfully illustrative of this. Despite the fact that gangs were not responsible for orchestrating them, the British state has still made gang suppression a key aspect of its post-riot social policy agenda (Hallsworth and Brotherton 2011).

Whereas moral panics by their nature rarely last long, in the case of the contemporary one surrounding the gang, I argue that this might be one folk devil that bucks the usual trend. To understand why, however, we have to understand the interests of what I term the new gang industry that has emerged allegedly to suppress gangs but which paradoxically has a vested interest in sustaining the very phenomena it exists to eliminate. The gang, I conclude, is too useful to too many constituencies to give up on at any time soon; which also helps explain why gang talk has become what I define as a form of social lubricant, oiling the wheels of the control effort, allowing its constitutive cogs to mesh seamlessly together.

Part Three

If the fears respectable society has about urban street gangs in its midst owe more to a rich and disturbing fantasy life than they do to the concrete reality of street life, this still leaves unanswered the problem of urban violence and the nature of the informal street organisations that produce it. In the third part of the book my aim is to move decisively beyond gang talk in order to rethink how we think about and interpret violent street worlds.

In Chapter 5 I take on a thesis that holds considerable currency among gang-talkers, including many of the academic variety. This thesis holds the gang to be an entity that has some form of fixed immutable essence that can be unproblematically measured and dissected, rather like a creature pinned to a vivisectionist's table. This tendency is well established among positivistic gang-talkers and is particularly evident in their autistic obsession with reducing the complex, messy reality of urban street gangs to desiccated clusters of dehumanised not to say decontextualised risk factors through the application of what Jock Young memorably describes as 'voodoo statistics' (J. Young 2007). This tendency to essentualise the gang is also evident in another fallacy endemic to many gang-talkers, and that is to presuppose that the informal world of the street can be grasped conceptually by imposing upon it the categories that describe formal organisations. This tendency is particularly evident in the desperate attempt gang-talkers make to corporatise the world of the urban street gang by ascribing to them pyramid structures, elaborate divisions of labour, cybernetic command structures and clear and distinct borders.

This way of thinking, while beguiling and popular, is nevertheless deeply flawed and follows logically from the implicit acceptance of a paradigm that needs to be consigned to the dustbin of history. In Chapter 5 I draw upon the philosophy of Deleuze and Guattari in order to demonstrate why this way of thinking fails, but also in order to establish the parameters of an alternative ontology and one better equipped to help us comprehend the nature of informal street worlds and informal street organisations that simply cannot be corporatised. This takes me substantively to the study of trees and grass, or, in Deleuzian terms, arborealism and rhizomatics.

I begin this task of theoretical reconstruction by drawing out the differences between, on the one hand, the sedentary 'rooted' societies of the West and, on the other, the nomadic clans that traverse the vast steppes and deserts of the East. In the former we observe social formations that are governed by the principles of enclosure and territorialisation, while in the case of the latter we find societies in movement that are permanently deterritorialised and deterritorialising. I then explore the metaphors that Deleuze and Guattari deploy to help us understand not only the distinguishing features of these different and opposed social formations but also the thought systems that define and characterise them.

Western societies, Deleuze argues, are inherently tree-like or arboreal in nature. Not only does the tree figure heavily in Western cosmology, tree-like structures define Western forms of social organisation. As we have seen, Western societies are very much rooted societies and the metaphor of the deep tap-root with its proliferating offshoots branching out also stands as a potent metaphor for Western forms of organisation. The bureaucracy in this sense is tree-like and this way of organising prevails, from corporations to armies to the very form of the state itself. What is also characteristic of Western states is that within them power always moves from the top down; what also characterises Western arboreal society is that within it all flows are fixed while the very space the state occupies is striated.

There are, however, different plant systems to that of the tree, and the one Deleuze mobilises to capture the essence of nomadic life, and beyond that a range of forces that resist and stand in opposition to that of the arboreal state, is that of the rhizome. Grass is a rhizome, as indeed are many of the invasive plants (like bindweed) which we classify as weeds. Rhizomes do not constitute plants that evolve from any common point of origin like a seed, they reproduce laterally by throwing out subterranean and service offshoots. Unlike trees which are bound to a point, the rhizome has no centre and no predicable logic or direction to the pattern of its development. It occupies smooth as opposed to striated space and is composed of various nodes or plateaus, each of which can be connected to any other node (at least in principle). Rhizomatic structures are non-hierarchical and the plateaus of which they are composed are linked to other plateaus in diverse ways.

It is my conjecture that the informal street world of gangs, like the world of the street more generally, is of the rhizomatic form. To capture its nature in thought we therefore need a rhizomatic frame of reference or, in Deleuze's terms, a nomadology to grasp it. The problem with gang-talkers, I argue, is that they simply cannot recognise this because they are profoundly arboreal in their thinking and by inclination. At the end of the day they have trees growing in their heads which is why they only ever see trees even when the object of their enquiries is grass.

I conclude my treatise by drawing out the implications of this: How to rethink the street in ways that do not impose upon it the conceptual categories of arboreal formations; how to embrace ways of thinking like the grass itself, not from the top down but from the centre of things. I begin this task by showing that the street can never be fully corporatised even if it tries. By drawing on the work of critical ethnographers whom I read as intuitive rhizomatic thinkers I then articulate some propositions concerning how we might think about informal organisations from within a nomadic frame of reference.

If, in part, the problem of gang talk is that it reifies the street gang while negating the wider, more complex totality of which it is a part, how then might we begin to comprehend violent street worlds in ways that move beyond this exercise in reductive thinking? Here I suggest the need for a different framework of interpretation: one that no longer begins and ends with the urban street gang but which locates the gang back into the wider ecology of the street of which it is a part. This leads me in Chapter 6 to develop as an alternative approach which foregrounds the need to study street culture and the imperatives around which it is organised. Gangs, I contend, cannot be understood simply by looking at their internal dynamics as much gang research imagines, not least because what gangs predominantly do is reflect in their self-actualisation principles and repertoires of action already embedded in street culture.

To study street culture I identify the three core imperatives around which social action within it is structured. These I identify as the search for pleasure, the search for respect and the search for money. While the ends to which street life aspires are by no means specific to the street world itself, what is specific to it is the particular way in which these ends are realised. The role of edgework, action, violence and not least the hyper-macho norms that are specific to this world, work together to produce, I will argue, an inherently unstable world, one predicated quite literally on the self-destruction of its inhabitants

For the purveyors of the gangland UK thesis, the arrival of the urban street gang represents something close to what is typically read as a watershed moment in the history of urban violence. In Chapter 7 I consider what exactly has changed in its aetiology by considering both continuities and discontinuities in urban violence in the postwar period. I begin by examining what we might colloquially consider to be the regime of urban violence that accompanied the development of the welfare state. Here violence certainly occurred and was, not least, mobilised by groups of young working-class men who would no doubt today be classified as urban street gangs. Their violence, I argue, was largely an extension of leisure mobilised as a way of breaking free, at least temporarily, of the work-time disciplines they encountered in the school and then the factory. Violence was both culturally legitimated by working-class cultural norms (at least within limits) and by traditional notions of masculinity. For some working-class men, it was also a potent currency they could mobilise to assert themselves when confronted with middle-class institutions like schools whose regimes appeared established to fail them. While violence has always been part of street culture, in a sense it was delimited by street codes and would by and large end when young people concluded what for the majority would be an orderly transition into adulthood. For most this meant engaging in the world of paid manual labour which in turn would stabilise their personality structures as adults.

Though much is made of the novelty and unrelenting brutality of street violence today, there are many continuities which I then draw out. Things might be changing but traditional masculinities continue to prevail and violence still finds affirmation in the persistence of older cultural norms and in the wider society more generally. The crisis of the welfare state and the shift towards a free market neoliberal economy, however, have had a profound impact on the class structure, not to say opportunity structures more generally. And these changes, I conclude, are beginning to change the ecology of urban violence and in disturbing ways. With the rise of a low-wage flexible economy, navigating orderly transition to adulthood through gaining permanent paid work is no longer assured for many young people. Instead of drifting into crime and then out, they become enmeshed instead in an 'on-road' existence. This is particularly the case for members of the new burgeoning precariat. Colonised by the logic of ornamental material consumer culture while simultaneously alienated by neoliberalism's all to successful assault on the very gains the working class had struggled to achieve in the era of welfare, social arrangements today are producing the preconditions for the production of young men who, with justification, experience deeply internalised anger and resentment at their precarious situation. While most of the violence in which they engage is inwardly directed and self-destructive, as the English riots of 2011 demonstrated, and all too clearly, under certain determinate conditions their anger can be externalised outward and directed at the wider society.

In the concluding chapter I seek to reconnect my analysis of urban violence and gang wars with the world of contemporary policy formation. In a world where money has been made available to suppress gangs and where, as a consequence, it pays dividends to have a significant gang problem, I begin by examining what policy-makers need to do to ensure they have a suitably serious one. To help them in this I outline a useful seven-step plan, which, if followed correctly, would enable them to have as big or as small a gang problem as they might possibly need. On a more sober note I conclude by trying to show why a more proportionate and meaningful approach is necessary, one that needs to shift decisively beyond gang talk if we are to see the problems of violent street worlds correctly and in so doing to respond to the real risks they pose to their inhabitants.

So What is this All About?

Where do I situate my analysis? To begin with, it marks my response to the position staked out by John Pitts and his followers who see gangs today as the new face of youth crime and who, by and large, appear happy to blame them for everything. As will become clear, I have no time whatsoever for this position. I do not accept that gangs are the new face of youth crime; I do not accept that gangs today are large and corporate, and nor do I hold with other widely-held gang 'truths' as exemplified in claims to the effect that they coercively recruit members or are habitual rapists. The book is, then, in one respect at least, a wholesale challenge to contemporary gang orthodoxy that prevails today in that confused state called the UK.

However, if this is a book in which gangs figure it is not a book about gangs, at least as these are traditionally constructed in the genre of gang research. I do not spend any time at all in seeking to define the term and nor do I provide a detailed ethnographic account of a particular gang or a review of the extensive gang literature. Though I try and say something about the nature of informal organisations like gangs, much of this text is directed at a critique of the way the term 'gang' is deployed and used. It is thus a book in which gangs figure but not a conventional gang book insofar as it breaks free of the normal conventions governing gang research. That said, it is a text informed by 18 years' worth of

perience studying urban violence in its various forms, including that
rpetrated by gangs.

f my intervention here has salience it is to try and persuade
ng-talkers to leave aside their fixations and concentrate on the wider
ue of street culture. As this text makes clear, much of the violence
med on gangs is not gang-related. Many of the crimes blamed on
ngs can be explained in ways that do not require evoking gangs at all.
To see the world aright we need to get back to the study of the street if we
are to see the wood and not get lost among the trees. Only by adopting
this approach can we avoid the reification that gang-talkers trade in.
Only by looking at the wider ecology of violence can we begin to think
about more sensible and proportionate responses to urban violence.

Does this exercise in gonzo criminology fit easily into one of the usual
theoretical moulds? Hopefully not: the violent street worlds I study
here are multifaceted and the critical gaze we bring to bear to examine
them must reflect this. Indeed, it is precisely against the single-minded
autistic determination to reduce complexity to crude reifications, such
as that all-embracing transcendental signifier, 'gang', that this text is in
part directed. If the text has a conventional logic insofar as the chapters
follow a recognisable logical sequence, in a Deleuzian sense, the text
also takes off along a number of different lines of flight, each developing
different frames of interpretation. Applying, for example, a new
methodology here to address an old question in a new way; engaging
in hermeneutics and discourse analysis elsewhere; rethinking questions
of ontology somewhere else. As will become clear, my thinking is very
much influenced by the philosophy of Deleuze; by his rejection of what
he terms 'arboreal thinking', the tree-like thought systems characteristic
of our sedentary rooted societies; and by his embrace of what he terms
'nomadic' thought and thinking.

How, then, to think like grass?

It is, to say the least, a tall order, not least in the context of a
criminological discipline that is relentlessly arboreal in its fixations:
How to think without allowing trees to grow in our heads, thinking
not from the top down but from the centre of things. While the text
by and large following the predicable patterns of an academic book,
each chapter constitutes an essay in its own right. As we shall establish,
rhizomes are composed of plateaus, these are not linearly arranged
or orchestrated from some classificatory centre. So feel free to move
around from chapter to chapter because each is itself a plateau.

If this text represents a challenge to arboreal thought and sedentary
thinking, it is also, in its own way, an engagement with cultural

criminology and its focal concerns (Ferrell and Sanders 1995; Presdee 2000; Ferrell et al. 2008). On one hand it seeks to extend the analysis of cultural criminology into areas where it has often been loath to tread. In particular into the study of street worlds the nature of which are often socially destructive. In so doing, my aim is to suggest that while it is of course necessary to 'humanise the deviant' and, not least, recognize that their lives are not entirely miserable (J. Young 2011), not all cultures can easily be humanised, not least when their participants kill one another, often with reckless abandon. However, they do have a culture and this needs to be understood, not least if we are to understand how destructive they can be. While I remain sympathetic to the critique cultural criminology has posed against positivistic criminology, with its fetish for reducing complex worlds to desiccated numbers and voodoo statistics, it could be noted that this methodological critique has not been matched by a corresponding process of self-reflection into the ontology of informal street worlds. In this text I will suggest that an engagement with Deleuzian thought can help amend this deficit and enrich cultural criminology.

Part One

Gangland Claims and Gangland Realities

1
Gangs, Weapons and Violence

Recent years have seen the urban street gang establish itself in the eyes of many as the UK's premier public enemy. In this guise, as we have seen, the gang has been blamed for a wave of weapons-related violence that has left scores of young men dead. The urban street gang has become, apparently, a kingpin in the illegal drugs trade; it is responsible for the recent outbreak of dangerous dogs that now apparently terrorise communities; gang members, it has been claimed, systematically abuse women, and were, most recently, responsible for the wave of urban disorder that devastated cities across England in August 2011. Indeed, so dangerous has the gang now become, it has been identified by the government of 'breaking Britain' as destroying the very foundations of community life as we know it.

Unsurprisingly perhaps, this perspective on the gang, now positioned as the architect of twenty-first-century mayhem, has led many to suppose that the solution to the various pathologies listed above can be found in gang suppression now touted as the magic bullet that will save or mend 'broken Britain'. And this way of thinking appears to shape governmental thinking insofar as the Coalition Government has placed gang suppression at the centre of its law and order agenda; has created a dedicated task force to drive its gang suppression policies forward; and, not least, has devoted significant resources to confronting the evil gangs allegedly pose.

But is the urban street gang really to blame for the many sins of which it currently stands accused? Are they really to blame for the wave of shootings that have claimed the lives of so many young men in recent years? Do corporate gangs now control the drugs trade? Is the urban street gang to blame for the problems posed by dangerous dogs, sexual violence directed at women and urban disorder?

While not disputing that gangs (however we elect to define this vague and tricky term) are implicated variously in all of the above, the

19

evidence used to justify the link between gangs and the crimes they stand accused of often turns out to be very dubious when subject to sober inspection. Not only is the evidence linking gangs to various forms of urban violence weak, anecdotal and often outright suspect, gangs, I will argue, are not to blame for most of the crimes blamed on them which have causes that lie elsewhere. There remains, as such, not only an excess to the violence that is currently blamed on gangs which not gang-related, explanations for crimes currently blamed on gangs can plausibly be advanced that do not require foregrounding the gang as a key explanatory variable at all.

In what follows, by reference to five case studies, my aim is to challenge the gangland UK thesis. In so doing, my aim is to challenge both the assumption that gangs are the most potent social evil the UK confronts today and that to prevent this evil we need gang intervention policy. To develop my case I will consider five claims that have recently been advanced (and widely accepted) about the involvement of urban street gangs in array of violent and illegal acts. I will begin by considering the issue of illegal drugs supply and the alleged role of the gang as 'kin pins' in this sector of the illegal economy. I will then consider the wave of shootings typically attributed to gangs and their gang wars. The third case study concerns its role behind recent outbreaks of 'dangerous dogs'; the fourth, the role of the gang in the sexual abuse of women. I conclude by considering the role of the gang as the orchestrating force behind the urban disorder the UK confronted in 2012.

Kingpins in the Illegal Drugs Trade?

The idea that gangs exercise considerable control over the import and distribution of illegal drugs is a claim that saturates a lot of the gang talk that has grown up around the gang since its sensational rediscovery in the twenty-first century. John Pitts was one of the first to have identified this phenomenon in his study of urban gangs in the London Borough of Walthamstow (Pitts 2008). Not only does he position the urban street gang at the very heart of the drugs trade in the borough, the gangs responsible were, he contended, large and highly organised with clear hierarchical divisions of labour. In his terminology they were nothing less than 'super-articulated' and commanded such awesome power that they controlled all social life in the estates where they were based. Indeed, such was the degree of coercive control they exercised that they were able to forcibly compel young men to become gang members. These, the forcibly converted, he went on to term 'reluctant gangsters'.

The idea of the gang as drug kingpin would also appear confirmed by more recent research into urban gangs in London by other academics such as Delaney and practitioners like Harding and Toy (Toy 2008) who also identify highly corporate structures in the urban gangs they locate at the heart of the drugs trade. In this model we find leaders or generals located at the top of the gang pyramid, along with groups of 'elders' who then 'run' tiers of 'youngers' who in turn 'run' 'tinies' (very young children) as 'runners' in what remains a highly cybernetic model of gang organisation. 'Soldiers' apparently are also employed by the gang to act as muscle, protecting drug assets and the money they generate. And these in turn are surrounded by 'wannabes' eager to move up the drug hierarchy.

Whilst by no means innocent of involvement in the illegal drugs trade, this evocation of the urban street gang as significant players in the drugs economy needs to be treated with more scepticism than the authors cited above appear prepared to concede to it. And before we reach for the gang as a key player in the drugs economy, it pays to think whether there are ways of thinking about the organisation of this trade that does not require placing corporate gangs at the centre of the explanation. With this in mind, in what follows, I want to apply a criminological version of Occam's razor. In so doing it will be my aim to demonstrate that if we utilise the principle of theoretical economy, and avoid in so doing the sensational and seductive allure of gang talk, an altogether different way of thinking about the trade in illegal drugs begins to emerge.

By way of a preliminary observation it could be observed that if we study the literature on organised crime and trace its development over the last 20 years then one of the most noticeable transformations that has characterised the scholarship that surrounds it is its rejection of overly corporatist models of criminal organisation such as those which mobilise images of 'Mr Big' and his empire, or which read criminal organisations (as Cressey sensationally did with the Mafia (Cressey 1969)) as mirror images of formal corporations. Not only is this a tradition characterised by its rejection of corporate models of criminal organisation but by its acceptance that in what Castells long ago identified as the 'network society' (Castells 1996), drug trafficking is predominantly a networked endeavour. Indeed, so vehemently have some authors writing in this tradition been in rejecting the corporate turn, many have questioned the very idea of crime being organised at all (Edwards and Gill 2003).

A perennial problem with gang talkers, however, as Jack Katz observed long ago in his study of gang scholarship, is that they are often unified by a tangible failure to engage with non-gang literature, even when the object of study (in this case, drug trafficking) is similar (Katz and Jackson 1997). And this, I would suggest, is a serious omission because had these gang researchers taken the trouble to reference it, they might well have had to rethink their corporate turn.

Of course, in response, they might well claim that, yes, the corporate gang until recently did not stand at the centre of the drugs trade, but given recent changes in the organisation of crime, now it does. Pitts, for example, articulates this in his claim that gangs today have replaced older style traditional gangster firms. But does this thesis stand up to critical scrutiny?

One response to this would be to suggest that in many respects Pitts has overstated the degree to which the crime family has declined as a model of criminal organisation whilst overstating the degree to which new super-articulated gangs have replaced them. As John Lea argues, the family has always been a key variable in the organisation of crime because in the illegal marketplace trust matters a lot and family affiliation is one of the strongest ways to assure it. But questions can also legitimately be raised over the extent and degree to which gangs are corporate and whether corporate organisation is itself a viable way of distributing drugs.

To begin with, though, let us explore the various relations gang affiliated young people may have to drugs and the drug trade in order to examine this. Gang members may, in the first instance, be drug users. But this may have little to do with their gang belonging or 'gangness', but simply be part of wider cultural milieu of the street world they inhabit. Their drug use, in other words, is not a product of 'gangness' but something they and many other non-gang-affiliated young people engage in in a world where drug use has become increasingly normalised (Parker et al. 1999).

Secondly, they may deal and trade in illegal drugs to make money, but even when they do this there are different ways of thinking through such engagement without corporatising the gang or placing it at the heart of the illegal drugs trade.

They may, for example, engage in drug selling as an individual sideline. In this scenario they have their gang belonging and in addition they also seek to make their money by hustling drugs as individual operatives in the drug marketplace either through selling to a small circle of friends and acquaintances (in closed markets) or to strangers in open drugs markets. In the world of high unemployment, this is by no means unlikely. Speaking from my own experience, there was clear evidence of this in some of the estates we studied in Hackney, what is now referred to as a 'gang afflicted' borough in London. Indeed, this is precisely what Hagedorn found in his study of street gangs in Illinois (Hagedorn and Macon 1988). Less corporate hierarchies (as the police fantasised them) but participants in a wider hustling economy populated by many other participants than gang members alone; a finding also reproduced in the UK by Aldridge and Medina in their ethnographic research into 'gang city' (Aldridge and Medina 2005). Given that street youth command little capital, and given that most live parochial lives and are not well networked into the criminal underworld, it is difficult to see why most gang members would participate as anything other than small bit-players in the lower rungs of the wider street-retail sector of the drugs economy.

The response to this might well be that this argument ignores the very real fact that the drugs trade is huge in the UK, as it is everywhere, and somebody has to be organising all this. In other words, above the small fry stand the big fish, and large super-articulated gangs constitute the big fish. Time to rethink how we think about networks and time as well to differentiate between network models of organisation and corporatised models.

Let's compare the two. In the corporate model we have a pyramidal structure where power moves from the top down in a cybernetic fashion. Tiers stand above tiers with leaders at the top dictating to subordinate ranks beneath them. Just like an army. However, within the network we have an array of different connections between nodes that can include but take rather different forms that that implied by the corporate model. Let's look at some of these in order to substantiate the point.

1. An individual buys a weight of drugs from a higher-level dealer then sells them on to his own network either in a closed or open drug market.
2. A group pools resources to purchase a weight of drugs. They then split the proceeds and sell through to their own network beneath them, which also may sell on to others.
3. The gang is collectively employed to sell drugs by more established dealers. They sell the drugs, pass on the surplus and are paid for the services rendered. Again the most likely model here is that of each individual selling for personal gain, not for the collective. Why is this the case? For the simple reason that the possibilities of strife and issues of trust become more problematic the more organised a group becomes and the larger it becomes. Hagedorn, as always,

is wonderfully instructive here. Why, he wanted to know, did the gang he was interviewing not maintain their drugs house? Their answer is priceless but illuminating: 'too much hassle' (Hagedorn and Macon 1988).

In part, a serious problem with the corporate gang thesis concerns the overall functionality of the model as the best way to distribute drugs anyway. Given that dealing is a highly criminalised endeavour, making your drugs business known to everyone in the gang leaves the gang itself very vulnerable to leakage either to enforcement agents through their informants, or to other violent men or groups who might want to rob them. Which is why in the illegal drugs trade knowledge is kept relatively insulated to the players required to initiate a transaction. People below do not look too far up and those above do not need to look too far down. You most certainly do not need to orchestrate an entire network in all its complexity to make money. All you need to do is ensure that the node to which you are attached is articulated appropriately to other immediate nodes in the wider network.

Often, the nature of the articulation will take the form of subcontracting the moving and shifting of drugs, often to younger people by elder and more established gangsters; 'runners' or 'shotters' as they are referred to in the vernacular of the street. As a gangster in Hackney explained matters, if you want, for example, to move a case full of money or drugs you might well enlist the services of a younger person, gang-affiliated or not, to do the work. You detail the instructions and in return they are rewarded for successfully conducting the transaction. If they fail, then in true gangster fashion, they are liable to be punished. In this transaction you do not need or require that the subcontractor be a paid-up member of your gang, only that they complete a transaction.

In the case of the UK, questions can also be asked about the virtue of a model which fails to distinguish between what we might want to call urban street gangs typically populated by young people with a pronounced street presence who often live parochial lives and who have little capital, and more organised crime groups typically controlled by older professional criminals who do. From where I stand, typologies that blur this distinction, such as Delaney's or Pitts', suffer from the problem of over-generalisation insofar as these important distinctions are lost in what becomes a corporate gang model. Technological developments, not least of which include the internet and mobile phones, also work to obviate having to organise corporately in order to distribute or sell drugs. Today, drug transactions can be mediated through new communication technology between geographically distant players in the global drugs economy. Yes, these transactions require organising, but they are typically provided by an array of different actors in a distributed network.

Now none of this suggests that gangs might not be involved in any network only while they may constitute a node in the network, they do not control the network itself and almost certainly cannot. In societies where the state is strong and sovereignty from above is by and large successfully imposed, it could be observed that the capacity to develop complex corporate gang structures will be difficult to achieve anyway. Indeed, once a group becomes large and organised then invariably their activities are likely to come to the attention of enforcement agencies that will eventually decapitate the group. Size itself creates its own set of problems as well. Which is why it is far less likely to be the case that organised drug gangs will be found in in states like the UK where state sovereignty is overly strong. Which also explains why organised drug gangs are typically found instead in states that are weak and where counter-forms of 'governance from below' (Lea and Stenson 2007) are likely to be as strong or in some cases even stronger than the governance imposed from above by the state. This disjunction explains, for example, why we find large drug cartels in Mexico and Colombia or Russia but not in the UK.

If the corporate street gang as kingpin in the drugs economy is a thesis that lacks credibility, we might ask why the myth of the corporate gang as key drug-player continues to haunt the control imaginary. To a degree it is because forms of arboreal thinking infest gang-talkers, and we will return to the epistemological and ontological implications of this in Chapter 5. But for now two other reasons can be cited which might help us understand this phenomenon. In part, the problem here, I would suggest, is one of misinterpreting the evidence; in part it reflects aspects of what we might see as the 'Our man in Havana' syndrome.

If we inspect where the evidential base upon which the corporate drug-gang thesis is derived then it is typically based upon the a priori assumptions gang-talkers work with which holds that the drugs trade is organised, where the term 'organised' is taken to mean corporate/ bureaucratic. This view, it could be noted, is also held implicitly by many denizens of the street world, and why not as they also live in a society of bureaucracies? The consequence of this assumption is that when asked to narrate how they distribute drugs, what tends to happen is that a corporate narrative is provided or is read back into the testimony. This is particularly the case when street respondents talk about how drugs held by 'elders' get 'young uns' to distribute them whilst being protected by various 'soldiers'. This is immediately interpreted as prima facie confirmation of a corporate structure even when what is really being described may well be a distributed network.

Grahame Greene's novel *Our Man in Havana* helps us understand why this reading becomes more rather than less likely. The book narrates the history of James Wormold, a semi-alcoholic vacuum cleaner salesmen who unwittingly finds himself enrolled by MI5 to become a spy in pre-revolutionary Cuba. Finding the job distasteful but nevertheless wanting to please his spymasters (and keep the pay cheques rolling in), he feeds their insatiable appetite for intelligence about the Soviets by sending them detailed drawings of vacuum cleaner components. Without evincing any doubt over the validity of the absurd evidence they are being asked to accept, the spooks conclude that these are indeed sinister Soviet installations. In other words, they suspend any capacity to disbelieve the fabrications they are presented with (even when they are staring them literally in the face), and find instead conclusive proof of the fears and anxieties about Soviet intentions they already held. And so it is, I often suspect, with much gang research. Despite the general flakiness of the data, gang-talkers make up for knowledge deficits by finding in everything conclusive proof of the enemy they already presupposed they knew anyway. They already presupposed that the gang is corporate and so it must be. And so the idea of the corporate drug gang orchestrating drug sales comes to establish itself as the orthodoxy of gang talk.

Gangs and Violence

One of the key reasons why the gang has come to command such a pivotal role in the space of our imaginary is because of its alleged role as a key driver of urban violence in its various forms. In this capacity the gang is considered responsible for a wave of shootings that have left scores of young men dead; it is responsible for the rising problems associated with what are called 'status dogs', sexual violence and the riots. But just how central a player is it? And to what extent is gangness an explanatory factor in all of this. In this section of the chapter I will look at the issue of gang participation in weaponised violence and street robbery – both are offences in which gangs clearly have some involvement, but maybe not quite as much as we are led to believe by the gang-talking community.

Given that the gang is a group invariably defined by its relationship to violence we cannot be surprised that research will invariably uncover the unsurprising truth that violent men are more likely to be more violent than non-violent men. This is, however, simply a tautological argument. Because these groups are populated by violent men who occupy a violent street-based world, nor can we be overly surprised by the fact that the violence in which they engage is serious and weapons are sometimes used by these men to settle their conflicts. As the American gang research tradition reminds us, if you are in a gang you are more likely to be involved in violence than if you are not (see Klein and Maxson 2006). This research also tells us that gang-affiliated people have a higher propensity to engage in more serious violence than non-gang-affiliated people; that the gang tends to draw mutually violent people together, and that once a gang is formed there is a propensity for involvement in crime and violence to proliferate (Klein 1995).

While gangs therefore are more violent than non-gang groups and while it is evident they use weapons, it would nevertheless be a mistake to assume that violence in general and weaponised violence in particular can be reduced solely to an issue of gangs. Let us take involvement in street crime as an example. This is a violent offence often involving the threat of violence and sometimes its use to rob victims of their belongings. According to the Metropolitan Police Service, London gangs in 2012 perpetrated apparently 40 per cent of street crime in the capital, which would suggest gangs are major players in this offence category. Leaving aside for a moment the accuracy of the figures (gang membership, as we shall see, is a moving feast), they still tell us that people who are not in gangs commit far more street robbery. Given this fact, it would be difficult to conclude that gangs are responsible for street crime.

What these figures also suggest is that if street crime is a crime largely committed by people who are not in gangs; it is not gangness that explains their participation but other factors commonly shared across the population of street robbers which also include gang members. Which also tells us that solutions to street crime would clearly need to look beyond the gang if they were to be successful.

It could also be noted that street robbery, of which there is much in areas now labelled 'gang-afflicted' was already high in precisely these areas in the years before gangs were discovered. Brixton, a poor, multiply-deprived area in London, is an excellent case study. Street crime was already way above national averages in the area well before it became redefined as 'gang-afflicted'.

If we consider why street crime remains so high today, then rather than evoke the gang to explain it, more can be gained by looking at the same intersection of factors that explained why it rose in the borough in the first place, those I explored in my 2005 book *Street Crime* based on research conducted in the borough (Hallsworth 2005).

As my research brought to light, what we had in Brixton was a situation whereby a significant section of its poorest community was experiencing significant economic disadvantage, despite wider attempts to regenerate the area by regenerating its retail and night-time economy. This population, subject both to relative and absolute forms of deprivation, was materially excluded but at the same time culturally included into the culture of compulsory consumption around which contemporary capitalism is organised. This disadvantaged population of frustrated consumers would produce the motivated offenders who would rob a range of more affluent suitable victims, many of whom were drawn to the area seeking either affordable housing or entertainment in the area's night-time economy; victims whose suitability was enhanced because they carried precisely the desirable goods that offenders craved, particularly mobile phones. Coupled with deficits in the control response such as the failure of mobile phone suppliers to immobilise stolen phones, and the lack of a credible police response, street crime proliferated.

Interestingly, when I asked the street robbers I interviewed whether they were in gangs they answered no, even though many operated in groups. While I will not dispute that today many street robbers may now claim to be in gangs, it could be noted that the motivation to engage in street robbery does not require evoking the gang to explain why it is occurring. It is also interesting to note that whereas in 2004, the period during which my research was conducted, street crime received sustained media attention, it was not gangs but 'muggers' and 'jackers' that received attention. Nobody uses these terms any more. Isn't that strange?

While it is by no means unusual to find gangs armed with weapons (knives being more commonly carried and used than guns), many other young men, including those in peer groups, also carry such weapons. Evidence suggests, however, that the carrying of weaponry is principally for the purpose of defence, not principally from gangs but from street robbers more generally (and this trend again was also occurring before the street gang came to prominence). So let me hazard a conjecture: rather than blame the gang for the rise of knife-carrying, I would suggest that it was in response to the very real threat of being robbed that best explains the phenomena.

Guns have also been used to settle a range of conflicts and the fact that around 50 young men (many from the African Caribbean community) have been shot dead in recent years attests to the self-destructive violence these young men are capable of. While a certain proportion of this violence can certainly be attributed to gangs and 'gang wars', other factors also need to be taken into account that again take us beyond the gang. In some cases young men who are gang-affiliated may also use weapons in an individual capacity, *not* as part of their gang affiliation. London is also home to many gangsters who may use and carry weapons in their individual capacity and who are unrelated to gangs. The most serious forms of weaponised violence, however, are connected to the street retail trade in drugs like crack and heroin (Hallsworth and Silverstone 2009). As we have seen above, while gang members are involved in this trade so too are many other participants, including professional criminals and individual criminals (such as lone drug dealers and delinquent individuals) who aspire to rob them (see Jacobs 2000). Finally it could also be noted that while many fatal shootings are invariably being blamed on gangs, on closer inspection many transpire to be unrelated to gangs altogether, as we shall establish in Chapter 4.

Weapon Dogs and the Gang

In addition to the guns and knives gangs routinely carried, it has been argued by a number of commentators that gangs are now equipping themselves with a new kind of weaponry, what are often referred to as 'status dogs', 'weapon dogs' or 'devil dogs'. The dogs in question appear to be predominantly Staffordshire terriers, American pit bull terriers and various crosses between the two. In the words of an RSPCA briefing paper on the problem:

> Dangerous dogs are widely used by gangs and criminals to intimidate and cause injury to other people and also some animals. The possession of them is often closely associated with other worrying elements of ASB and gang culture, including knife violence and drugs. (RSPCA 2010)

Similarly, in the publication 'Weapon Dogs: The Situation in London' (Monks 2009), produced by the Greater London Authority (GLA), we are told:

> there is no doubt that a proportion of Pit Bulls and other 'weapon dogs' are being deliberately trained to attack people and for dog fighting.

Like many claims that have been made about gangs, these invite critical scrutiny.

The first point that could be made is that claims about the use of 'dangerous dogs' by gangs are not supported by any compelling evidence. The RSPCA paper provides no objective evidence to justify the claims it makes. What is presented in the GLA report is information regarding police and RSPCA activity, but activity alone cannot be taken as evidence of wider trends in crime. For example, we are told that 'the number of dogs seized by the MPS has increased 44% between 2007 and 2009'. As the reasons for this growth in seizures may have as much to do with policy changes (that is, the decision to create a specialist unit (Status dogs Unit) with a mandate to seize dogs and a policy shift to seize more dogs as opposed to fewer) it may be as much the police response to rising concerns about alleged 'dangerous' dogs, rather than changes in gang behaviour, that explains the extent of the problem.

While increases in dog bites have also been used to justify the alleged gang connection, these statistics do not separate domestic from non-domestic incidents; nor are the breeds that bite identified. If the goal of good policy is that it is evidence-driven, anecdotal and subjective evidence alone does not provide the grounds to develop evidence-driven policy. We cannot therefore treat as credible assertions also made in the GLA report such as:

> anecdotal evidence suggests that many residents do not want to leave their houses or make use of their local parks because of the intimidation and threats posed by dangerous and aggressive dogs and irresponsible owners.

So what is the nature of the threat posed by so-called 'dangerous dogs' and what if anything has this to do with gangs? As little systematic research has been undertaken, it is difficult to answer this question. If we apply common sense to what the available evidence shows then the picture that emerges is rather different from the alarmist headlines the public typically receive.

At first sight it might appear that the relationship between 'dangerous dogs' and gangs is very real given widely reported gang-related violent incidents in London in 2009 (see Calahan 2008; Metropolitan Police Service 2010). In this case a dog was used to attack two people and in the assault that followed the victim received a number of dog bites. It was human-inflicted stab wounds, however, that were ultimately responsible for the victim's death. While this case attests to a gang connection, it was also reported that this was the first case of this kind, which is also why it received so much media coverage. This case alone certainly cannot be used to justify the reduction of the problems posed by 'dangerous dogs' to a question of gangs, or to establish that gangs are now using weapon dogs to 'solve their conflicts', as claimed by the RSPCA.

While many gang-affiliated men may own or aspire to own 'status dogs' like pit bulls and Staffordshire terriers, many other young people in working-class estates in London (including a number of young women) do as well. So too do a number of adults, including the author of this book (this is not 'paws-off' research). This suggests that these breeds are popular and that many want to own one, not just gang members. The population of 'status dog' owners, in other words, is not homogeneous and gang membership remains relatively small in the population at large (gang surveys, for what they are worth, tell us that between 3–6 per cent of respondents are in gangs). Nor is ownership for 'status' pathological, as owning dogs for 'status' or 'reputation' is an historic phenomenon, whether it be the reputation associated with German shepherds, labradors or Staffordshire terriers, most 'pure-bred' animals are acquired either for status or for enterprise/employment.

While it could be the case that owning a dog like a pit bull occurs because of the 'hard' image it is associated with (its extrinsic appeal), it could also be the case that such dogs make devoted pets and are by nature very tractable with humans (their intrinsic appeal). Indeed a significant number of gang-affiliated young men interviewed in recent research by Mahler and Pearpoint claimed that it was specifically the issue of companionship that defined their relationships to their dogs (Mahler and Pearpoint 2010). None of the dog 'experts' interviewed in this research made any reference to this issue. In rare cases where proscribed breeds have been involved with human fatalities, these typically involved dogs that had been abused or under-exercised and left in proximity to young children with no adult present. These cases all occurred within a domestic setting, and family pets, not 'gang dogs', were involved.

When dogs are interdog-aggressive it by no means follows that they are human-aggressive. In fact, a trait in the breeding of most dog-fighting breeds is that they are bred not to be human-aggressive. Turning them into human killing machines as such requires considerable effort and skill as it opposes their basic instincts, and most young people (gang-affiliated or not) are unlikely to possess refined dog-training capabilities of this kind. Rather than define the many real problems posed by 'status dogs' as a problem of 'gangs', a less sensational interpretation probably has greater explanatory power. The problem here is likely to be one posed less by innately psychotic dogs trained to attack humans on command by organised gangs settling their conflicts; the issue is more likely to be posed by young, immature people owning powerful dogs that they buy on a whim and then sell on when they get bored with them (which happens quickly), are under-exercised, badly trained, often neglected, and that are not kept under effective control by their owners (Hallsworth 2011b). While humans can certainly be bitten and intimidated by such dogs, the problem here is not 'gang dogs' but the irresponsible ownership of such dogs by a growing number of young people. This would also help explain why growing numbers of these dogs are being abandoned as young people quickly discover the old truism 'A dog is for life, not for Christmas'. This interpretation is certainly more likely than alarmist claims to the effect that the abandoned dogs are those which are not aggressive enough for the gangs (see Davis 2010; BBC News 2009).

While it could be the case that criminals use dogs, the context in which they do so varies. To begin with, they may use them to protect criminal property such as drugs. (One elderly drug-dealer we interviewed, for example, defended his house with a Rottweiler and a pit bull, and a CCTV camera placed above his front door which also had a large iron-grilled door set before it.) But this is not a new tendency in criminal circles. In fact, the motive here is no different from that applied by legal companies who also employ guard dogs to protect valuable goods. It could also be the case that the ownership of dogs such as pit bulls occurs not because of a desire to own a 'weapon dog' to 'terrorise a neighbourhood' but because it is part of the wider cultural fabric of the street community. Like wearing branded clothing, it is something you do to affirm and cultivate your status relative to others. It could be remarked that legal dogs like Alsatians are better equipped with the instincts that allow them to be trained as human-aggressive rather than dog-fighting breeds like pit bulls, legally defined as 'dangerous' (and thus deserving of death under the UK's draconian Dangerous Dogs Act) even when most are not.

While some people illegally breed dogs such as pit bulls, prior to jumping to the conclusion that they are being bred for gangs and as weapons (as argued recently by Harding 2012), a more sober appreciation of the facts may suggest other motives. To begin with, in a society where the demand for these dogs is high, breeding them can make money. If you are poor this may be one way to address the problem. As evidenced by increasing dog ownership of these breeds, many people want to own these dogs and it is likely that the gang member is only one of many customers. It seems unlikely that gang members, like other individuals, would in fact want to own a dangerous and unpredictable dog which may attack its owner or their companions, though it must be said that the idea that they do want to own 'bad pits' has much currency among gang-talkers (see Harding 2012). To date there is no evidence to substantiate claims that dogs are being bred to be aggressive to humans or that gang members in fact desire psychotic animals. Although the increase in ownership of bull breeds has been linked to the rise in gang culture, such an assumption is erroneous.

Rather than blame gangs for the increase in the ownership of bull breeds, more can be gained by examining the unintended consequences of the Dangerous Dogs Act which was introduced with the explicit aim of eliminating dogs like pit bulls as a breed. As Mathiesen argued, deterrence only works if you are likely to be deterred (Mathiesen 1990) and it is by no means clear that many of the pit-bull-owning fraternity fall into this constituency. Many distrust law enforcement and few know much about the Dangerous Dogs Act. As Kaspersson argues, by criminalising these dogs the Dangerous Dogs Act has paradoxically worked to enhance their reputation and increased their appeal to the very people the state was actively trying to discourage from owning them, while also creating the preconditions for an illicit market that trades in these breeds. While there certainly exists a small subculture that breeds dogs for dog-fighting purposes, as yet no evidence has been presented that connects this subculture to the wider gang situation in London.

Although there is evidence that fear of such dogs has increased, this may well be a result of a media and enforcement-driven moral panic rather than the dangerousness of particular dogs. The media in this sense not only increasingly writes about dogs like pit bulls but does so in a way such that unusual and atypical cases are now presented as the norm.

Although assumptions have been made about the association between gangs and these dogs, the ownership of such animals may well be attractive to gang members for the same reasons they are to non-gang-affiliated people.

Gangs and Sexual Violence

In addition to mobilising 'weapon dogs' as their 'preferred weapon of choice', gangs, it is alleged, are now mobilising sexual violence against women in the form of group rape and sexual exploitation. According to the Deputy Children's Commissioner, Sue Berelowitz, currently fronting a two-year inquiry into gang-related sexual abuse, the problem is endemic.

> As one police officer who was the lead in a very big investigation in a lovely leafy rural part of the country said to me [a policeman speaks, it must be true ...]: 'there isn't a town, village or hamlet in which children are not being sexually exploited. This is what is going on in some parts of our country. It is very sadistic, very violent, it is very ugly.'

Never one to knowingly understate a problem, she continued:

> There are parts of London where certainly children expect to have to perform oral sex on line ups of boys, up to two hours at a time at the age of eleven. And it is quite common for girls to be lured via internet chat rooms to meet a friend only to be met by a group of boys and raped in a park. Then another group of boys come, they take her to another part of the park and she is serially raped again.

In response to what is being constructed as a national epidemic, the government has made over £1 million available to support the victims of such violence. As with 'dangerous dogs' and gangs, however, the link between gangs and sexual violence also requires careful scrutiny.

If we consider the evidence that has been presented to substantiate the connection, then leaving aside the sensational rhetoric of the tabloid press and not least Ms Berelowitz, little systematic research appears to have been conducted, while much of what has is of very dubious provenance. If we inspect what has been written, however, as with many of the other sensational claims made about gangs, the evidence for the gang-as-sexual-predator thesis does not stand up to critical scrutiny.

Responding to wider fears about what the tabloids like to term 'gang rape', the Metropolitan Police Authority (MPA) conducted a review into multiple-perpetrator rapes (defined as sexual assault involving three to eight suspects). These increased from 73 in 2003/04 to 93 in 2008/09 – conclusive proof for some that the gang rapists had arrived.

However, when you inspect the data compiled by the MPA establishing the link between multiple-perpetrator rape and gangs becomes altogether elusive. The report systematically profiles the age, ethnicity and gender of perpetrators and victims; it examines the boroughs where this offence appears to occur, and the relationship between deprivation and sexual offending is also profiled. Unlike much that has been written about gangs, the report acknowledges the difficulties attached to defining the term 'gang' and concludes that connecting such rape to gangs is difficult to establish.

When examining rapes committed by multiple perpetrators it should be noted that the number of offenders involved and the methods used by assailants vary. Analysis on such offending is primarily based on victim testimony and any other supporting evidence, so links to 'gangs' cannot necessarily be established. These offences are complex in nature ranging from allegations of consensual sex between the victims and a known party, followed by non-consensual assaults committed by associates, to stranger attacks involving large groups. (MPA 2010)

In other words the connection is not proven.

If the MPA report presents findings which follow from a commendable review of the available evidence, the same cannot be said of 'research' conducted by ROTA into gangs and sexual violence which has generated considerable media coverage and which, not least, provided the evidential justification for the ongoing investigation by the Children's Commission (Firmin 2010). Based upon interviews and focus groups conducted with 352 women who, according to the ROTA website, were 'friends, relatives, victims or perpetrators of gangs and gang violence', the report found clear and seeming unambiguous proof of the link between the gang and sexual violence. As the report concludes:

Sexual violence and exploitation are significant weapons used against females associated with, or involved in, gang violence. Rape has become a weapon of choice, and used against sisters, girlfriends and on occasion mothers, as it is the only weapon that cannot be detected during a stop and search.

And if this was not bad enough:

Girls who carry firearms and drugs for their boyfriends often live in areas that are not perceived to have a 'gang-problem', may attend grammar or private all-girls schools, will rarely be under any form of surveillance or be known to any specialist services such as children's or youth offending services, have their own bank account where their boyfriend can store his money.

Taken together with the MPA report, these findings implicate the gang in serious sexual abuse of women; a form of violence which, as the ROTA report intimates, has not been treated as seriously as the male-on-male violence that gangs are usually associated with. But how strong is the evidential base from which these claims are derived? While this research raises important issues, as we shall now see, clear gang connections to sexual violence cannot be easily established. Tellingly, nor does the evidence presented remotely justify the sensational conclusions reached.

Let's begin with the claim that rape is now a 'weapon of choice' of gangs. A nice soundbite and one we have already seen, used in relation to dogs. However, if you go through the report, evidence confirming this is hard to come by. Ten case studies of girls connected to gangs are presented; however, only in one case does the woman in question claim to have been raped. This is hardly conclusive. As to the claim that gangs are now routinely raping mothers, one of the 'key findings' of the report, then apart from one woman who 'claims' to know mothers who have been raped, no evidence at all is presented to substantiate the thesis by, for example, mothers who have been raped. (It could be noted that the gang member as mother-rapist appears to have disappeared as an issue by the time the Children's Commission started to report its findings.) As to the 'key finding' that gangs are targeting grammar and all girl schools, no evidence is provided to substantiate this claim at all. None of this of course means that gang members might not target grammar school girls or that immature grammar school girls may be attracted to 'bad' men, only that stronger evidence must be presented if such a claim is to be taken seriously.

Despite claiming in its website that the report involved *'face-to-face research with 352 friends, relatives, victims or perpetrators of gangs and gang violence'*, on inspection it transpires that 43 per cent of the women interviewed had no involvement in gangs and only 25 claimed they were gang members. As the report contains no systematic attempt to define what they meant by the term 'gang' where it appears the term was self-defined by the women interviewed, it is difficult to know precisely what kind of group is being referred to and the degree to which they can legitimately be termed 'gangs'. In a report based almost wholly on opinion and hearsay rather than grounded personal experience, none of the claims made are remotely substantiated by the evidence presented. Despite the fact that this second-rate piece of 'research' lacks anything that resembles validity and integrity, it has nevertheless been widely cited as providing definitive proof of the 'gangs as rapists' thesis.

Given that men who are violent populate gangs it might well be the case that the sexual abuse of women by gangs does occur, but to suggest that rape is a culture or 'weapon of choice' of gangs is to advance a claim where exceptional, atypical cases are problematically extrapolated to define the gang norm. To put this another way, some gang members sexually abuse women, ergo all gang members are sexual abusers. This becomes clearer if we look beyond gang talk at the wider context in which rape and sexual violence occurs.

Again, if we apply the principle of theoretical economy, a different picture emerges. We can begin by noting that the overwhelming majority of rape cases that come to the attention of enforcement agencies are perpetrated by individuals and duos, not groups or gangs. The overwhelming number of cases typically involve family or friends known to the victim, and 'stranger rape' is very rare. As we have seen above, while multiple-perpetrator rapes do occur, it is by no means the case that the groups concerned meet the criteria necessary to be termed 'gangs'. As Horvath and Kelly (2009) point out, there is currently 'no evidence to suggest that perpetrators with these [gang] characteristics make up the majority of multiple perpetrator rape suspects'. As recent cases testify, other groups of men, such as professional footballers, have also been implicated in such abuse (see Hindley 2005; Horvath and Kelly 2009). It could also be observed that offenders who commit multiple-perpetrator rapes might not be part of a 'gang' 'group' (as groupings may also form spontaneously). A recent study by Hauffe and Porter (2009) also suggested that the relationship between young people and multiple-perpetrator rape is similar to that of other youth co-offending. This age group spends more time in groups, are vulnerable to peer pressures, lack the skills to negotiate dysfunctional group behaviour and/or use their peer group to develop social identity and status.

More importantly, we should be careful not to reduce the explanation of sexual violence, routinely proliferated by men from all sectors of society, to that of 'gang culture'. Such conjecture and reductionist thinking negates the real issues involved, and by so doing obscures an examination of the basis for such behaviour. Far from being progressive, such analysis panders instead to the worst aspects of populist tabloid prejudice and simply becomes yet another aspect of that denuded discourse I propose to term 'gang talk'. Reframing sexual violence as a gang-related issue may therefore be counterproductive to effectively addressing the very complex issue of sexual abuse and rape because by scapegoating the gang we take our eyes off the real source of the problem (see Naffine 1997; Warner 2004).

Rather than lay the blame for multiple-perpetrator rape and the sexual abuse of women at the door of the gang, far more explanatory power can be gained by seeing the issue as one that pertains to highly problematic gender relations and sexual mores at play in a highly gendered not to say patriarchal society; one which produces an excess of young men who, as Tara Young's work shows, are literally programmed to desire sex and lose their virginity, but who live in a world populated by a dearth of young women who, fearful of reputational damage (and the risk of sexual violence that might follow from this), do not provide them with the sex they desire. To reduce these complex relations to a problem of gangs is consequently misguided and dangerous. For interventions to be effective, policies need to reach beyond the gang to target the wider population of young people (young men, but also women) who are socialised into what remains a pathological system of gender norms. As with the claims that have been made about 'weapon dogs', the relationship between sexual violence and young people warrants systemic, not to say balanced and proportionate, assessment of the evidence, not alarmist headlines produced by sensation-seeking, irresponsible populists such as the Deputy Children's Commissioner.

Urban Disorder

Over four days in August 2011, Britain's inner cities exploded in a wave of violent public unrest unprecedented in recent years as thousands of young people took to the streets: violence predominantly associated with, but not exclusively perpetrated by, its most powerless citizens; in particular those who inhabited the poorest areas of its metropolitan cities – areas that, in turn, would experience much of the worst violence. At its conclusion lives were tragically lost and stores were looted, whilst swathes of England's urban landscape were reduced to the status of a devastated wasteland. These events have provoked, and with justification, a sense of deep collective trauma as the search for explanations has gathered momentum: How to account for a wave of destruction that reached from London to cities as far apart as Birmingham, Liverpool, Nottingham, Manchester, and Salford?

As we saw in the introduction, condemnation as opposed to explanation defined the immediate political response as the government and the mass media sought to translate the disorders into a narrative fit for public consumption. Someone had to be blamed and it was not going to be government policy. Step forward the urban street gang which, within 24 hours of the first riot in Tottenham, was already being singled out as the direct cause.

Evidential support for the claim that gangs were behind the riots was subsequently justified on the basis of a statement released by the Metropolitan Police claiming that around a fifth to a quarter of the people they had arrested in relation to the riots were 'gang-affiliated'. This would provoke newspapers like the *Mirror* (Myall 2011) to bizarrely read this as conclusive evidence that gangs were therefore behind the riots. Leaving aside the status of how accurate such gang designations are (which I return to consider below), it could be noted that if this indeed reflected the composition of the population involved in the disorders, these figures meant that three-quarters of the rioters were *not* 'gang-affiliated'. Whilst this suggests that the gang members played a role in the riots, what these figures also tell us is that they played a limited role. In short, the riots were not only about gangs or indeed mostly about gangs, a fact belatedly noted in a Home Office report which observed:

In terms of the role gangs played in the disorder, most forces perceived that where gang members were involved, they generally did not play a pivotal role. (Home Office 2011: 19)

This, of course, assumes that the police figures on gang affiliation are themselves robust and accurate and, as such, can be trusted. But can they? The first point that needs to be made in relation to this is that gang identification is *not* an exact science. On the contrary, it is an interpretive process replete with many problems; not least of which are the subjective assumptions on which they are based and the definitions used. What we can be clear about is that the police attributions are not made on the basis of self-ascribed designations by gang members; nor, as the Home Office itself acknowledged, was any consistent definition of the term 'gang' used by the police forces from whom the figures are collated. Police attributions, rather like those of the media, are made by those with the power to label and make their labels stick. The problem with labels, however, is that they are not infallible.

This is not an insignificant issue of semantics. The issue of defining when a gang is a gang is a real issue by no means settled in criminology where it has been debated the most (Jankowski 1991; Klein 1995). From the perspective of media pundits who kept evoking gangs in TV studios following the disturbances, it was easy to get the impression that the term 'gang' was being deployed to describe just about everyone hanging around in the context of a riot dressed a particular way. This, it could be observed, is not too far from the usual media trick of describing just about every group that is felt to be causing trouble to someone as a 'gang' (Hallsworth and Young 2008). Given that gangs and non-gangs wear the same ubiquitous street uniform, it could be observed that distinguishing between gangs and non-gangs in the context of a riot is as difficult a task as distinguishing between them on the street.

With this in mind let us now consider the term 'gang affiliation' more closely. What precisely does this term mean? Does it mean gang member (that is, from perspective of enforcement, someone who meets the criteria necessary to be formally labelled as a gang member)? Or does it mean someone who has been seen by police officers associating with other 'gang-affiliated members'? The term is vague and vague terms need to be treated with considerable scepticism. As most young men who live in the areas where the disturbances occurred will know and often interact with gang members who are themselves integrated into wide friendship and kin networks (Gunter 2008), it would not be at all difficult to define most as in some sense 'gang-affiliated'.

Let's further consider the evidence linking gangs to the disorder; in particular the claim that the sheer volume of gang members arrested constitutes overwhelming evidence of significant gang involvement. In a telling demolition of the way gang statistics were used to sustain the 'gangs caused riots' thesis, Roger Ball and John Drury show how problematic this assumption is. Gangs, they observe, were very quickly identified by the mass media and others of orchestrating the riots. Given that the police already have extensive databases on gang members, it was this population that the police went out of their way to arrest along with just about any other prolific offender on their records. A fact, not least, confirmed by Metropolitan Police Commissioner Tim Goodwin, who observed that as his officers went through the CCTV files to identify suspects the ones they knew were the ones they went out of their way to arrest ('we have lots of images to go through and obviously the ones that you know are going to be arrested first' (cited in Ball and Drury 2012)). As Ball and Drury observe (ibid.), given the fact that the arrested population was populated by people police had already labelled as gang members, this means it is impossible to generalise and extrapolate from this skewed figure (as the media and government did) that the arrested population represented accurately the population of rioters.

Let's pause here and apply what is lacking in all this madness, and that is something called common sense. Whilst not disputing that gangs can organise, the idea that they would sit down and plan the disorder that occurred across England also implies degrees of organisation that appear to fit the implausible world of James Bond and Dr No more than they the reality of English street-life. The idea of criminal masterminds organising and planning the riots also ignores what history has to teach us about urban disorder. Far from being planned with precision, the characteristic of urban disorder is that they are events that are typically spontaneous, insurgent, instantaneous, dramatic, spectacular, mobile and improvised.

The lesson of this is that we need to be very careful when we want to identify gangs and, beyond that, place them at the centre of any criminal conspiracy. Adjudicating who is 'gang-affiliated' on the basis of a vague concept, imprecise measuring instruments, often dubious intelligence, in the context of a society whose way of imagining gangs owes more to a rich and disturbing fantasy life than informed understanding, must leave room for considerable doubt as to the merits of the gangland UK thesis as a plausible explanation for the riots.

Conclusion

In summary, while by no means disputing that gangs can be involved variously in all the offences described here, it would be amiss to think that this involvement provides any clear confirmation of the gangland UK thesis. What this discussion has also sought to highlight is that in each one of these case studies, while gangs might have some involvement, it is by no means as significant as gang-talkers like to imagine. Not only is it the case, then, that gang involvement is heavily overstated, to truly understand the offence in question you would have to look beyond the gang to find an explanation. To put this another way, explanations advanced to explain any and all of the phenomena discussed above not only need to go beyond the gang but do not actually require foregrounding the gang as a key explanatory variable. This does not mean that we should simply forget about gangs, but we should regain some sense of proportion about them and their role in the aetiology of urban violence and crime. What this means on the one hand is not capitulating to variations of the worst-case scenario where some gang involvement in an offence leads to the offence in question being wholly blamed on gangs. It also means not falling into the trap of capitulating to populist gang-talking discourse which, as we shall see in Chapters 3 and 4, invariably functions this way. Most of all, it means putting gangs in their place, which is also an exercise in the art of not reifying a phenomena to the exclusion of other variables that possibly have greater explanatory potential – by no means, I accept, an easy act to perform in a society of paranoid gang-talkers.

2
The Fists and the Fury:
My Life in a Sea of Gangs

'Where have all the bootboys gone'
(Song lyrics by Slaughter and the Dogs, 1978)

It was not the first time I had been mugged but it was the worst. The crime location: a small back alley running off the Columbia Road in Shoreditch, London. Time: around 9pm in the evening of a brisk autumn night in September 2008. I was returning to my flat and the alley constituted a short cut. I didn't stand a chance. There were about ten of them, the oldest aged around 16–18 – but I recall seeing younger faces as well. Who were they? Bangladeshi boys, I suspect, from a local council estate.

'Give me your phone', demanded one of the older ones as they surrounded me. I remonstrated but to no avail. They weren't in the mood for talking. They had violence on their minds. Things happened quickly after that. I felt blows to my back and a fist in my face. I dropped to the ground and curled up; experience told me that this wouldn't last long. Kicks rained in but it was over quickly enough. They ripped my coat pocket open and stole my phone, my wallet and, in a spirit of pure malfeasance, the keys to my house. Then they ran off.

I stumbled to my feet, shaken, more in shock than pain, but bleeding quite heavily from my nose. I made my way to a nearby newsagent and the shopkeeper called the emergency services. A paramedic eventually arrived, looked at me and concluded what I already guessed; my nose was indeed broken and would need treatment. The police arrived but there was not much I could tell them. As they left to look for the culprits, one confided to me that when they caught up with the 'scumbags', they would leave them looking like me. I found myself smiling at the thought, which was reassuring because it told me my sense of humour was still intact – even if grinning was painful. I was subsequently taken to the local Accident and Emergency at Whitechapel Hospital to be deposited in a room full of other victims of London's brutal street world, many in a state far worse than mine. I waited for about three hours before a doctor found the time to tell me that, yes, my nose was indeed broken and would need reconstructive surgery at a later date. I was then told to leave. Would they at least help clean the blood off of me (I was covered in the stuff)? He agreed and a pleasant nurse turned up to help. I was then evicted on to the streets of the East End at around 2am with no house keys and in a considerable state of shock. But I was no longer their problem so my problems were no longer their concern.

I looked terrible. I had bloodshot eyes; heavy bruising around them, and my nose was pointing in altogether the wrong direction. Truth to tell, I resembled a street fighter, only not a particularly successful one. By a strange coincidence it was Halloween and in celebration young people across the city were dressing up in ghoulish apparel to mark the occasion. I didn't need to do anything as I looked quite scary enough; indeed, so scary that people actively moved out of my way as I approached them.

How, you might wonder, did I react to this? Did I feel vengeful? Had my liberal sensibilities evaporated in the face of this brutal, unprovoked assault? I knew from the moment I regained my feet, dripping blood, that I would need to make an existential choice. Either I would let anger and rage consume me, in which case, I reasoned, my assailants would have won. Or I wouldn't. I wasn't prepared to let them get to me and nor did I, so I let it go and got on with my life. My friends, I found, expressed instead the anger and indignation I was not prepared to allow myself to feel. I was touched.

Taken at face value this incident would certainly appear to provide pretty conclusive proof that urban street gangs exist today and more than that pose a serious risk and not only to themselves. Some may also find in this sad incident stark confirmation that gangs are indeed the 'new face of youth crime', as argued by John Pitts (2008). My victimisation, taken together with that of many others today would certainly confirm that group-based violence is a real and potent threat and needs to be taken seriously.

But just how novel and just how new is the gang threat? Was I confronting something new or have we been here before? As the work of Geoffrey Pearson reminds us, the British have a wonderful capacity for historical amnesia (Pearson 1983). A capacity, that is, for forgetting that the bad things we experience as novel today often have a long and established prehistory behind them; that the dystopian reveries that shape our representations of the present are also present in a past that is never quite as peaceful and pacific as fugitive memory discerns. When caught in the 'infinite novelty' of the present the wider continuities with the past are too often lost. And so it is, I will suggest, with the gangland UK thesis today.

One entirely legitimate way of demonstrating this would be to embark on a Pearsonesque journey of enquiry. To revisit the past and show how journalistic accounts of group deviance and delinquency in the postwar period were often explained as 'gang-related' at the time; or, alternatively, showing how group-related deviance in the past was experienced as presaging the arrival of terrible outbreaks of gangland violence the like of which British society had never witnessed before. This, for example, was certainly the case with the arrival of the Teddy boys in the 1950s, as headlines from the newspapers of the time will confirm. The arrival of the Rastas in the 1970s was also interpreted the same way.

But this is not the approach I intend to adopt here. Instead, my aim will be to present an auto-ethnography detailing my experience of growing up as a young man negotiating his way through environments where not only are 'gangs' a perennial part of the street furniture but where the risks of being beaten up by them constituted a very real and ongoing risk.

Before we get to this, however, a brief preamble on auto-ethnography, a method by and large absent from criminological enquiry but which commands a growing body of supporters elsewhere in the social sciences and humanities. Auto-ethnographies can be understood as a qualitative research method that aspires to combine the characteristic features of ethnography with that of autobiography. In conducting ethnography, researchers observe the lives of others in order to study their meanings, values and practices and, through this, their culture (Geertz 1973). Methodologically, this process involves taking detailed field notes, listing observations and conducting interviews with their research subjects. In an autobiography authors instead:

> retroactively and selectively write about their past experiences. Usually the author does not live through these experiences to make them part of a published document ; rather these experiences are assembled using hindsight ... Most often auto biographers write about 'epiphanies' – remembered moments perceived to have significantly impacted the trajectory of a person's life. (Ellis et al. 2011)

In an auto-ethnography the practices of autobiography and ethnography are combined in so much as auto-ethnographers 'retrospectively and selectively write about the epiphanies that stem from, or are made possible, being part of a culture and/or by emphasising a particular cultural identity' (ibid.). As in an autobiography, the researcher assembles elements of their past but with the proviso that, as with an ethnography, the elements assembled are subject to the rigour of social scientific conventions to ensure that when subjective experience is documented it is examined analytically (Ronai 1992).

As with any other historical survey, auto-ethnographies provide a record of past events, except that, whereas traditional historical approaches are written from the perspective of an outsider looking in, an auto-ethnography presents a similar narrative but with the addition that this is written from the perspective of the insider – the subject who experiences them. If we accept – as we should – cultural criminology's injunction that crime is a dramatic lived experience that requires deep phenomenological excavation (Ferrell et al. 2004), the auto-ethnographic method, as Ferrell notes, is a viable way of producing thick accounts of crime and deviance that foreground and recognise precisely this fact.

It could, of course, be objected here that a whole genre of crime-writing exists that is wholly biographical but which remains of dubious provenance given that its authors are often ex-gangsters. What makes their work interesting but questionable is that such accounts are typically written in ways that invariably sensationalise their subject matter and, not least, the lives of their narrators. There is also a tendency in such biographical accounts for the narrator (invariably the hero of their testimony) to reconstruct their biography in order to narrate a redemption narrative. In such accounts the hero's past life is invariably saturated with violence and sin before some life-transforming event propels them towards a future state of redemption. Could not the same problem reproduce itself in the case of auto-ethnographies such as the one I propose to conduct here?

While this is a relevant critique and one that needs to be addressed, the answer is no. As will become clear in the narrative that follows, the testimony I provide is not that of a hero but predominantly a (suitable) victim. Nor is this a redemption narrative or, indeed, a narrative that has any sense of a beginning, middle and end. I appear in the text as a spectator and participant in the events I describe, but most certainly was not an author of the violence that emanates from the groups that constitute the key focus of analysis. When I appear, it is rather like the tumbleweed that rolls across the desert, blown here and there by the winds of chance. My narrative simply records my contact with groups that have the hallmarks of gangs (as they are defined today) as I encountered them on my journey from childhood to adulthood, beginning in a village and then widening out to a number of different cities. I begin aged nine, growing up in a West Country village in England in the late 1960s. The narrative ends as I enter adulthood in Peterborough, a relatively small New Town in Cambridgeshire, in 1980. It is not my aim to sensationalise the world of gangs I describe or in any way to claim that my experiences are somehow unique and exceptional. Far from it. My account, I will hazard, will resonate with many young men, particularly those who derive from or live close to working-class areas and schools and who, in all probability, have also had to navigate their way through the same treacherous and often hazardous landscape that I will try and describe below. It is precisely in the mundanity of my experiences that the validity of my narrative and its criminological relevance will be revealed. Memory also plays tricks but my recall of the events, I would contend, is accurate. A good sociologist is invariably a voyeur by nature and inclination. I was always an avid spectator on the madness of the world and this preceded my formal training as a sociologist.

In the Beginning

I first became aware of gangs having been formally 'groomed' and then 'recruited' at the tender age of nine into the MMM, a self-defined street gang that had formed under the auspices of Monkey, its self-styled leader. I was at primary school at the time and the year would be 1969. The MMM claimed as its territory a patch of wasteland on the edge of Wick, a small village situated midway between Bristol and Bath. At the centre of its territory could be found a large corrugated-steel barn upon whose roof we would periodically assemble.

Well this is how my entry into the world of gangs would read if I were to adopt the vernacular of contemporary gang talk. The reality was somewhat different. A school friend of mine suggested one day that I might like to meet up with him and his mates near the barn where I could become a member of the MMM (or Monkey's Mighty Marauders, to give it its full title). I duly arrived to find several youngsters from the village milling around, most of whom were about my age, Monkey a few years older. The term 'Monkey', by the way, was a nickname accumulated on the basis that its owner had vaguely simian features. He did not appear to mind. My nickname at the time, for what its worth, was 'Boz' or 'Bozzle' and this was ascribed on the basis that a consensus had been reached that I read too many books (Bozzle Bookworm (obviously)). What exactly did this gang do? As I recall events, the answer to the question was: very little. We hung around the barn pondering deeply on what the destiny of the MMM might be and what its initials stood for. 'Monkey's Mad Men', I recall, was another alternative.

The life and times of the MMM, however, were shortlived. As I went to school one day I was approached by a local lad who lived in a council house at the end of our road which was otherwise dominated by small privately-owned bungalows, one of which I knew as home. He wanted to know if the MMM were prepared to do battle with the Mendip Hill Boys, so-called because they inhabited another council estate nearby on a road called, unsurprisingly, Mendip Hill. I can't remember the details of the conversation but it seems I somehow agreed to the challenge which I then subsequently forgot all about and which, to my everlasting shame, I never mentioned to the rest of the MMM. The Mendip Hill boys duly arrived that evening and duly trashed the MMM who put up no struggle. We were the soft products of the petty bourgeoisie, while the Mendip Hill Boys were tough working-class lads. In the melee that ensued (dominated by a lot of running away on my part) Monkey was kidnapped and beaten (but not too seriously). And that was the end of the MMM.

I was, I have to admit, a gauche, provincial child with absolutely no street awareness at all. And this innocence, I think, helps explain what happened when next I encountered the world of gangs. There was a disco at the local village hall and my friend Dave suggested I went along. The year is now 1970. When I arrived I found myself confronted by a group of young men who would not let me enter the Hall until I divulged my gang allegiance. Was I a supporter, they demanded to know, of the skinheads or grebos. I was, I have to admit, flummoxed, as I had no idea what a skinhead or a grebo was. Boxing clever (or so I thought), I asked them which group they were affiliated to. 'We're skinheads', they replied. Unsurprisingly and very quickly I also found myself to be an avid supporter of the skinheads. Only this was the wrong answer. 'Were not skinheads, we're grebos', they replied. I duly received a kicking and a lesson I would never forget into the mendacity of the grebo. Nor had the grebos quite finished with me. But before we get to this instalment in my life I must digress here and describe my entry into secondary education because it is entirely relevant to this narrative.

The Joys of Adolescence

I had the dubious honour of being a member of the first generation sent to what was known as a comprehensive school. The school in question had previously been known as Oldland Common Secondary Modern but had now been rebadged Sir Bernard Lovell Comprehensive (after the famous astrologer who had lived in the area but had not attended the local school), given a new set of buildings, and high hopes for the future were had by all. But as the American expression goes, 'You can take a child out of the ghetto but you can't take the ghetto out of the child', so the same applied to the school. As a secondary modern its mission was less the pursuit of academic excellence so much as providing a holding pen for the local working-class youth who lived on the huge council estates adjacent to the area; until, that was, they were old enough to be claimed by the local factories. Though the ethos was supposed to change now that we were part of the brave new world of comprehensives, this tradition still endured in what was, at heart, a tough working-class school.

The scene still remains engrained in my mind today, the vision I encountered in my first walk into the playground of my new school. Where, there, in the very middle of it, a group of bootboys adorned with Bristol Rovers football scarves, stood singing popular terrace anthems of the period with gusto, including the following, relayed in a broad Bristol accent:

When the red, red, robin comes bob, bob, bobbing around
Shoot the bastard, shoot the bastard

And:

We hate Bristol City and we hate T-Rex
We love Bristol Rovers and we all love sex
Walk with a wiggle and wiggle and a walk
Doin' the Tote End, Boot Walk ...

Concluded by way of a glorious finale (accompanied by clapping):

You're goin' to get yer fuckin' heads kicked in.
You're goin' to get yer fuckin' heads kicked in.

This group, which varied in composition on a day-to-day basis, were variously part of the youthful cohort of the Tote End Bootboys (the football hooligan element of Bristol Rovers); simultaneously, the younger element of the Banjo Island Boys, so named because at the heart of the local council estate from which the school predominantly drew its pupils, could be found a park shaped like a banjo. But their territorial affiliation could also extend to the school itself, which was in an eternal state of conflict with another local comprehensive known as the Grange (and every other local school, come to think of it). A perennial state of conflict also existed between the boys and the teachers whose tragic destiny it was to contain their innate propensity for violence to, at least, within manageable proportions.

This group, aged between 12 and 14, were aspiring to be mirror images of the older Banjo Island Boys who had built up quite a notorious reputation in the local area and beyond. They were the idols whose defiant pose they emulated and whose exploits they exalted. My first glimpse of this group, or part of it, also occurred shortly after I joined the school. I remember seeing a group of older lads walking menacingly across the playing fields, two swinging bog chains in their hands; what in contemporary gang talk would be considered their 'weapon of choice'. For the uninitiated, the 'bog chain' was so named because most public toilets then had cisterns high above the toilet and to flush them you pulled a chain. Given that they often had weighty handles attached, they also made excellent weapons for self-styled bootboys.

I also had a chance to witness the elders at our school in action, the context being away trips to various schools in order to play rugby. We were, to be frank, absolutely hopeless and lost miserably each time. But sport, I was given to understand, was not where the fun was to be had. On one occasion I remember standing outside one local school after yet another summary pulverising, when a group of our older boys arrived having left the changing rooms. We were briefly free from adult supervision and they took immediate advantage of the opportunity gifted to them by trashing the neatly planted flowerbeds nearby while heartily singing 'Tiptoe Through the Tulips'. I can't recall the lyrics, but they had been changed.

It was around this time (1972) that the Banjo Island Boys elected to invade my village in ostensive pursuit of the Mendip Hill Boys. I remember coming across them in the vicinity of the local village pub. Fortunately for me, a number of the younger people who had come along with them were from my school and vouched for me – which was a relief ('He be alright, Boz is a good un'). They had arrived in cars which indicates that the age range extended beyond 18. I clearly recall seeing one guy sitting in a car with a shotgun in his hands, the epitome of a 1970s gangster. Others hung around nearby: some carrying chains; some, clubs. Violence had been anticipated and they were ready for it. Fortunately, the Mendip Hill Boys had melted into the ether, so nothing subsequently happened.

By way of phenomenological detail these young men were dressed in the height of 1970s bootboy fashion: longish tangled hair and thick sideburns (for those that could grow them). Wide-lapelled shirts with strange designs; baggy leather jackets with wide lapels, large baggy trousers with side pockets with four- and sometimes five-button waistbands; and invariably Doc Martens or Chelsea boots. This really was 'life on Mars'. I know because I lived it.

Life then, as it is today, was nothing if not territorially grounded. You were known by reference to the area you came from, and being from the wrong area or, alternatively, in an area claimed by someone else, could entail violent repercussions. On one occasion, my friend Mark and I, whilst returning from a Rovers football game, were jumped by a group of young men from the St George's area of Bristol. Our error was simply to have strayed into their turf. More amusingly was the time I received a good kicking from a group of bootboys who cornered me after I left a nightclub in Keynsham Centre, an area adjacent to Cadbury Heath where my school was based. I would have been 16 at the time.

I found myself in the unfortunate position of being surrounded by a group of about six young men who again had violence on their minds. 'Where are you from?', they demanded to know. I told them 'Cadbury Heath', to which one responded that the Banjo Island Boys had beaten him up. This was clearly said with the implication that I was going to be made to pay. Sensing that someone from the moon would have beaten him up if that had been my home, I challenged him. 'Come on', I said (bravely), 'I'll take any one of you on in a one to one fight.' Without even pausing to consider my entirely reasonable offer, one immediately responded: 'We fight as a team.' Then they pounced. I received a good kicking and one that left me with two black eyes.

Summer and Easter holidays were times when people travelled, a few to hot and distant climes, while most stayed in their locality or went to nearby holiday resorts such as Weston-super-Mare. My mother instead took us to stay with our cousins in Birmingham. The city was then an industrial one and its core business was making cars. To signify its status as an important metropolis its city centre had been reconstructed in the spirit of postwar modernist brutalism, and in the shadow of the Bull Ring (as it was called) strange tribes proliferated.

One day (we are now in 1973) I found myself playing by the side of a canal with my cousin Martin and several of his friends. We could have been no more than 12 or 13 years old at the time. Out of nowhere a young man appeared breathless and in a wonderful Midlands accent relayed the dreadful news:

Better run, the grebos are comin'.

Exhibiting what I would like to think of as a fledgeling interest in the sociology of deviance, instead of running away (as everyone else was) I moved towards where he had told us the threat was coming from. There in all their glory, sure enough, was that tribe now lost to memory: a gang of grebos. There were about twelve in number, walking towards me in a single, flat, extended line. They also had violence on their minds. They wore a very distinctive uniform. Blue flared jeans, long greasy hair, white T-shirts, black biker jackets and biker boots. As soon as they saw me the chase was on. They were about three or four years older and I was quickly captured. They also grabbed my cousin. We were knocked around a bit but not too badly. Then they made off looking for more victims. They also took my cousin's bike, which we found a little later having been partially dismantled and well and truly trashed. This upset Martin who had recently been given it brand new as a birthday present. I was beginning to hate grebos ...

Jock Young has recently argued that one of the problems with criminology is that it paints an unduly dark picture of the lives of young working-class men who are often its object of analysis (J. Young 2011). Where, he demands, is the recognition of youthful pleasure; recognition of the humour and fun that saturates the lives of deviants who are never quite as miserable and excluded as much criminology suggests? So let me set the record straight here. The boys whose lives I describe were not desperate, nor, for the most part, was their violence driven forward by psychological defects. Yes, they could be violent and clearly many sought to accomplish proficiency in its exercise. Their masculinity demanded it; working-class culture meanwhile excused, reproduced and legitimated it. But there was generally a good-humoured rumbustious aspect to the violence they inflicted. Yes, they would give you a good kicking, but there was typically a sense of humour attached as well. Their violence was not so much wilful crime, it was a leisure pursuit, a space where they found a welcome break from the mundane disciplines imposed within institutions such as the school and the factory through which their lives predominantly unfolded. In their violence a liminal space was created where they could spectacularly break free from the routine monotony of everyday life; here they could embrace and excel in what Jack Katz terms 'the ways of the bad-ass' (Katz 1988). And by and large their violence was contained. Established codes of the street typically precluded the idea that you would continue to kick someone when they were down; hitting girls was frowned upon; fists were used more than the weapons they sometimes sported, and 'beef' was largely contained to each other.

Get Pissed, Destroy

We are now in 1977; punk had arrived and within its extended family I had finally found myself a home. Punk was not some movement I joined, nor was it ever something I was 'recruited' to. I experienced my participation from the beginning as a vacation. Its aggression and anarchic impulses resonated immediately with my own sense of alienation from a society whose authority structures and pointless rituals I was already beginning to detest. Johnny Rotten's enigmatic sign-off line at the end of 'Anarchy in the UK' just about said it all:

Get pissed, destroy.

It was a liberating mantra. It distinguished us totally from the wreckage of the 1960s 'summer of love' along with all the 'hippy shit' that surrounded it; it also put us head to head with the strange, weird, fucked-up place I knew as England. And it was pretty fucked up, at least to my way of reasoning. A pointless queen was going to celebrate a pointless jubilee, and a nation of pointless people wanted to celebrate it with her in the context of a society that was at that time quite literally falling to pieces. The British, I came to reason, were born to be slaves and this active complicity in their own subjugation just about summed them up. I hated it all. I hated them all.

Trouble was, where to live and how to avoid the threat of violence that being part of a subculture whose *raison d'être* was to piss everyone else off left as its legacy. Straight society would ban us from its pubs and clubs; gangs of bootboys, Teds, skinheads and squaddies, meanwhile (true to their calling), would attack us on sight, and not least try and disrupt gigs, a number of which would terminate in horrendous violence. I can vividly remember seeing a sign posted on the side of local clubhouse called the 'Slab' then used by the local Hell's Angels chapter. It carried an uncompromising message: 'Any punk found on these premises will be shot.' I also recall a pitched battle between the proto-feminist punk band the Slits and a group of bootboys who had invaded their gig.

Strange as it might seem, it would be the Hell's Angels who would resolve the question of where I was going to live (at least for a while), while also providing me with the opportunity to reflect on the structure of drug-dealing gangs of the 1970s. But let me give a bit of background here to explain how things came to this strange impasse.

My dad had been made redundant in 1977 and in pursuit of work had taken up a position in Peterborough, a small provincial town I had never heard of, and, to be honest, didn't want anything to do with. I, meanwhile, had just enrolled on a course of A levels at my local school. Given that relations with my parents were already pretty tense, they agreed to let me stay at the home of *aged distant relatives* in Bristol while I completed my studies. Retrospectively, it might not have been one of their best decisions. Testosterone was kicking in and punk had arrived. My life was changing and new priorities beckoned. Ian Dury and the Blockheads would encapsulate them superbly in their classic 1977 anthem:

Sex and drugs and rock and roll
It's all your brain and body need
Sex and drugs and rock and roll
It's very good indeed.

The immediate problem I faced was not that of recognising how necessary these infinitely desirable goods were but – more pressingly – how to gain access to them. Sex was never quite the readily available resource my adolescent self desperately aspired to gain access to and disappointment haunted my fumbling endeavours far more than the occasional success that came my way. Rock and roll was fine, only I never had any money to afford the records. Drugs certainly appealed, but where to get hold of them in a cultural milieu where drug use was by no means normalised?

Step forward my wonderful bohemian friend Melissa and her friends the Hell's Angels. The background context, my being evicted from the home of aged distant relatives for indescribable behaviour that need not detain us further. This situation had the unfortunate knock-on consequence of rendering me homeless in Bristol. So there I found myself one evening, one day, in a local hostelry musing tragically on my future (or lack of it) when out of nowhere appeared Melissa. She suggested I came to stay with her. She was then living with an older ex-Hell's Angel. Having no other option available to me, I readily agreed.

I subsequently met her partner, who appeared (strange as it might seem), well disposed to me; as indeed did the tribe of biker boys and Hell's Angels who variously lived in his house (there were comings and goings all the time in what was a very mobile and shifting population). Though they were very much a group of outsiders (in Becker's (1964) sense of the word), by and large the truth of the matter was that this was a group that had fallen on hard times. Their lives as glorious outlaws riding stripped-back Harley-Davidsons across the highways and byways of England was by and large over; only the myth of the good times remained. Middle age was beckoning and none of them had jobs or wanted them. They lived off benefits and exploited the welfare system to the limit. In a low-wage economy they supplemented their meagre income through hustling and engaging in various scams. One involved selling household goods to bored housewives on the basis that the disabled had produced the goods. I was quite good at this. But far and away their greatest source of extra income came through drug dealing. They also consumed a great deal of the produce that they traded with which, I suspect, diminished their profit margins considerably.

One direct consequence of this entrepreneurialism was that I, a 17-year-old punk, found myself spending the best part of two months totally stoned and permanently high-wired. It was a hell of an education but not quite of the kind that would see me through my A levels. It was also an education in the art of drug dealing. First off, these were not high-level dealers. They sat somewhere in the lower-middle tier. Marijuana was the key drug of choice, though at times they also dealt acid and speed. Though I think it fair to say that Mellissa's partner commanded the most authority, he was not in any real sense an active leader. It was more a cooperative affair. Though much is made today of new corporate-style gangs (with elders running youngers, running tinies) (Pitts 2008), the group I was living with had no corporate structure at all. Nor, looking back, can I imagine why they would need one. As is the case today, they were a loose network plugged into a larger distributed network that defined Britain's then burgeoning drugs economy.

Though at the group's edges people came and went, there did appear to be a core group present most of the time and this group spent a lot of time trying to identify where next to score. They did not rely on one source but potentially many. Issues of availability and cost were key factors in the decision to pool money together to purchase a weight of dope. This was then cut and sold on down the drug chain, mostly to known users in what remained at heart a closed, as opposed to open, marketplace. Though dealing was regular and brought in an income, it most certainly was not enough to raise the standard of living of this group beyond their bohemian roots.

This all occurred in the days before skunk had been invented along with the hydroponic revolution that made it all possible. Dope in the 1970s by and large came in three forms. At the bottom of the tree could be found Moroccan hash. The best of this was known as 'Sputnik'. In the middle was Red Lebanese, so called because of its red hue. It was more pliable than Moroccan, which tended to be quite hard. Top of the tree was Afghan Black which was black and very pliable. Together with Jamaican Semsimilla and Asian opiated Tie Sticks (which occasionally appeared), this stuff at its best could induce something quite close to a hallucinogenic trip. Today Afghan Black and Red Lebanese no longer figure in the UK drugs market. The Israelis destroyed the dope industry when they invaded Lebanon. Thereafter, the Bekka valley where the dope had been produced harvested opium. The same went for Afghanistan, now a net exporter of heroin to the Western markets.

Into the Eighties

Not long afterwards, devoid of money, A Levels, and any sense of what I was going to do in life, I made my way to Peterborough. Eventually I found a job and rented a flat prior to an eventual move to Brixton in London. Peterborough then was a small provincial market town that was reinventing itself as a New Town. To signify its new status, its enlightened planners literally ripped the heart out of its old city and build a huge not to say brash new shopping mall in its place. This would provoke local punk band The Now to release their superb 1977 single 'Development Corporations' ('they're changing the face of the nation'). As with Birmingham, strange tribes proliferated in the shadow of its regenerated centre. A walk on Saturday morning in 1980, for example, would bring any would be flaneur directly into contact with a spectacular array of British subcultures, and these veered from the ornate and flamboyant to the far more dangerous and lethal varieties.

Occupying the city square were the biker boys (with motorbikes) and their grebo cousins (without bikes). Long hair, leather biker jackets and jeans – this was their uniform. Not too far away, standing in the vicinity of the Eight Bells pub (and within it) you would find the local skinheads. They came shaven-headed and wore the ubiquitous uniform of rolled-up straight jeans, Ben Sherman shirts, Doc Martens boots, braces and Harrington jackets. Both of these subcultures had a capacity for violence; the skinheads a highly developed capacity, as we shall see. Enveloped by the new mall was another of Peterborough's pubs, known as The Still. It had a number of bars. Hippies and various survivors of the 1960s' generation occupied one of the bars and the punks another. In its car park an interesting piece of graffiti remained for many years which read 'The Destructors kill music'. The Destructors were another punk band and they did indeed 'kill music'. The punks were far and away the most creative and flamboyant of the various tribes and their local music scene was, to say the least, vibrant. Members of this tribe plus local drug-takers could also be found in the vicinity of the Gladstone Arms mingling with the local Rastas. Various New Romantics could also be found in the vicinity, many heavily influenced by David Bowie. Walking through the city centre, clutching Adidas bags and wearing outrageously baggy pants, were the soulboys, preparing to head north to Wigan where, strung out on amphetamine, they would dance the night away. The year is now 1980 and the sheer biodiversity of subcultures was startling.

Another group also needs to be added to the mix here; this is not a subculture but it deserves a mention given the focus of this chapter, which is on gangs. Again, resident in a number of the local pubs could be found groups of squaddies home on leave. They also sported short haircuts. They also moved in groups. They were also trained in violence and in my experience were prepared to mobilise it against anyone and everyone who looked remotely different.

It is important not to overstate the number of young people involved in these subcultures; they certainly stood out, but the numbers involved were generally small. They lived out the round of their lives in the vicinity of the straight world of 'normal' people, who strangely enough looked pretty strange given that they were also adorned in the height of seventies fashion. Flared trousers, wide-lapelled shirts and jackets, to list only some of the abominations in this, the decade that style forgot. Against them, the punks, despite the spikey haircuts and bondage gear they sported, were an altogether more stylish outfit; and it would be their penchant for straight or drainpipe trousers and thin-lapelled jackets that would set the style scene for the next decade.

At this point some might well be wondering why I am describing subcultures here when the subject of this chapter is gangs, but there is a reason for this. If by 'gangs' we mean discernible groups known to themselves and to others and for whom crime and or violence is, in some crucial sense, intrinsic to their identity and practice, then in my mind there is no doubt at all that many of the groups I have tried to describe here fit this definition very clearly – even if they did not see themselves and were not at the time formally defined as gangs.

Take the skinheads as a case study. They congregated in groups and these groups were, at heart, street-fighting units. They certainly affiliated to the far right (some more than others) and Holocaust denial came as part of the package, as indeed did a pronounced animosity to migrants. But violence was the crucial currency in which they traded and they valorised it. Their very social presentation of self was cultivated in a way that left you in no doubt at all that these were people you did not want to mess around with. And their violence could be explosive.

My first real encounter with skinhead violence took place at one of the many Anti-Apartheid Festivals in London in the late 1970s. I was still in Bristol at the time and had travelled up in one of many coaches to take part. I remember finding myself standing near a group of Chelsea skinheads when the Tom Robinson Band took to the stage and sang what remains one the great protest songs of the age 'Glad to be Gay'. The skinheads went berserk, attacking the people around them while aiming a barrage of beer cans and bottles at the stage. Later in Peterborough I watched them attack the fans of another New Wave band called The Lurkers. There was nothing political about it, violence is what they did and they enjoyed doing it. It was their currency, their stock-in-trade.

Their propensity for violence was brought powerfully home at an event I was also instrumental in organising entitled 'An Alternative Evening', which we convened at the local theatre in Peterborough. We sought to bring together avant-garde, New Wave bands of the time including Sudden Sway and Ersatz, with Art House cinema and, if I recall matters, poetry. The event was very successful and attracted an audience primarily drawn from the cities more flamboyant subcultures. The local Drug Squad also put in an appearance but unfortunately their attempt at anonymity was rather spoiled given the fact that they stood out like a sore thumb as they were anything but alternative. Unfortunately, the skins also put in an appearance and brought the event to a halt when they initiated their own riot, having taken offence at some of the shop mannequins we had assembled. They were black.

Later that year, together with some of my friends, we went into the Eight Bells pub in the city centre as part of a wider pub crawl in celebration of Christmas. I was standing at the bar waiting to be served and found myself next to a skinhead. He was half-cut but friendly. 'Come on,' he said, 'have a drink.' I said no, but he took it personally. He was, he said 'only being friendly'. I accepted. He wanted me to join his friends. It was Christmas, after all. Gripped by the weirdness of the situation I relented, thinking 'Whatever.' His friends were also skinheads, by no means people I would ever willingly elect to have anything to do with. There were five of them and they were well on the road to inebriation. They were also friendly, albeit in a way very peculiar to the skinhead.

I drank my whisky, thanked them and got up to leave. I was told I needed another drink. I remonstrated, but one of the skins sitting next to me put his arm around my shoulders and sat me down. 'We're all friends here', he said, but with a vague tone of menace. So there I sat while another skin went to bar and came back with another round. The same thing happened when I tried to leave, with the consequence that I felt compelled to sit through three more rounds bound to this band of brothers by the implicit threat that leaving their company just might be read as an honour slight. I began to feel desperate and somewhat concerned for my safety. How in the name of hell was I going to escape the clutches of this bunch of psychopaths who were now trying to explain to me (now a dear friend and supporter of the skinhead movement worldwide) how I could access men with guns in London? As we were drinking neat spirits, the rate of inebriation escalated. Eventually they brought a final round, then, at a signal, ran drunkenly for the exit, lacking the money necessary to pay for their drinks. I escaped in the melee that ensued. Johnny Rotten once famously observed, 'Never trust a hippy', to which I would also add 'Never take a drink with a skinhead.'

As I observed above, the biker boys were not adverse to a bit of the old ultra-violence. Shortly after I moved to Peterborough, I helped organise a series of discos at a local village hall. This enterprise came to a dramatic halt when a group of bikers turned up in a van which they then parked across the door of the entrance (so nobody could leave). They then invaded the hall, kicking all and everyone that opposed them. They had come in search of someone who had crossed them. They kicked him unconscious with the result that an ambulance was required to take him to hospital. The place was covered in blood.

Finally, in the context of a country that appears to be witnessing an unpleasant surge in militarism as this chapter is being written, let me conclude this narrative by saying something very briefly about the squaddies and my contact with them. In many respects they were not that different to the skinheads. They also sported short haircuts, they banded together in groups, they were innately reactionary and, like the skinheads, also valorised violence. And like the skins, you didn't need to do anything ostensibly wrong to provoke it.

I had a rather unpleasant experience with squaddies at another gig in Peterborough when my friend and I were threatened by three of them. They had, they explained, just arrived back from Northern Ireland. They had taken offence to the fact that we were wearing American-style combat trousers. We were lucky: things didn't kick off, but it was a close-run thing. The New Wave band that was playing at the time was not so lucky. The squaddies subsequently attacked them and two of its members were hospitalised. I subsequently ran into one of the thugs responsible. He was, he said, 'sorry', but in justification claimed that he and his friends were upset because two of their army colleagues had recently been shot dead by the IRA. As a technique of neutralisation, it didn't really wash.

Periodically things went the other way. I recall finding myself walking out of a chip shop with Rob, a New Wave friend of mine who was dressed at the time in a spectacular zoot suit and who sported died orange hair. A group of biker boys walked up and stood in front of us, blocking our way. 'Give us a chip, punky', one said to Rob. Looking the biker in the eye he slowly put a chip into his mouth, chewed it for a moment and spat it onto the ground in front of him. 'Eat that, sucker.' To this day it remains one of the coolest things I have ever seen. We were lucky to escape with our lives.

Conclusion

What, then, is the criminological significance of this exercise in gonzo criminology? Do my impressionistic reminiscences count for anything? Can this subjectivist account even be trusted?

Let me deal with the last point first. There is, I would contend, no reason not to trust them. I have not tried to narrate anything other than events I personally witnessed and experienced. I have not tried to sensationalise these events nor am I making any claim at all that in any sense they were exceptional. As I hope would have become clear, I am not a hero. For the most part I am a victim or a witness to other people being victimised by groups of young men for whom collective violence constituted part of their everyday reality. And I must emphasise here that there is nothing glamorous or exciting about the violence I witnessed. The perpetrators may well be experiencing some of the 'seductions of evil', but as victims of it, we, by and large, were not.

Auto-ethnographic accounts have gained respectability in areas such as the performing arts and humanities. It has gathered a momentum in sociology more generally but remains very much a minority pursuit and a contested one; often rejected as soft, subjective and as lacking rigour and objectively by positivists, and by some ethnographers as little better than a lazy exercise in navel-gazing (Madison 2006). This indeed, was precisely how Jeff Ferrell's auto-ethnographic work on scrunge culture was received – condemned by some as little better than pure subjectivism (O'Brian, 2005).

Criminology, however, has much to gain by engaging with it and cultural criminology leads the way here (Ferall 2012). Its use would certainly help some criminologists of the present think more carefully about the uniqueness of present events before advancing claims to the effect that gangs represent the 'new face of youth crime'.

While Pearson has recently sought to challenge this thesis on the grounds that we are looking today at little more than a contemporary reiteration of fears about gangs that echo 'respectable fears' that have a long prehistory (Pearson 2011); and while historians have pointed to the presence in the past of large organised gangs that appear to resemble contemporary gangs in crucial respects, this has not been the approach I have sought to adopt here. By adopting instead an auto-ethnographic method, I have sought to show that, far from being a unique product of our present, the kinds of group-based violence today being identified as gang-related, constitute a longstanding, perennial, deeply embedded feature of street life in British society. Its contemporary novelty, as such, is significantly overstated.

In this respect, at least, Malcolm Klein is right when he argues that European societies are in denial of a gang problem that has always been around (Klein 2001). Yes, indeed, they have always been present, as my endemic exposure to and experience of territorially-affiliated street-fighting groups over the space of two decades, signifies. Nor are the groups I have tried to describe here rare. As I have tried to show, by relaying my experiences of them in three cities over two decades, such groups constitute an intrinsic part of working-class culture and working-class street life in England. There are, in other words, far more continuities as opposed to discontinuities in urban street life.

If we take the various facets of gang life and culture currently identified as novel, then for the most part it is not. Take violent territorialism. This is reported today as new and disturbing phenomena. It even has a new label to describe it: 'postcode wars'. As I have documented above, however, variations of this have always been around. The language used to denote it might have changed but that is all. As my experience of living with the bikers also demonstrates, drug dealing was also a commodity that was traded in by groups that today would, without doubt, be described as gangs. As to the idea that gangs are now targeting schools in new and sinister ways, then again as my experience of growing up in a working-class school testifies, groups of street-fighting kids with violence on their minds were always already there. Finally, are the groups described as gangs today more violent than their historical predecessors? The issue of weapons I will touch upon below. In relation to issues of prevalence and inclination I would suggest that the gangs of skinheads I encountered were every bit as violent as the violent urban street gangs that rove the streets of our inner cities today.

So what explains this culture of denial? A number of reasons need to be posed to address this. First off, we are living through a moral panic about gangs (Hallsworth 2011a) which we will subsequently explore in Chapter 4. In such times a sense of proportion is evicted in a world where gang-talking fantasies prevail while the reality principle gets lost (Cohen 1972; Hall, Critcher et al. 1978). It could also be the case, however, that the sheer ubiquity of the groups and the violence they did paradoxically helps render them invisible. As Alfred Schulz observed long ago, we tend not to notice and easily overlook what is always present in our everyday life-world (Shultz and Luckmann 1973). Taken together with the fact that many of the groups I have described were not described as gangs, nor for the most part saw themselves as gangs, this helps explain in part the historical amnesia British society is currently experiencing.

None of this is to suggest that the gang situation as we experience it today is not in some respects different. Between the 1970 and 1980s the groups I describe wore highly distinctive uniforms, and ones that clearly distinguished one subculture from another (Hall and Jefferson 1976). Today, the aesthetics and styles of black ghetto culture predominantly shape and define the uniform and style of urban street gangs today. While the groups I have described were certainly capable of ultra-violence, by and large their violence was delimited by established street codes with longstanding histories in what remained, until recently, stable working-class communities. My suspicion (based on significant research) is that today, this situation has changed and is changing.

As working-class communities have fragmented and as the new precariat has grown (Wacquant 2008), the moral force of established street codes has withered to the extent that violence is no longer delimited to the same extent. As one young man in Hackney explained,

'The thing about violence rules is that there aren't any.' (Hallsworth and Silverstone 2009). More weapons such as guns are also making their way into the hands of volatile, immature gang-affiliated young men, and this coupled with their engagement in the ultra-violent retail end of the heroin and crack economy has created, I would suggest, the preconditions for a surge in lethal violence that was not routinely seen in the past (ibid.).

Finally, whereas the group-based violence for the young men whose lives I have tried to document here constituted an extension of leisure in a world where their will to violence would be contained and end as they entered the world of work, I am not sure the same applies today in a post-full-employment society where such orderly transitions of adulthood are no longer assured for the burgeoning precariat (Standing 2011). For some young men, there might not be an orderly transition into adulthood; more a prolonged drift between adolescence and adulthood in a low-wage, low-skills economy, where the presence of stabilising forces such as stable working-class jobs are notable by their absence (Hall et al. 2008). In such a context the violence I predict will become more volatile and potentially lethal. In a world where more people than ever before carry valuable goods like smartphones, I will also predict that violent street robbery will be the form through which much of the violence is channelled. Gangs will invariably be blamed.

By contesting the alleged 'novelty' of the gang situation today through the vehicle of an auto-ethnography, my aim has both been to introduce a new method into a discipline which could, I will suggest, gain much by embracing it. At the same time, in reflecting on my personal experiences of growing up and around groups that have all the hallmarks of being gangs, my aim has been to contest in a new way the current debate about the alleged novelty of gangs today.

Part Two
On Gang Talk and Gang-Talkers

3
Deciphering Gang Talk

We are back in England yet again, it's August 2011 and London is burning. The police have managed to shoot dead yet another black male in dubious circumstances and across the city thousands of people have taken to the streets. The resulting disorder unfolds for a further four days as the riots reach out beyond London to take hold in cities across the country. It would be the worst outbreak of urban disorder England had witnessed in decades. Someone or something had to be blamed and it was not going to be the police. Within three days of the riots the Prime Minister, David Cameron, convened a press conference and identified 'gangs' as the criminal masterminds responsible for organising the riots, and 'gang culture' the background cause. Put together, these were responsible for what he went on to identify as a 'major criminal disease that has infected streets and estates across our country'.

> At the heart of all the violence sits the issue of the street gangs. Territorial, hierarchical and incredibly violent, they are mostly composed of young boys, mainly from dysfunctional homes. They earn money through crime, particularly drugs and are bound together by an imposed loyalty to an authoritarian gang leader. (Cameron 2011)

Lets go back in time now to 2007 where Hurricane Katrina, obeying every prediction that had been made about such an event, swept into New Orleans, breaching its levees, burying the city beneath an avalanche of water. If this was a tragedy for the city it was an even greater tragedy for the city's poorest black community whose neighbourhoods were devastated by the resulting floods that would also go on to claim many lives. Only this would be a tragedy with a difference because within 24 hours of the levees being breached, the worst humanitarian crisis the United States had experienced in recent decades became discursively reconstructed instead into a crisis of law and order. Instead of recognising the black population as victims cruelly abandoned by a federal government seemingly impervious to their plight, a dominant theme in the reporting of Katrina was of black looters, armed black gangs on the rampage and black rapists. And the power of this 'gang talk' was so powerful that when the authorities eventually returned to the abandoned city; it returned more as an invasion force than a rescue effort.

Two very different events, but each unified by the fact that, in both cases, versions of 'gang talk' were mobilised to make sense of them. Not only did gang talk establish the definitional narrative, as we have seen, reality was then (re)ordered around it: in the case of New Orleans, troops were sent in to reclaim the drowned city from its gangs, while, in the immediate aftermath of the riots not caused by gangs, the British government developed a gang-suppression policy as its response

These two cases are graphic but by no means unusual examples of events where 'gang talk' has come to provide the interpretative grid by and through which divergent social problems are rendered legible, even when the events in question are by no means solely or even remotely gang-related. In the US the gang has been equated with the terrorist threat, the illegal drugs trade, and global crime more generally. In the UK, media hysteria has seen the gang blamed for everything (as we have seen) from outbreaks of dangerous dogs, to the mass rape and sexual abuse of women, to most shootings and, not least, the organisation of the illegal drugs trade.

The sensational and often hysterical coverage the gang has received has by no means remained absent from the radar of critical scholars. Dwight Conquergood was one of the first commentators to draw attention to the criminalising rhetoric at play in the way gangs were being represented and the criminalising functions such a discourse performed.

> In the public sphere, the label gang is a thickly layered represen-
> tational screen onto which powerful and contradictory images are
> projected. The term gang powerfully cathects and conjures middle
> class fears and anxieties about social disorder, disintegration
> and chaos, that are made palpable in these demonized figures of
> inscrutable, unproductive, predatory, pathological alien Others
> lurking in urban shadows and margins, outside the community of
> decent people. (Conquergood 1991: 4)

In his own reflection on the way the gang was represented, not least, within the academy of American gang researchers, Jack Katz also observed the disjunction between the way the gang was being narrated in official discourse and a street reality that was very different (Katz and Jackson 1997). The 'gang', he argued, appeared less a descriptive term identifying groups out there in the street, but appeared instead as a 'transcendental evil' into which wholly disparate social problems could be unproblematically folded. In the UK, Claire Alexander has also pursued a similar theme. The term 'gang', she observes, is one heavily saturated with a cultural and not least racial baggage from which it is difficult to disentangle (Alexander 2008).

Given the seductive appeal of gang talk and the sheer variety of social problems it is now deployed to explain, a case could be made for exploring its nature further, and this will constitute the focus of this chapter: its aim, to build upon and develop the insights of Conquergood, Katz and Alexander by seeking to decipher the enigmatic discourse, gang talk. To explore this 'garrulous discourse' the chapter addresses two questions: 'What are the defining characteristics of gang talk?' and 'Why is this discourse so seductive?' It concludes by looking at some of its unintended consequences.

Gang talk, I will argue, constitutes a free-floating discourse that can operate wholly independently of gang realities as these unfold in any street context. In constitution, it can be considered a *conspiracy discourse* produced by those who do not live gang realities but have a vested interest in gang lives and gang worlds. Gang talk is thus a discourse that reflects what, following Lefebvre, I propose to term *representations of the street* not *street representations* as gang members produce them.

Gang talk is a discourse that possesses a determinate structure. It constitutes, as such, what Wittgenstein would designate a 'language game' replete with its own vocabulary and rules of composition; rules that gang-talkers intuitively iterate and reiterate in the gang talk they produce. Gang talk is organised around several common self-reinforcing tropes about gangs and how they are imagined to develop, and these can be narrated and recognised by gang-talkers without any of them ever having to have met a gang member or a gang in their lives. Gang talk, then, can reveal the 'truth' of 'gangs' wholly independently of any empirical confirming evidence.

Gang talk is seductive precisely because of the performative role it plays and by reference to the primal and powerful archetypes it harnesses. This is not a discourse that lends itself to disconfirmation because, as we shall establish, gang talk operates through iteration and confirmation. It is seductive precisely because it is performative. It is popular because the archetypes it trades in are timeless and because it provides a seemingly plausible narrative about the way things are. At the same time it is also a discourse of power and must also be understood in terms of the ideological role it plays in stabilising a post-welfare neoliberal security state and its constituent social relations.

Defining Gang Talk

By 'gang talk' I mean to designate a discourse about gangs that has wide currency. It is a discourse that operates to make meaningful the world of gangs both to those who produce this discourse and to others who are receptors of it. By and large, the producers of gang talk (hereafter 'gang-talkers') are those with a vested interest in gangs (of some sort) but who are not of the world of gangs they talk about. They may be journalists looking for a good story about them, enforcement agencies that want to suppress them, practitioners on the hunt for gang suppression money, the public who are scared of them, academics wanting to study them, or policy-makers who have been given the mission of developing anti-gang strategies.

These are people who, by and large, do not belong to the street world of gangs they want to talk about and who, consequently, have a distance from this world. They produce, as such, and to evoke the language of Lefebvre, *representations of the street* not *street representations* as those who live gang realities produce them (Lefebvre 1991). This disjunction is important but often lost on gang-talkers who imagine *their* world and the world of gang members is, in some sense, cognate. It is not. Gang-talkers, therefore, occupy a very different discursive space from those who live *gang realities*. Those who live gang realities at the same time live their gang realities in very different terms than the gang talk that gang-talkers produce about them. Gang talk as such constitutes a discourse of power because gang-talkers are primary definers of deviance and their interpretations predominate over street representations which are silenced or alternatively translated into versions of gang talk.

Just as it is important to distinguish *representations of the street* from *street representations* so it is important to distinguish the order of representations from the world of *street practices* (see Figure 3.1). This is a material reality populated by social relations within and between groups (gangs and others), relations that are in perpetual movement. This order is not directly legible either to those who live gang realities or to gang-talkers who want to comprehend the street world where gangs dwell. Gang talk does not capture this reality because what it typically trades in are idealistic representations of the street. While gang-talkers might well respond that they in fact trade in street representations, having spoken to gang members, their epistemological illiteracy blinds them to the fact that when asked to narrate their gang realities ('Tell me about your gang please') what they tend to get back is more gang talk.

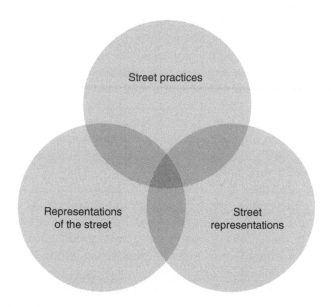

Figure 3.1   Ontologising the street

Source: Author.

Rather than engage with gang talk as a discourse that is mistaken about its object (they are wrong about the gang for this or that reason), or see it as the product of a moral panic that exhibits moral panic features (over-reaction to an event, sensational coverage, the pathologising of an enemy (Cohen 1972; Goode and Ben-Yehuda 1994)), I would suggest that more can be gained by examining gang talk as an imaginary discourse that best exhibits the desire production of its producers. Gang talk, at least as I intend to approach it, can thus best be read and studied as a collective control fantasy that reveals the predilections, anxieties and desires of its producers more than the truth of the street it aspires to represent.

Reading Gang Talk as a Language Game

If we consider the literary genre of fantasy-writing, evoked in novels and cinema such as *The Lord of the Rings* trilogy, then what we find distinctive about it is that the worlds in which the novels are set are not just fictional but literally fantastic (Butler 2009). These are imaginary worlds often populated by imaginary beings set in parallel worlds or worlds set in some remote time. These are magical places populated by magical beings, but at the same time they also possess recognisably human attributes which are what make them familiar to us.

Gang talk, I would suggest, is not unlike the fantasy genre insofar as it does not capture the reality of gang practices, but rather a fantasised representation of them. These are found materialised in various journalistic accounts, press releases, academic articles, reports and statements about gangs. Gang talk, like fantasy fiction, is an imaginary construction which reflects gangs less as they are, and more how they are imagined to be; where what is imagined represents the phantasmagorical desires of gang-talkers. This is why, as we shall see, the gang, as gang talk constructs it, has a sensational appearance that has little to do with a material reality that is often more mundane. As we shall also observe, gang talk is also populated by similar tropes to those reproduced in fantasy fiction, particularly in its evocation of a world reduced in Manichaean terms to Evil subterranean multitudes that are on the rise and which must be vanquished by those of the Good.

To study gang talk then we need methodologically to treat it as a self-enclosed, self-referential discourse that has a distinctive structure we need to interpret. To study this we need to look at how the gang is imagined and positioned within this discourse. The first point to note is that gang talk is a conspiracy discourse; one that coalesces around a perspective on gangs where they are presumed to be a potent threat and one that is growing. Gang talk, then, is an unending paranoiac rumination about the evil gangs represent and pose in the process of their mutant development. Within this discourse, as we shall observe, seemingly innocuous events and activities assume the most sinister dimensions. In this world gangs do not spontaneously form, they 'recruit' and 'groom' instead; they do not communicate, they engage in 'branding exercises'. In David Garland's terms, to study gang talk is thus to engage with what he terms 'the criminology of the other' because it is as 'Other' that the gang is imagined (Garland 1996). The question I now want to pose here is what precisely is it that is 'Other' about them?

To address this, it pays to think of gang talk as a language game in Wittgenstein's (1953) sense; that is, as a primitive language defined by common terms and bound by common rules that define the permissible moves that any player (gang-talker) can make in the gang talk they produce. As a language game, gang talk is composed of a series of mutually self-reinforcing tropes. Each reflects a particular 'truth' about the gang and the alleged pattern of its development. There are, I will suggest, six that require consideration (though that said, there may well be many more). These may be studied under the following headings:

- *Novelty:* They were not here but now they are and we have never seen their like before.
- *Proliferation:* They were few but now they are many. Now they are multitude.
- *Corporatisation:* Until recently they were disorganised but now they are organised and organising as we speak.
- *Weaponisation:* Their violence was once manageable but as they organise they appropriate and possess ever more terrifying 'weapons of choice'.
- *Penetration:* They may emerge in particular areas but over time they expand to penetrate and colonise new settings (they are out to get us!!!).
- *Monstrousness:* Gang members may look like 'normal' people but they are essentially different. 'Here be monsters ...'

For the most part the evidence I adduce to explore and substantiate these elements of gang talk is derived from the UK experience. As a case study the UK is relevant because it has been undergoing a moral panic about gangs for some years now. As with other moral panics, the gang has found itself at the centre of moral outrage from a state that has now delegated an array of alarming coercive powers to enforcement agencies; many taken 'off the shelf' from the US. The media continue to report the gang in sensational terms while enforcement agencies, in what has becoming a burgeoning new anti-gang industry, have produced an ongoing blizzard of gang-talking reports about them.

In what follows I will draw, albeit selectively, on a range of different gang-talking texts. Most, it could be observed, present themselves as serious documents composed by serious commentators seeking to reveal the terrible truth about gangs; a number even claim that the 'truth' revealed is based on empirical research and constitutes a 'realist' analysis of the gang phenomenon. Here, without exception or apology, I treat them as fantasy constructions.

Novelty

British history is rich with groups that might well be said to constitute what we today call 'gangs'. In the Middle Ages they were known as 'canting crews'; in the seventeenth century the notorious highwayman Dick Turpin belonged to what was known as the Essex Gang (Hallsworth 2005; Harris 1971). In his novel *Brighton Rock*, Graham Greene narrates the tragic history of would-be gang member Pinky, set in Brighton during the period between the First and Second World Wars (Greene 1975); while in the novel *Clockwork Orange*, written in the 1960s, Anthony Burgess paints a dystopian vision of a British future overrun by gangs (Burgess 1962). Gangs, in other words, have always been around and the public have always been fascinated by the lives of gangsters.

Despite being a perennial feature of street life in many neighbourhoods (as we saw in Chapter 2) gang talk constitutes the gang as an entirely new phenomenon, the like of which has never been seen before. As Geoffrey Pearson observes, in imagining the gang as eternally new, the public is caught up in a form of historical amnesia about a past characterised as invariably benign and peaceful (from which gangs are absent) which is then set against a bleak dystopian present (Pearson 1983, 2011) now apparently overrun by gangs. Captivated by the shock of the new; the idea that they have discovered something the like of which has never been witnessed before, gang-talkers produce a fantasy of the present characterised by an immense rupture with the past. Evidence of the hold this way of thinking exercises is nowhere more clearly exemplified than in the widely held claim that gangs in the UK today represent nothing less than what Pitts terms 'the new face of youth crime'.

That similar refrains about youth groups exist back through the twentieth century (and beyond) becomes, unfortunately, lost in this exercise in negation.

Proliferation

It is not just that the gang is here where until recently it was not, gang talk also coalesces around the idea that the gangs are now proliferating; where they were once few, now apparently they are multiplying and are now many. And, of course, it is getting worse all the time. This narrative is often bound up with a representation of gangs and gang culture imagined as some form of infectious disease or virus that gestates in one group before migrating to another, which then becomes 'infected' by this mutant 'criminal disease'. This refrain became popular in the aftermath of the riots of 2011, not least after the appearance of celebrity historian David Starkey on a primetime news programme, who argued that a gang culture that had gestated in the black community had now reached out to infect the culture of the white working class.

Most gangs are populated by young men and most gang offending, according to the available evidence, is male (Klein 2001). None of this, however, has prevented various journalists from recurrently discovering girl gangs populated by hyper-violent 'she-male' gangsters who, we are asked to believe, have become as dangerous or even more so than their male counterparts. Though, as Tara Young's (2009, 2011) and Susan Batchelor's (2009) careful and detailed demolitions of the 'she-male gangster thesis' attest, the evidential basis for such claims is weak, headlines nevertheless proliferate: 'Mob Violence: The Rise of Girl Gangs' (Lee 2008), or 'The Feral Sex: The Terrifying Rise of Violent Girl Gangs' (Bracchi 2008).

Nor is it only young women you have succumbed to the gang infection. According to other reports, gang members are getting much, much younger. Hail the rise of the 'tinies' as they are known, young gangbangers aged no older than three, armed and dangerous and on a street near you (Clements and Roberts 2007).

Corporatisation

Not only are the gangs multiplying, the gang today is evolving and organising in ever more lethal directions. The narrative runs something like this: 'Once upon a time the groups were disorganised and posed a relatively small threat we could deal with; but now they are organising as we speak, and now pose terrible threats to us all.' At its most developed this (hysterical) aspect of gang talk works by conceding to the gang bureaucratic attributes that best describe the structure of corporations and armies. In this projection, a street reality which is most often composed (as we shall subsequently see) of loose, amorphous, fluid and, in a Deleuzian sense, rhizomatic networks (Hallsworth and Silverstone 2009) becomes reconstructed in terms that best describe the organisations that gang-talkers typically inhabit. And so the gang is ascribed with elaborate divisions of labour and a complex vertical, hierarchical structure.

This attempt to *corporatise the street* by projecting upon it attributes that best define formal social institutions is by no means new. To return to the Middle Ages the Canting Crew was imagined in organisational terms that corresponded to that of the medieval guild. Entry to the

Company of Thieves required a solemn oath while the Canting Crew was imagined to possess twelve subdivisions (the Canting Orders) presided over by the 'Dimbler Dambler', the Prince of Thieves (Harris 1971). Moving forward to the 1960s and the same process could be observed in the US, nowhere more brilliantly worked through than in Cressey's evocation of the Mafia as a shadow corporation (Cressey 1969). This fantasy of organised crime as a criminal corporation involved conceding to it a pyramidal structure presided over by the Godfather, supported by a company lawyer (the 'Consigliere'), run by various middle managers (the Lieutenants) who control the street 'soldiers'. The same process can also be seen at work in the UK today, in accounts of gangs that rework street terms like 'elders' (older gangsters), 'youngers' (younger men), 'tinies' (young children) and 'wannabes' (would-be gangsters) and transforming this into a full-blown bureaucratic gang structure (see Pitts 2008).

This attempt to corporatise the gang also reflects a key trait about gang talk more generally. Again, to revert to the language of Deleuze, gang talk is constructed from within an arborescent (tree-thinking) perspective and this is nowhere reflected more than in the pronounced tendency to approach the gang in the same way sociologists traditionally studied bureaucracies and to deploy a managerial language to describe their features (Deleuze and Guattari 1988). In the words of Jonathon Toy, for example, a practitioner musing on the gang situation in London, 'organisational gangs', as he terms them,

> are well structured, profit led businesses. They are led by entrepreneurial, dynamic individuals, capable of creating high levels of loyalty with dividends being paid to the board of directors as a reward for success. They have a strong recruitment policy, akin to headhunting, and are willing to fire people who do not perform or who go against the ethos of the business. (Toy 2008)

Weaponisation

As the attraction of gangs is bound up ineluctably with the violence that gang members do, it is unsurprising that a key focus of gang talk condenses around the weapons gang members allegedly carry. To a degree, this aspect of gang talk is also bound up with the idea that as the gang becomes more organised, gang members are more likely to carry weapons, while the weapons they carry become ever more lethal.

In the UK, the gang-talking narrative that surrounded the contemporary (re)discovery of the gang exhibited precisely this narrative.

Gangs, it was alleged, were no longer fighting each other with fists; they were now carrying knives and were increasingly arming themselves with guns to sort out their 'gang wars'. If that was not enough, the gang was also beginning to innovate by using what the media and other right-thinking people like to term 'new weapons of choice'.

As we saw in Chapter 1, they have quite a lot of these, including dangerous dogs such as pit bulls which have now become 'a weapon of choice for gang members, drug dealers and street corner thugs' (BBC News 2009); while according to ROTA, 'Rape has become a weapon of choice, and used against sisters, girlfriends and on occasion mothers, as it is the only weapon that cannot be detected during a stop and search' (Firmin 2010).

The idea of the gang imagined as an armed, insurgent unit perhaps also explains why they were so quickly identified and blamed for the urban disorder in the UK in 2011. After all, they have been blamed for every other inner-urban problem in recent years, so why not riots? This also helps to explain why they can be identified with the capacity not only to cause riots but also to destroy community life entirely; a sentiment expressed clearly by government minister Iain Duncan Smith, a self-styled expert on gangs, in his reflections on the causes of social breakdown:

> Gangs have created no-go areas and made impossible the very things that could help deprived neighbourhoods to rejuvenate, such as community action and business development. Gangs are both a product of social breakdown and a driver of it. (Duncan Smith 2011)

Penetration

Fears about the 'new weapons of choice' are compounded by various fears and anxieties about the gangs' capacity to extend themselves through space. They begin as always in the inner-city estates where they emerge, but, over time, they reach out to colonise other settings which they dominate and control. This fantasy is expressed variously in the idea that super-gangs have developed which now exercise total control over social life in the estates where they are found (see Pitts 2008), to fears and anxieties over what are often referred to by gang-talkers as the 'recruitment strategies' of gangs, and in particular the corrupting role they play in 'grooming' vulnerable people and enticing them into a life of vice and crime.

Gang members often groom girls at school and encourage/coerce them to recruit other girls through school/social networks. There is also anecdotal evidence that younger girls (some as young as 10 or 12) are increasingly being targeted, and these girls are often much less able to resist the gang culture or manipulation by males in the group. The girls often do not identify their attackers as gang members and tend to think of them as boyfriends. They may also be connected through family or other networks.

Girls are often groomed using drugs and alcohol, which act as disinhibitors and also create dependency. Girls may also be used as mules to transport drugs, which frequently involves trafficking within the UK. (London Serious Youth Violence Board, 2009)

Nor are gangs today geographically bound to the estates which they apparently control. In such narratives the gang is imagined as a mutant force that invades new territories in order to feed upon ever new categories of victims. They have, apparently, invaded the prison system. Apparently radical fundamentalist Islam gangs are not only rampant in the penal system, they are forcibly converting young men to Islam within them (Beckford 2012).

If this isn't bad enough, it gets worse. The gangs apparently are also seeking to target posh girls-only schools in leafy suburbia, at least according to the findings of the self-defined 'watershed' ROTA report:

Girls who carry firearms and drugs for their boyfriends often live in areas that are not perceived to have a 'gang-problem', may attend grammar or private all-girls schools, will rarely be under any form of surveillance or be known to any specialist services such as children's or youth offending services, have their own bank account where their boyfriend can store his money. (Firmin 2010)

Note what is being evoked here: the world of childhood innocence corrupted; a world where decent girls who attend privileged schools in 'good' areas, are targeted by evil gang members from the ghetto who force them to carry their weapons and hide their criminal goods. That the report was based, as we have seen, predominantly upon opinion, much of it garnered from people who had no gang affiliation, where the term 'gang' was never defined, escaped notice. As for the claim that gangs were targeting grammar school girls, the report (in common with most gang talk) produces no evidence at all in support of the sensational claim being made that everyone else then unquestioningly accepts.

Monsters

If we consider the way in which gang members are described in gang-talking narratives, what comes across is a vision of a population who are not only systematically dehumanised but rendered absolutely Other. In this guise they appear as violent psychotic outsiders, driven by depravity to crime; wholly devoid of recognisably human attributes.

If we consider further what it is that is monstrous about the gang then one of its most evident features is that its members are almost always imagined to belong to or come from a minority ethnic group. The legacy of deeply inscribed racism, it could be observed, invariably reflects itself in gang-talking narratives not least when produced by white middle-class gang-talkers. And this explains why, in the UK, the gangs are invariably black or Asian. This also explains why group offending is never found in predominantly white middle-class suburbs, though fears of wealthy areas being penetrated by gangs forms a potent trope within gang talk, as the idea of the gangs targeting privileged schools reminds us. Like the undead in *Buffy the Vampire Slayer*, the gang member is conceived as someone who is essentially different from the indigenous (white) population. And like the undead in *Buffy*, this is a population that cannot be reasoned with but only coercively controlled.

Monstrousness is also bound up with the idea prominent in gang-talking discourses that the gang member is essentially different from 'normal' members of society. They may be born different or, once subject to the fatal embrace of the gangs or that wonderfully nebulous term 'gang culture' (having been 'groomed' or 'recruited'), they become different. Here are the signs and symptoms that define those who have been subject to such a process of conversion, at least as fantasised by the authors of a report into serious youth violence in the UK – a report which, to define a typical and recurring feature in the gang-talking literature, adduces absolutely no evidence at all to support its claims:

Gang identifiers:

- Child withdrawn from family;
- Sudden loss of interest in school. Decline in attendance or academic achievement (although it should be noted that some gang members will maintain a good attendance record to avoid coming to notice);
- Being emotionally 'switched off', but also containing frustration rage;
- Started to use new or unknown slang words;

- Holds unexplained money or possessions;
- Stays out unusually late without reason, or breaking parental rules consistently;
- Sudden change in appearance – dressing in a particular style or 'uniform' similar to that of other young people they hang around with, including a particular colour;
- Dropped out of positive activities;
- New nickname;
- Unexplained physical injuries, and/or refusal to receive medical treatment for injuries;
- Graffiti-style 'tags' on possessions, school books, walls;
- Constantly talking about another young person who seems to have a lot of influence over them;
- Broken off with old friends and hangs around with one group of people;
- Associating with known or suspected gang members, closeness to siblings or adults in the family who are gang members;
- Started adopting certain codes of group behaviour, e.g. ways of talking and hand signs;
- Expressing aggressive or intimidating views towards other groups of young people, some of whom may have been friends in the past;
- Scared when entering certain areas; and
- Concerned by the presence of unknown youths in their neighbourhoods. (London Serious Youth Violence Board 2009)

In reading the above, continuities can be established between the way the gang member is being identified today and older myths and stereotypes reproduced about dope fiends in the 1940s and 1950s; everyday stories about how decent, well-behaved kids from respectable families became demented and depraved addicts having been forced to take the evil 'weed' by a drug dealer. As with the dope fiend, we find signs of dropping out of the good society as a marker of gang belonging ('broken off with old friends', 'dropping out of positive activities'), as we do signs of entry to a new monstrous gang order (adopting certain codes, a new nickname, and so on).

Monstrousness is also evident in the eternal fascination gang-talker's exhibit towards what are often imaged as the evil induction rituals gang members indulge in. Initiation ceremonies often garner considerable and salacious interest. And several circulate, though evidence attesting to their reality is often difficult to find, as research into this issue attests

(Decker and Van Winkle 1996). For some gangs, apparently, rape is used as a rite of passage, while other gangsters, it is claimed, apparently require wannabes to randomly shoot or stab a stranger as a price for belonging.

Taking the idea of the gang member as abnormal monster to its logical conclusion, images of an atrophied brain were presented by members of the Wave Trust, a proselytising organisation steeped in biologically reductionist theories of crime, at practitioner conferences and seminars about gangs in the UK, with the implication that this is what the brain of a gang member looks like. The brain in question was that of a seriously neglected three-year-old Romanian orphan.

The Seduction of Gang Talk

None of this disputes the fact that gangs exist and can be dangerous, however we elect to define this vague and elusive term. There are gang realities and we need to comprehend them. Moreover, gang lives fit certain aspects of the ascribed archetypes which help to confirm the gang talk that gang-talkers do. Guns and knives are not discursive constructions, not least when used by gang members to shoot each other. Gangs, as such, are not, as Aldridge and Medina (2010) observe, spectres or chimeras of the control imaginary. That said, when gang-talkers attempt to engage with the reality of the gang, it is not the reality of *gang practices* that they engage with, what is produced instead is an imaginary set of representations about gangs that take the archetypical forms described above, and it is these that take precedence when gangs are being evoked by the wider gang-talking fraternity.

In such representations any sense of proportion is invariably evicted. Rare instances become indicative of the norm; the exception defines the rule. Complex, messy lives in this process are reconstructed into evil caricatures; a pornography of violence prevails in which only the most extreme representation is allowed and heard. In this highly essentialised construction complexity simply has no place, all gang members are ubiquitously alike and each and every one embodies every pathology the gang-talking fraternity identifies. In the evocation of the gang as the harbinger of all evil the gang literally becomes what David Brotherton terms 'everyman's other'.

The archetypes around which gang talk is assembled are deeply ingrained in the social imaginary. They are not, as such, new; all that gang talk does is reassemble them. The image of the gang, in this sense, parallels archetypes about fearsome outsiders everywhere. Historically, elements of these can most certainly be found in the folk literature and fairy tales; they also provide the stable of much fantasy literature that also hinges on the arrival into the good society of dark subterranean forces that mean it harm. In our insecure age, primordial fears about the Other continue to enjoy wide dissemination. Fears about the terror threat represent yet another manifestation. So too does gang talk, which also articulates long-established perennial fears about outsiders everywhere.

Gang talk, it could be noted, is never a neutral discourse, but one bound up with a racial subtext from which it cannot be disentangled. This helps explain, not least, why gangs have been so sensationally rediscovered in British society. The fact that they were associated from the beginning with black youth, an already criminalised population, has a lot to do with it. For Conquergood, gang talk is itself bound up with what, following Said, he identifies as 'orientalism' (Said 1978); only in this case the 'other' being evoked is no longer the exotic colonial subject abroad, it denotes instead the 'new postcolonial natives of the urban jungle'.

> The inner city and suburbs are polarised sites within a new economically articulated geography of power and domination that remaps the colonialist axis between capital and colony. The 'inner city', like Joseph Conrad's Congo, is spatially imagined as a journey into a dark interior, the penetration of a cavity, an orifice, an absence, a moral decent into an urban heart of darkness'. (Conquergood 1991: 5)

In gang talk then we find a world reduced to a fundamental binary between the healthy 'included' (white) middle-class society and, confronting it, (black) feral gangs that threaten to overwhelm it (unless beaten back). In a recent paper McGuire explores further what it is about the Other than constructs it as such (McGuire 2011). To arrive at this, he argues that we need he argues a science of abnormality, a teratology; in effect, a science of monsters. Gang talk, I suggest, is one of society's most potent teratologies, a treatise on the imagined deformed and deforming nightmare that white society imagines is taking root within the inner-city 'heart of darkness'.

Why are these teratologies continuously resurrected in the space of our contemporary and consumed so avidly? The answer to this is that they are performative; they provide an interpretative grid through and by which murky, difficult chunks of reality may be readily comprehended. They offer a ready-to-hand vocabulary that puts messy reality into context and place. Not least, gang talk provides a vocabulary about gangs that everyone can quickly recognise even if the producers of gang talk have never met gang members or gangs. Gang talk also chimes well with the arborescent horizons of control agents. By corporatising the gangs and locating them into their various offices, so a reality is constructed (as opposed to discovered) that they believe they can manage and control.

In a postmodern, hyper-real culture, where the signified and the signifier have long departed company (Jameson 1984; Harvey 1989), gang talk is ready-made for narrating the 'reality' of a world which, in Richard Rorty's terms, is already 'well lost' (Rorty 1972). In the 'society of the spectacle' (Debord 1994), gang talk establishes the reality of the gang but as simulacra; as an identical copy of a reality that never existed (Baudrillard 1981).

But there is also an ideological function to gang talk that needs to be acknowledged. In the post-welfare, neoliberal state where penal-fare as opposed to welfare increasingly defines the way in which poverty is managed (Waquant 2009); gang talk helps establish the terms in and by which the global precariat, the losers in the neoliberal, winner-takes-all society, are now defined. Together with underclass thinking more generally, it reconstructs the lives of the urban poor as feral outsiders; as a population to whom pain dispensation appears necessary and not least just. It constructs them in Nils Christie's terms as a *suitable enemy* at the same time as it establishes the included society as a *suitable victim*. In Conquergood's terminology, gang talk as such 'functions as discursive apparatus for controlling and containing difference, managing the problem of diversity' (Conquergood 1991: 7).

In part, this ideological function is realised precisely through the visceral emotions that gang talk evokes. Gang talk is not a neutral discourse or one that operates only at the level of explaining *What the Gangs are Doing Now*. What gang talk does is simultaneously appeal to deeply-inscribed fears, phobias and anxieties the good society has about its monstrous outside that are ignited in its very evocation of it; fears grounded on primordial ontological insecurities about dark strangers violating penetrating and invading the body of society that gang talk mobilises, harnesses and then translates into fear, indignation and rage. In so doing, gang talk establishes the emotive register then comes to define the control response. Fears easily translated through media amplification spiral into the demand for coercive action against enemies reduced to terms of absolute, essentialised difference.

Collective fantasies are not merely fictions that can be discarded if they have been falsified. People cling to them with faith. In this, they behave rather like scientists attached to paradigms that have been falsified but who refuse to accept the failure of their science (Kuhn 1962). And so it is with gang talk, the Philistogen theory of the street. It produces a self-referential reality that everyone readily comprehends and into which everything gangs do or are imagined to do can be condensed and folded: knives, dangerous dogs, shootings, muggings, riots, the drugs trade, social breakdown, and so on. Given this, what gang-talkers want to find is not evidence that challenges the gang talk that constitutes the orthodoxy of their conspiracy discourse, so much as a further iteration of the archetypes and thus a confirmation of the orthodoxy.

Let me take this argument further. Academics who undertake respectable gang research, whose findings either challenge the orthodoxies of gang talk or which fail to deliver the sensational truth about the gangs which gang talk demands and trades in, are those most likely to be ignored. This has certainly been the situation in the UK, and I suspect the US as well. If, however, the researcher appeals directly to the archetypes embedded in gang talk (novelty, proliferation, corporatisation weaponisation, and so on) then the findings will almost invariably be celebrated and widely reported – and funding is likely to follow.

And when we come to study policy formation in respect to gangs, the same logic applies. Gang suppression is less a rational proportionate response to a threat whose nature is carefully identified in a world dominated by 'evidence-driven policy'; it conversely takes the form of a set of knee-jerk responses, where overwhelming force is used to address the problem of the gang, when the only evidence being marshalled is that typically produced through gang talk and its constitutive archetypes. And this also helps explain the often wildly disproportionate responses that gangs attract. 'Wars' declared against an imagined evil, rather than a proportionate response to social problems posed by unruly groups among multiply disadvantaged populations.

Unforeseen Consequences

But gang talk can also produce unforeseen consequences in its othering. To understand this, however, we must return to the insights of Labelling theory as this was articulated in the work of Becker and Goffman many years ago. As Becker argued, labels are potent, they exist not only as vehicles through and by which deviant groups become classified as deviant by those with the power to label them as such; they determine both how agents of social control respond to and perceive the rule-breakers; they also shape the way rule-breakers subsequently perceive themselves, often in the manner of a self-fulfilling prophesy (Becker 1964). Gang talk in this sense is a potent way of labelling groups; it defines what they are, it establishes the magnitude of their difference; and the appalling nature of their crimes. It establishes them as a public enemy and legitimates their coercive treatment. Living with the burden of stigma is difficult, insofar as it often forces those stigmatised to acquire the deviant personality they have been ascribed (Goffman 1963).

The gang talk that saturates the US is illustrative of this process. By classifying entire generations of ghetto youth as a public enemy, and treating them as if they are, so the preconditions have been created where the ghetto responds by coming to accept the demonic labels used to classify them. These are then thrown back in the face of the excluding society. 'We will become the nightmare you imagine us as' arises as a predictable response. This, not least, was a fact recognised by organic intellectuals within the hip hop movement. One exemplar would be the group Public Enemy; Tupac Shakur's 'Thug Life' and Outlaw Immortalz also play on this refrain.

And the same process it seems to me is also at work in the UK today. In a world where gang talk saturates public and political discourse, groups of young people in poor areas are not only being labelled as gangs, they are also being treated as if they are. Many reject the demonic labels they find imposed upon them; but as Cohen's work on the Mod phenomenon and Jock Young's early work on 'drug takers' many years ago demonstrated, some may well come to assume the persona of the folk devil into which they are being interpolated (Cohen 1972). And this leads me logically to the final irony: *the unintended consequence of gang talk is that it constitutes the Other it designates.* The deviant, as always, is less discovered but produced.

Conclusion

Trying to have a reasoned debate on gangs in any society is difficult. The object of enquiry does not lend itself to easy definition as the academic gang-literature attests. And the task of studying worlds that are themselves closed to and often hostile towards outsiders is inherently difficult. But attempting to get to the reality of the gang is also bedevilled by gang talk of the kind I have tried to identify here. The 'truths' in which it trades are not those of the gang realities it claims to narrate but partakes instead of the phantasmagorical elements I have tried to describe here. A paranoid hyper-real, conspiracy discourse that proceeds wholly separately from the street world it claims to represent. A collective fantasy that has its own rules of constitution and combination, as we have seen, and which, like most fantasies, does not lend itself to falsification. While it might appear that this populist discourse belongs to the world of the mass media, the foolish and the ignorant, this I fear is to underestimate the seductive allure of this discourse that also continues to infest and infect the academy. The question I want to pose, but leave unanswered here, is, how far can the pitfalls of gang talk possibly be avoided? Indeed, can they?

4
Moral Panic and Industry

'This sure doesn't look much like Kansas City.'
(Dorothy to Toto her dog on entering the Land of Oz)

As we saw in Chapter 1, the gang has been blamed for a range of contemporary social problems and continues to be blamed even when a more sober and proportionate assessment of the evidence suggests that the gangland UK thesis is significantly overblown. As we saw in Chapter 3, the powerful hold the gang exercises on the social imaginary has, in part, a lot to do with the conspiracy discourse with which it is associated and the capacity of gang talk to mobilise, harness and articulate powerful primal fears about enemies organising against the good society invariably positioned as a community of victims. This certainly helps explain the seductive allure of gang talk but it says little about the conditions of its production and the temporal trajectory of its creation.

If gang talk can be considered a symphony, then in this chapter my aim will be to consider the orchestra that produces it and the orchestration that surrounds it, and this takes me away from an analysis of the gang problem as it unfolds variously in the street to consider instead the social response its discovery has provoked in the UK. Only, in this case, rather than consider the internal dynamics of gang talk considered as a language game, I want to consider instead the constituency of gang-talkers who are its producers and the sequential development of gang talk as this has unfolded in recent years.

In examining the social response that gangs have provoked following their discovery in early years of the twenty-first century I will, in the first instance, draw upon moral panic theory. The reason for adopting this line of enquiry follows straightforwardly from the fact that the social response to the gang very closely fits the process model of moral panic development initially described by Stan Cohen in his analysis of the response to the Mods and Rockers in the 1960s.

> Societies appear to be subject, every now and then, to periods of moral panic. A condition, episode, person or group of persons emerges to become defined as a threat to societal values and interests; its nature is presented in a stylized and stereotypical fashion by the mass media; the moral barricades are manned by editors, bishops, politicians and other right-thinking people; socially accredited experts pronounce their diagnoses and solutions; ways of coping are evolved or (more often) resorted to; the condition then disappears, submerges or deteriorates and becomes more visible. Sometimes the object of the panic is quite novel and at other times it is something which has been in existence long enough, but suddenly appears in the limelight. Sometimes the panic passes over and is forgotten, except in folk-lore and collective memory; at other times it has more serious and long-lasting repercussions and might produce such changes as those in legal and social policy or even in the way society conceives itself. (Cohen 1972)

While the moral panic that has grown up around the gang helps us understand why the gang has established itself as the contemporary folk-devil par excellence of our time; and while such theory also helps explain why the gang has been blamed for many crimes not of its making; there are nevertheless some limits to this approach that need to be recognised. As moral panic theory informs us, such panics tend by nature to be relatively intense as they develop but are typically short in duration (Critcher 2003). While this model of development describes well the moral panics that have surfaced in the UK in recent decades, it does not appear to fit closely the contemporary panic that surrounds the gang which shows no sign of disappearing or dissipating any time soon. To understand why this is we need to look more closely at what I will term the developing gang industry and its vested interests, and consider the functions which gang talk now performs in the emerging post-welfare security state.

In what follows I will explore the development of this moral panic. I will begin by examining its emergence in the first decade of the twenty-first century. In so doing I will examine how gangland realities gradually became reconstructed into a fully-fledged gang-talking fantasy by the mass media and other right-thinking people. In examining this flight from reality through an examination of the 'media inventory' that surrounds the gang, we shall see how all the hallmarks of moral panic: distortion, exaggeration and symbolisation (Hall, Critcher et al. 1978) are exhibited in the coverage the gang has received. In so doing we shall see why the gang has come to be positioned as a key public enemy and blamed for the many crimes of which it now stands accused, even if most are not, as we have seen, of its making. I will then show, by reference to two cases studies (the response to the English riots and discovery of the gang as a sexual predator), how gang-talking fantasies then come to establish the very templates around which reality itself, in the form of the social response to gangs, is being organised. I conclude by looking at the industrial logic of gang production. A new gang industry, I contend, has now been assembled and it has a vested interest in sustaining precisely the very phenomena it claims it wants to curb.

Emergence

The rise of the 'gang' within public consciousness appears to 'fit' with the moral panic model well. Up to 2002 there was limited interest in 'gangs'. In fact they simply did not exist as an issue in a society that was far more concerned about street crime and mugging. Not, it could be observed, without good reason, because between 2000 and 2003 street robbery appeared to have bucked the downward trend in crime and had risen sharply, particularly in areas subject to multiple deprivation and disadvantage, areas today now defined as 'gang-afflicted' (Hallsworth 2005).

A tangible consequence of this was something of a re-run of the 1970s moral panic around the 'mugger' with street crime now commanding sensational front-page coverage by the mass media. They, in turn, were responsible for placing enforcement agencies and, not least, politicians under intense scrutiny, demanding that something be done. As with most deviance amplification spirals, this particular episode began to fade as a consequence of the level of resources that were subsequently thrown at preventing it. Over time, enhanced police tactics began to have an impact and street crime rates lowered (though there still remained a lot of it around). Ever in search of a new story, the media eventually lost interest in the mugger, and coverage of street crime disappeared as a public issue as the media-driven issue attention cycle focused elsewhere

It was at this moment, just as wider social interest in and coverage of street crime was waning, that the gang was discovered as a public issue. The immediate catalyst was the murder of ten-year-old Damilola Taylor after being stabbed in the leg on the stairway of his home on a council estate in Peckham, a multiply-deprived area of London, in November 2000. (Two brothers aged 12 and 13 were subsequently convicted of manslaughter.) This was immediately identified as 'gang-related' even though, as we shall see, the gang connection was heavily overstated. In the next two years a small but steady stream of fatal shootings, many involving young black men, began to be reported as gang-related and these began to establish the idea of the gang as a new social problem. It was, however, the shocking drive-by shootings in 2003 of two young women in Aston, Birmingham – Charlene Ellis, aged 18, and Latisha Shakespeare, aged 17, who had been attending a New Year party – by men who clearly had gang connections that confirmed what would become read by the media as compelling evidence of a new and burgeoning social problem; one that the media would begin to describe in sensational terms as, quite literally, out of control.

Moral panics are always responses to a social problem, which, is also to say, that the folk devil identified is not simply a chimera. Britain's inner cities have always had their share of groups that have all the hallmarks of gangs (as we saw in chapter 2) but until recently it was the violence that the groups engaged in, particularly street crime, that constituted the focus of social attention, not the group itself. Indeed, even though the 'muggings' that commanded so much media attention in 2002 were largely perpetrated by groups that have all the hallmarks of gangs (though when I was studying them in 2004 it could be observed they did not define themselves as being in gangs), the focus of attention then was on the 'mugger', not the group itself. This changed. From 2005, no one spoke any more about 'muggers' or 'jackers', or indeed street crime, attention became focused solely upon the phenomenon of the group responsible now formally identified as a gang. To a degree its sensational rediscovery was certainly (in my mind) bound up with the racial connotation that this was all somehow to do with black youth who had now migrated from individual robbery to group-based counter-insurgency; which is also to say that without this racial connotation the current moral panic over gangs would certainty not have developed in the same way.

Given that the de facto uniform of inner-city youth was now being shaped by the fashion and aesthetics of American rap culture, reconstructing the problem of urban violence as a problem of new, burgeoning, American-style black gang culture appeared to many an entirely plausible phenomenon. After all, most kids on most estates where now wearing the uniform of the American ghetto defender.

Evidently this must be read as indicative of the rise of the gang. Given that a number of fatalities were gang-related, and given that a number of street groups were consciously embracing the 'gang' label, so the seeds were set for the development of what has become a fully-fledged moral panic about them.

By 2004, enforcement agencies across the UK were waking up to the phenomena of the urban street gang. Manchester was one of the first cities to establish a dedicated Gang Unit (MMAGS) and one of the first to commission academic research into its gang situation. The subsequent report, authored by Nick Tilly and Sandra Bullock, identified a number of armed and highly violent urban street gangs in Manchester's inner city (Tilly and Bullock 2002). It advocated, as a solution, a model of gang suppression based on the American 'Boston Ceasefire' model.

It was around this time that Andre Baker, then head of the Serious Crime Directorate at the Metropolitan Police Service (MPS) in London, established Operation Cruise, a body formed with a remit to pool intelligence from across the force on the gang situation in London. Shortly after it had been established, I became involved as its academic adviser. Together with my colleague, Tara Young, we were subsequently commissioned in 2004 to provide the MPS with an assessment of the gang situation in London (Hallsworth and Young 2005). Mindful of the fact that the media were already beginning to deploy the 'gang' label in a wildly permissive way, and mindful too of the racialising dimensions of the label, not to say its criminalising ones, we provided the MPS with a definition of a gang which we read as a group for whom crime and violence was in some way integral to its purpose and identity. In so doing our aim was also to suggest that few of the groups currently being labelled as gangs quite met this criterion and could better be understood as peer groups. We also sought to distinguish urban street gangs from more professional groups of criminals we termed 'organised crime groups'. Our objective then was to counter what we were beginning to recognise as the beginning of a media-driven panic about gangs.

Our work was conducted against a backdrop of criminological indifference to gangs. However, as the nation began to become sensitised to the presence of gangs through media reporting, this situation would change. Judith Aldridge and Janos Medina subsequently received Economic and Social Research Council (ESRC) funding to conduct a two-year ethnographic study into gangs (Aldridge and Medina 2005); while in London, John Pitts was commissioned to study gangs in

Walthamstow (Pitts 2007). Subsequently the Centre for Social Justice, a right-wing think tank established by Iain Duncan Smith, conducted its own analysis (Antrobus 2009) with John Pitts as an academic adviser. While never denying that gangs exist or denying that the street world from which they came was a violent one, Tara and I were nevertheless sceptical, from the outset, of the claim that all the problems of violence now being laid at the door of the gang were necessarily gang-related; nor were we convinced by the idea that the gang had suddenly arrived. We were even more sceptical of the claims being made which suggested that gangs today were somehow large, corporate and organised. While other writers beginning to study the contemporary gang phenomena such, as Claire Alexander (2008), also adopted a sceptical position in relation to discovery of the contemporary street gang, this more tentative approach ran against the grain of what was now a gang-talking society and one that had come to believe it was facing a gang threat of unprecedented proportions.

It was against this background that John Pitts sensational discovery of the gang *as the new face of youth crime* came to prominence (Pitts 2008). Not only were the gangs on the move; they were, he argued, large, very organised and, if that wasn't bad enough, were forcibly coercing young people to join them. Nor was this a rare event insofar as he was able to calculate (with such amazing certainty) that around 30 per cent of gang members were what he termed 'reluctant gangsters'. His report was an instant hit, at least with the mass media and sections of the practitioner community, who were by now also waking up to gangs and the possibility of gang-related work.

This gang-talking narrative also provided a template that others would subsequently embrace and successfully emulate. No time for doubts now, the gang was here and people needed to be made aware of its terrible nature. In what remains one of the most academically mediocre reports ever written on the subject of gangs, Carlene Firmin of ROTA identified gangs as inveterate sexual abusers who were now using 'rape' as a 'weapon of choice' against girlfriends and mothers (Firmin 2010). The report made headline news. Subsequently the author was given an MBE in record of her services to the nation while the *Guardian* invited her to become a columnist. A deluge of gang-talking narratives was subsequently published identifying various other 'weapons of choice' that gangs were now apparently embracing, while providing a conveyor-belt procession of policy responses documenting how the threat should be removed.

From Reality to Gang-Talking Fantasy: Reflections on the Media Inventory

There is little doubt that the media reporting that began to surround the 'gang' had all the hallmarks of 'exaggeration', 'distortion', 'prediction' and 'symbolisation' that Cohen (1972: 34) identified as the 'media inventory'. It began with the permissive application of the 'gang' label to describe any and all groups of young people with any street presence. Given that urban-based, street-based groups often wear the same ubiquitous street uniform, it wasn't that difficult to establish the illusion that gangs were everywhere. Whilst there were certainly cases of gang-affiliated men killing other young men that helped provide the evidential basis for the gangland UK thesis, it could be noted that several of the fatal cases subsequently identified by the media as 'gang-related' were not.

Take the case of Damilola Taylor, a young man allegedly killed by a gang in Peckham, a deprived area of London. Damilola was in fact murdered by a duo, brothers Danny and Ricky Preddie, not a gang. The boys, aged 12 and 13 at the time of the murder, were allegedly members of *two* gangs, the Young Peckham Boys and the Out to Bomb Crew (France and O'Shea 2006). Indeed, according to a report in the *Guardian* newspaper, the brothers were at 'the apex of the rigid pecking order that bound their gang' (Laville 2006). Leaving aside what amounts to an unsubstantiated assertion, there is no reliable evidence linking the Preddie brothers to either group; nor is it clear what, if anything, their relation to these gangs had to do with the murder of Damilola. He bled to death on a stairway having been stabbed in the leg by a broken bottle in what appeared to be an assault that went badly wrong. What we do know about the two boys who stabbed him is that they lived very chaotic and disturbed lives and it is this, rather than their gang-belonging, that best explains their actions. Take another widely reported case, that of Toni-Ann Byfield, a three-year-old murdered with her father in 2003. She was what one media report described as 'the youngest victim of gang violence' in the UK (Muir and Ellinor 2003). The newspaper strapline does not, however, accurately portray what actually happened. It transpired from evidence presented in court that Toni-Ann and her father, a convicted drug-dealer, were shot dead by Joel Smith, a lone gunman who made his living robbing drug-dealers (*Daily Mail* 2004).

Not only were gangs now taking control of the inner city, they had brought, it was argued, a new corrosive 'gang culture' with them. Though never explicitly defined, this culture was now apparently taking root among the nation's youth where it was seemingly spreading in the manner of an infectious disease. Rather like the living dead in a Romero movie, those touched by what was often referred to as 'the' gang culture, were instantly transformed into mindlessly violent gangsters. The *Sunday Times* in 2005 captured well the tone of the day in its claim that Britain's inner cities have become 'Sin Cities' awash with warring gang members (McLagan 2005). Indeed, so pervasive had the 'gang culture' now become that Britain's school inspectors from Ofsted, not previously known for their criminological expertise, felt qualified to note in their 2005 annual report on the state of British schools, the development of an ominous and seemingly burgeoning 'gang culture' in the school playground (Ofsted 2005).

By imposing, without any reflection, a framework of reference that begins with and always returns to the gang, so the media began to create an interpretive grid around violent street worlds that permitted only one interpretation: it is the gangs that are responsible. And so gang talk became the order of the day. In this narrative the gang threat was unprecedented and new, they were growing, they were becoming more organised; they were arming themselves with new 'weapons of choice'; they were indeed threatening the very foundations of social order itself.

Any attempt to counter this media-driven juggernaut by interjecting into the mix less sensational and more plausible interpretations was doomed to failure. And this, I think, helps to explain why the more nuanced attempts to understand 'gangs', ones that have cast considerable doubt on any notion of an organised counter-force confronting the 'good society' (Aldridge and Medina 2005; Alexander 2008), were easily ignored by the media and political elites who, after all, wanted their fantasies of the street confirmed rather than challenged – which also helps explain why the work of Pitts and Firmin gained such widespread coverage in the media; after all, the idea of forcibly converted gangsters and gang rapists resonated with populist appeal far more than more plausible attempts to describe gang life in terms such as 'messy networks' (Aldridge and Medina 2005). It was not only that gang talk became the hegemonic discourse that explains why the urban street gang became transformed into a folk devil, it occurred against a backdrop where any alternative voice was effectively silenced. And so the stage was set for what Jock Young, in his recent reflections on moral panics, observes as the flight from reality to into fantasy life (T. Young 2011).

If we now consider how the media do their gang talk then a variety of journalistic devises can be observed at play in the construction of what we might term the 'gang myth'. The first tactic deployed has been

...ons of which he claimed were 'sick'. This would be coupled with ...ghly punitive response that would begin with specially convened ...rts meting out draconian sentences to the rioters. Unsurprisingly, ...ey component of this punitive response would entail 'a concerted, ...out war on gangs and gang culture', the inspiration for which ...meron found in US gang-suppression policy. To signal his 'get tough' ...dentials, Cameron claimed he was seeking policy advice on precisely ...ese issues from the architect of zero-tolerance policing in America, ...l Bratton.

The political establishment and the mass media had no reservations ...n taking up the gangland UK thesis. In a range of broadcasts various ...elebrities, media pundits and self-styled 'gang experts' were invited to ...hare their opinions – even though it was evident that many had never ...ncountered a gang in their lives. Within hours of the violence, Britain ...ound itself in the grip of *gang fever*, and *gang talk* quickly became the ...dominant narrative from which answers to the questions posed by the ...disturbances would be found. For those who had the temerity to suggest that the causes might just be a little more complex than 'gangs', their fate was to be shouted down by partisan interviewers who accused them of 'excusing the violence'. Criminologists and sociologists were noticeable by their wholesale absence from this debate. In a field consequently freed from any commitment to evidence, the collective wisdom of media columnists, politicians and celebrities assumed centre stage, each competing with one another in the gang talk they produced.

Without taking time to reflect on what 'gangs' are or what a 'gang culture' might be, a consensus was quickly reached that gangs were indeed the criminal masterminds behind the disturbances. Their presence was also identified at the heart of the violence and looting. The gangs were seen simultaneously (if contradictorily) as both calculating architects as well as being responsible for what the media were quick to identify as 'outbreaks of mindless criminality'. As for explanations that evoked issues such as austerity, class and deprivation, these were given short shrift; the riots were essentially about criminality and this quickly became the only permitted narrative.

Even though mindless violence by its nature precludes explanation, someone or something had to be found to account for why so many people now appeared to be involved in it. The answer would be found in a narrative that would instead incriminate 'gang culture'. This, apparently, now defined the way of life of young black men everywhere. Worse, its influence had now spread away from its black heartlands to

to apply the 'gang' label more or less permissively and uncritically to any group that appears to occasion social disquiet to somebody. This goes hand in hand with a tendency to simply assume that the gang is the problem even when the evidence linking it is very tenuous. People interviewed about gangs are rarely challenged about their knowledge or understanding and are literally presented with a pre-scripted narrative which they are then asked to follow and agree with (it's all about the gang isn't it?). Leading questions, uncritical acceptance of often completely absurd testimony and the time-tested procedure of treating atypical exceptions as rules confirm the picture. For good measure, having terrified the wider population, self-defined 'gang experts' are then pulled in demanding that urgent measures to suppress the gang need to be initiated, which law-and-order politicians are happy to cater for. It is, I would suggest, the wide reporting of these incidents in the context of an insatiable 24-hour news culture which has helped incubate 'gang talk' and forge a consensus that the problem of the present is the problem of the gang. Let's look at a number of recent examples.

The screening of documentaries such as *Gang Wars* (*Dispatches*, Channel 4, 8 June 2003) and *Rude Girls* (BBC2, 9 December 2003) mobilised a number of these tactics. The *Dispatches* exposé of the hidden world of Britain's dangerous youth gangs involved filming a group of defiant kids (and their self-styled leader Danny (aka Taba) hanging menacingly around dark streets and asking them about the 'gang problem' – which they happily confirmed. *Rude girls* tracked the lives of three girl-gang members profiling the criminality in which they engaged. While this documentary certainly captured an antisemitic, aggressive and prejudicial dimension to the lives of the young women interviewed, as with the *Dispatches* documentary, what we were being presented with were narratives that hinged for effect on the entirely dubious premise that gangs were on the rise, there are more of them than we imagine; they are dangerous to the general public; not enough is being done to curtail them, and the police and politicians have a societal duty to do so. In both of these exposés the 'gang' label was applied to messy realities that were far more complex than the term 'gang' could possibly encompass. In both these exposés, the testimonies of the young are never meaningfully challenged (although in *Rude Girls* the reporter uncovers that one gang member is not quite the prolific and notorious 'gangster' she makes herself out to be). Whilst both documentaries highlighted the hopelessness and pessimism of young people and the real fears and dangers they faced, no attempt was made to contest the idea that the problem might be wider than the gang or that the groups in question might not, in any technical application, be considered gangs.

An excellent example of journalistic overkill concerned the imputed rise of a new gang in south London called the Muslim Boys, which, according to a report in the *Independent* newspaper (14 August 2005), now numbered around 200. What made this group so attractive to the media was that not only was this a gang but, allegedly, a violent fundamentalist Muslim one at that, with a *suspected* connection to al-Qaeda. This was a gang that would allegedly forcibly convert young men to Islam, and imams were apparently being woken in the dead of night to open mosques for this purpose. Resistance could entail death, and this was indeed what appeared to happen in the case of Adrian Marriott, who was reportedly shot in the head when he refused to convert.

In his hard-hitting exposé of the group for the *Evening Standard* newspaper (3 February 2005), reporter David Cohen interviewed a gang member called 'Winston' conveniently photographed wielding a meat cleaver in one hand and a knife in the other. His testimony certainly made good copy, though the application of common sense might suggest that it would be unwise to take it at face value as the media evidently did. Knives, as far as Winston was concerned, was not where they were at:

> 'Knives is fuck-all. Later, my bruvs will be back from their robberies with our skengelengs [guns] and cream [money]. Later there be MACinside-10s [sub-machine guns] all over the floor, laid wall to wall. And moolah! We count it – 10 grand, 20 grand. Then, after midnight,' he adds, matter-of-factly, 'me and my bruvs go to mosque to pray.'

When told that the Muslim clerics were not overly pleased with Muslims such as these, Winston remarked in true gangster style, 'Fucking cheek! Mocking us. There'll be retribution for this!'

In an article subsequently printed in the *Independent*, Lee Jasper, the Mayor of London's (then) adviser on race and policing, declared the Muslim Boys to be *'the biggest criminal phenomenon'* he has ever witnessed in the UK. According to Jasper, the group was *'sworn to bring a criminal jihad to Britain'*, and he warned that this group *'does not only do law-breaking, they do it, apparently with militant Islamic vengeance'* (*Independent*, 14 August 2005). Whilst not disputing that there is a group of young men known as the Muslim Boys who may well be linked

to a number of violent crimes, the terms in which reported epitomise less a rational evocation of an more an overly-sensational exercise in 'journalise' of unsubstantiated claims and stories. No imam ha (publicly) to verify the story of being forced to open far, no other young men have been identified who converted. As to the alleged al-Qaeda link, so far thi unsubstantiated. It could be observed that if the M the *'biggest criminal phenomenon'* yet seen on the shore would expect much more to be reported about them and Since the trial for the murder of Adrian Marriott took they have literally disappeared from the media radar.

The Journey Back: Reshaping Reality in the Imag Fantasies

The study of how gangland realities became reconst. gang-talking fantasies constitutes a rich vein of research ar is replete with so much subject matter as to constitute a own right. One could look, for example, at how problems su posed by pit bull terriers and other officially designated 'dange also became spuriously articulated to the gang menace. The se discovery of girl gangs and 'she-male' gangsters apparent dangerous than their male brothers also deserves study in its ov One could also talk about the 'tinies' in this inventory of gang stupidity. One could go on in this vein but here I want to cc my investigation into the moral panic around the gang by exar two cases studies: the social response to the English riots of 201 the sensational discovery of the gang as a sexual predator. Both again reaffirm the key elements of the media inventory: exaggera distortion and the translation of reality into a fully-fledged gang-tal fantasy. What these case studies also illustrate, however, is the ov side of the moral panic, the concomitant reconstruction of mate realities in the image of the gang-talking fantasy.

The riots

As we have seen, on the basis of no evidence at all, the English riots were immediately blamed on urban street gangs by government ministers including the Prime Minister, David Cameron. Cameron subsequently went on to call for a campaign of re-moralisation in a society some take root in white working-class communities whose young people are also, or so we were told, 'infected' by it.

It would be the celebrity historian David Starkey who would project this highly racial discourse into the public arena in an appearance on the BBC TV flagship news programme, *Newsnight*. Being a medieval specialist, some might wonder quite where his expertise lay in pronouncing informed judgements on contemporary urban disorder, which he had never studied. But in the context of a programme that had squandered any claim to serious journalism, ignorance was clearly its own qualification. When asked to provide his interpretation of the disorders, he identified a 'violent, destructive and nihilistic black culture that had corrupted too many of Britain's youngsters'. He went to argue:

A substantial section of the chavs have become black. The whites have become black. Black and white, boy and girl, operate in this language together which is wholly false, which is a Jamaican patois that's been intruded in England, and this is why so many of us have this sense of literally living a foreign country. (Starkey 2011)

For good measure he then added that Enoch Powell was right in warning, more than 40 years ago, that immigration would ultimately cause conflict in the cities of the UK. For those who cannot remember, Powell evoked the image of 'the River Tiber foaming with much blood' and called for migrants to be repatriated. Many supported Starkey, including *Mail* columnist Tony Sewell. The looting, Sewell argued, arose as a consequence of a 'gangsta culture' to which young people of different races were committed. In its celebration of 'bling', this culture provoked a 'raw acquisitiveness' that would lead them to target 'specific stores that are cherished in this culture, such as those selling mobile phones, trainers, sports clothes or widescreen TVs' (Sewell 2011). For those who had the temerity to complain about Starkey's comments, these were condemned for stifling 'free speech' in the name of 'political correctness' (Delingpole 2011).

This interpretation, it could be observed, occurred within days of the riots. However, as became quite apparent and quite quickly, gangs were by no mean to blame for events which evidently had causes that lay elsewhere. The Home Office subsequently released data that showed that the overwhelming majority of rioters were not in gangs. Such a reality check, however, did not prevent some papers – such as the *Mirror* and the London *Evening Standard* – from citing the involvement of some gang members as conclusive proof that gangs were indeed behind the urban disorder (Myall 2011). And even when government ministers publicly acknowledged that gangs were not as involved in the riots in quite the way Cameron claimed, this did not prevent the government from still making gang suppression a key aspect of its policy response to riots which, even it had to admit, were not caused by gangs.

At this stage in our investigation into the moral panic around gangs we arrive not only at a situation where complex reality has been translated into a full-blown gang-talking fantasy (gangs were responsible for the riots), we see now how reality itself (in the form of a the resulting policy response) is shaped by the fantasy. Within a month of the riots the government hosted an international conference on gangs. Bill Bratton was invited to attend (much to the chagrin of the police service). For some media pundits and Conservative MPs, his gang-busting credentials also made him perfectly equipped to lead the Metropolitan Police Service as its new Chief Commissioner. Fortunately, this never happened. However, a new task force was established in the wake of the riots and £30 million was made available to fund it. Its dedicated remit was to 'end gang violence'. As part of the initiative, 100 gang 'experts' were invited to join the task force.

Advent of the Gangbanging Motherfuckers

We are back now in 2006 and Tara and I receive an urgent request from the Metropolitan Police Service to attend a meeting of Operation Cruise. One of their researchers had produced a report of rape in London and its findings seemed to suggest that group rape is on the increase, and that young black men appear over-represented in it. With justification, the police were concerned. The MPS, after all, is quite a leaky institution; journalists were already pushing for information. And let's be clear here, black gang rape would indeed make for a powerful tabloid scoop. We agreed to look at the data from which the findings were extracted. It was, to say the least, somewhat flawed. It only profiled group engagement in rape and no attempt had been made to profile or compare this with data on individual rape or rape conducted by duos (who perpetrated the vast majority of rapes) which meant the report was, to put it mildly, rather unbalanced. The researcher's mistake had been to over-egg her case, which was to foreground one serious form of rape at the expense of others which were far more numerous. As always in our work, our aim was to try and address a serious problem proportionally.

Gang rape, however, was by no means going to disappear as an issue. Race on the Agenda (ROTA) began to 'research' the issue and in 2008 a 'Girls and Serious Violence Conference' was convened by the

Network Alliance in London. Gangs were subsequently identified at the conference as sexual predators. In 2010 ROTA released its report. On the basis of interviews conducted with 320 (allegedly gang-affiliated) women, it identified 'rape as a weapon of choice of gangs' where it was used regularly against, it was claimed, 'girlfriends and even mothers'. Despite the wholesale absence of meaningful evidence to substantiate these sensational claims, the story made headline news across the country. Its author was commended for her sterling work. A second report was produced by ROTA, not much better than the first. But by now we were living through a deviance amplification spiral and issues over mere matters such as the evidential basis from which these sensational claims were made were simply ignored. The only truth worth countenancing, and the only view that the media and most others appeared prepared to countenance, was that gangs were indeed habitual sexual predators and that was all we needed to know. It chimed perfectly well with the gang-talking narrative that now prevailed everywhere and no one, by and large (with the exception of myself), challenged the findings (Hallsworth and Duffy 2010).

Meanwhile, over at the MPS an eager Superintendent, demonstrating commendable entrepreneurial flair, put together a bid through the EU DAPHNE funding stream for money to confront the menace posed to young women by sexually predatory gangs. On the basis of absolutely no compelling research findings that suggested such groups actually existed, she was given £600,000 all in all, a fair bit of money to counter the sexual perversions of the gang. Good money if you can get it. By now, Britain was awash with gang fever and in this context the gang was beginning to be blamed for just about every urban malaise, and a range of new moral entrepreneurs began to enter what was now becoming something of a congested gang landscape. Step forward the Deputy Children's Commissioner of England and Wales, custodian of a quango dedicated to the laudable pursuit of protecting children everywhere and also the author of a highly favourable Foreword to Carlene Firmin's second research report into the sexual violence of gangs. Time now, evidently, for a two-year fully-fledged commission with a dedicated remit to investigate and confront the very real threat posed to women by urban street gangs.

The commission was duly established. Carlene Firmin was subsequently employed to provide strategic advice. John Pitts, fresh from having discovered his 'reluctant gangsters', was also employed to discover the gang rapists. Evidently not one to take many chances he deployed a definition so wide as to include just about every kind of group there is, including those with names like 'brethren' (ergo friends), 'mandem' (ergo friends) and 'brothers' (ergo friends). At the beginning of the project Tara and I were also invited to some of the opening advisory meetings. Then we were not. Far from approaching the issue of sexual violence on the part of gangs as a conjecture that needed testing, the commission made it very clear, very early on, that this was in fact an established fact and one that the rest of society was in denial about. Before any research had even commenced the convenient figure of 10,000 young women were identified as victims of these gangland predators. In what was essentially an inquisition, Carlene Firmin's role was little more than that of Witchfinder General. John Pitts' job was simply that of coughing up a suitable amount of gangsters by way of trying to get this exercise in populism redeemed as scientific.

And the moral of all this? Here again we have seen strong claims about gangland UK that have been universally accepted and rarely challenged, even though the evidential base from which such claims are derived remains weak and questionable. Nevertheless, adulatory headlines flow; conferences are organised to discuss the issues; the Home Office has been assiduous in getting in on the act by establishing its own working group on girl gangs, and resources follow. In 2011 the government announced that as part of its ending-gang-violence strategy it was going to make £1.2 million available to help support the victims who had been sexually violated by gangs. Coupled with European Union money and the costs accumulated to the taxpayer by organising and funding a commission, it means that huge sums of taxpayers' money has been expended upon a problem the reality of which is still open to question. You simply cannot make this up. Once again, we are faced with a reality reconstructed in the image of a gang-talking fantasy.

The Industrial Logic of 'Gang' Production

Moral panics tend by nature to be relatively intense but short in duration. Eventually they fade away as 'solutions' are developed by control agencies and/or the media lose interest and, in time, turn attention to an alternative 'folk devil'. While the 'discovery' of the 'gang' certainly fits with the developmental cycle of moral panic as this has been articulated by theorists such as Cohen (1972, 2002) and Critcher (2003), its demise appears less certain in the short term. Indeed, it is more likely that violent street life – engendered by multiple forms of marginality in polarised cities – will continue to feed the gangland UK thesis. Nor is it only 'gangland killings' that sustain such fantasy. The term 'gang' is now so nebulous, fluid and elastic that it is randomly applied to just about any group of young people 'hanging around'. The fundamental idea that society is facing an organised counter-force – as distinct from a self-destructive mess – ensures that the focus of attention remains on the 'gang' rather than on the social and economic conditions that tend to produce violent street worlds.

The continued rediscovery of the 'gang' also meshes well with the needs of the emerging post-welfare security state that requires a tangible object on which to focus. Conceptualising the street as an amorphous, messy reality is too complex, fuzzy and uncomfortable for most control agents. It unsettles and challenges their explanatory universe that is typically constructed in arboreal terms. If the street world can be reduced down to a readily-defined 'office' and neatly organised divisions of labour – 'lieutenants', 'soldiers', 'aspirants' and 'wannabes', for example – to particular group identities allocated 'risk' scores and, ultimately, to coercive control, it lends itself to convenience, whereby multiple, intersecting and extraordinarily complex phenomena are simplistically encapsulated by the problem of the 'gang'. The term 'gang' might also remain popular because of its intrinsic growth potential. As we have seen, it is an elastic construct that can be mutated, blurred and hybridised at will. The term is pregnant with possibility. New 'gang' typologies can be readily created – such as 'girl gangs' – and blended with other weird labels such as 'knife crime' and 'gun crime' in a proliferation of bizarre, hybridised, gang-talking stupidity.

As Christie (2000) reminds us, where there is crime there is also an industry that feeds from it, and in this case there is also an industrial logic to the reproduction of the 'gang menace'. Until recently the UK had no established 'gang' experts and certainly little by way of a developed 'gang control' apparatus. But this has all changed and there is now a burgeoning industry that, on the one hand, claims to suppress the 'gang' whilst, on the other, paradoxically feeds from it and accordingly has a vested interest in discovering and maintaining precisely that which it ostensibly aims to expunge. Ultimately, a stage has been reached where too many people have too great a vested interest in the 'gang' to surrender the gangland fantasy.

At the general level, 'gang talk' operates like a lubricant oiling the control apparatus in ways that allows its constituent cogs to turn and mesh together. 'Gang talk', in this sense, animates the system. It provides a clear and common focus around which the control apparatus – and its various vested interests – works. Take, for example, the research community who have had a field day: discovering 'gangs', defining 'gangs', producing 'gang' typologies and, not least, proffering views and informing 'action plans' pertaining to what needs to be done. This is now big business. Whereas, until recently, few academics were researching this issue, 'gang' studies has now mushroomed into its very own subdiscipline.

The political community is equally, if not more, implicated. By doing 'gang talk' politicians have found a powerful tool they can deploy to demonstrate governing competence within the emerging security state. Indeed, in the run-up to the elections for the office of the Mayor of London in 2012, gang suppression was used as a regular motif in the elections. The Metropolitan Police's newly appointed commissioner was happy to support the campaign, both by creating yet another dedicated gang-busting unit (in effect rebadging the one he already had), and by orchestrating highly-visible gang crackdowns involving dawn raids against 'known' gang offenders. OK, many of the people being targeted weren't actually gang members, but that wasn't really the point of what remains a highly-visible public relations exercise in symbolic policing. In the spirit of 'We're all in this together', a photo-op was organised in Trafalgar Square in London featuring the police chief, the Mayor of London and various representatives from the emerging gang industry.

It is not just that the gang has become the suitable enemy par excellence, insofar as it represents an enemy whose social construction as such no right-thinking person can possibly disagree with, it has become a very convenient scapegoat upon which an insecure society can vent righteous indignation and rage. As a state, Britain has never recovered from the economic crisis bequeathed to it by its financial elite, a bloc composed largely of privileged white men who operate in corporate gangs, schooled to crime in boardrooms and prestigious universities. As this book is being written, the country is sliding into a triple-dip recession, its economy has literally flatlined and youth unemployment has rocketed. For the burgeoning precariat, life is particularly hard in a world where stable work is rare, where wages are low and where welfare support is being dismantled. Far from reading the crisis of the poor as a crisis of the neoliberal state and its perverse economics, social breakdown has instead been blamed on the gang, which, in the words of government minister Iain Duncan Smith, is both a symptom and a driver of social breakdown in communities.

One of the core beneficiaries of the government funding that has followed its gang fixation is the practitioner community. This has found common purpose in 'gang' suppression. By becoming 'gang' experts and – in some cases – chairing or establishing various 'anti-gang' committees and task forces, many practitioners' career prospects have prospered even if the scale of their 'expertise' is open to question. Others have created 'anti-gang' programmes with the aim of attracting funding from central and local government. The practitioner community is by no means a homogeneous community. It is certainly populated by a constituency of good people. Many have found that unless they also do 'gang talk' they are unlikely to receive the necessary resources needed to sustain services for the troubled young people with whom they work. It is also a constituency rife with fantasists and chancers.

Additional beneficiaries are the army of moral entrepreneurs and right-thinking people who have nobly taken upon themselves the right to pronounce informed judgements on the gang situation and propose, of course, solutions. This is, by and large, another weird constituency unified by the fact that it is typically composed of those whose lives rarely intersect with those of the gangs they talk about with such authority. This constituency is again nothing if not eclectic. Where to begin? We can go back in time to when the then-new Mayor of London, Boris Johnson, desperate to parade his anti-gang credentials to the public, hosted a press conference attended by Ross Kemp, an actor who had once played a gangster in a popular soap opera, and on the basis of this now ran a popular documentary series on gangs. Who better to pronounce solutions on gangland Britain? What gang members need, he opined, were military role-models.

In 2009, I (also a participant in this circus) was asked to attend a seminar at Downing Street chaired by the then Prime Minister, Gordon Brown. We had been invited to talk about gang violence. Also present was the head of the Racial Equalities Commission, Trevor Phillips, someone I hadn't as then figured as a gang expert. An article was subsequently published on the front page of the *Guardian* informing us that he was in fact going to take a strategic lead in confronting the gang situation. His informed opinion on what needed to be done next was as idiotic as that of Ross Kemp. Gangs need military role-models. Sitting next to him at the Downing Street conference was a representative of the Wave Trust, an organisation that pedals a biologically reductionist theory of crime. Yes, gangsters' brains, he declared, are different from those of normal people and the differences can be identified at the tender age of three. I subsequently saw him again at an 'expert' conference on gangs hosted by the Mayor of London. John Pitts and Carlene Firmin also spoke. In his presentation he presented the audience with a picture of two brains. One looked like a walnut. This, he insinuated, was what the brain of a gangster looked like.

Cashing in on the 'gang', Channel 4 launched a project grandiosely entitled 'The Commission'. Chaired by Cherie Blair, the wife of the ex-Prime Minister, Tony Blair, it bought together a panel of people who would then interview various gang 'experts'. The panel subsequently recommended super-gang Anti-Social Behaviour Orders (ASBOs) as part of its 'solution'. Now, self-evidently an accredited 'expert' on gangs, Cherie Blair subsequently appeared before a parliamentary inquiry into gun and weapon crime to provide evidence about them. The ravings of David Starkey we have already considered. But in many ways the appearance of this, a celebrity historian, on Britain's premier flagship news programme during the riots, just about sums up the state of play in British society today. But in all fairness he was one of many self-styled 'gang experts' who appeared, most of whom I have never heard of in my life. No sociologist or criminologist was interviewed. Welcome, then, to the strange world of Metropolitan 'Othering'. Listen to the privileged talking about the powerless, the included talking about the excluded, the wealthy pontificating about the poor. The infinite drivel of the chattering classes.

Conclusion

While it is evident that gangs, however we elect to define them, have always been around, it is wholly impossible to make sense of the contemporary rediscovery of the gang independently of examining how it has been represented. While this does not obviate the need to examine what is actually going on in a street context, as this and the previous chapter has tried to establish, what goes on there and the way it is represented through gang talk by the growing army of gang-talkers is an altogether different matter. One lesson that can be derived from this is that any attempt to examine and interpret violent street worlds has to consider both sides of the issue. To return to the ontology sketched out in the last chapter, it is, of course, important to study street practices, and to get to those we need to engage with street representations. But at the same time it is also important to study the way that this street world is represented and socially constructed, typically by those who live lives distantly from it. The final lesson – and I consider this an important one for academics who consider themselves to be critical – is be careful. In the context of societies where the tendency towards media excess is well established, it is imperative that they refrain where possible from making the mistake of buying wholeheartedly into such representations. In fact, and going further, if you find your work chimes directly with the media inventory, or indeed is helping shape it, you are (a) not a critical criminologist and (b) making a serious mistake somewhere.

Part Three
Getting Real about Violence

5
Arborealism and Rhizomatics: A Treatise

How do we understand and make sense of informal organisations such as gangs? For gang-talkers, this is not a question that appears to present any serious epistemological and ontological challenges. Gangs, from this standpoint, are simply considered criminal organisations with clear determinate features that can be established and measured. Considered this way, they are imagined to possess fixed essences, the compilation of which provides an understanding of the whole. This tendency is wonderfully exemplified in the quantitative tendencies at play in the American administrative gang-research industry. It is particularly evident in their autistic obsession with reducing the complexities of informal street organisations to denaturalised and decontextualised clusters of risk factors from which the truth of gangs is then discerned (Klein 2001).

The tendency to essentualise, however, does not stop here and is also evident in another characteristic feature of administrative gang research. It is particularly evident in the tendency to presuppose that the organisational forms and structures of gangs not only parallel those of formal organisations but can be described in the same terms. This tendency is particular evident in various attempts to corporatise the street; to ascribe to it the hierarchical bureaucratic features typically found in armies and corporations. This way of approaching the gang has many adherents. John Pitts in the UK established his gang credentials by discovering super-organised gangs of this sort, and the tendency is also reflected in the US in the work of Jankowski (Jankowski 1991; Pitts 2008). Indeed, looking beyond academia this trait is the dominant characteristic of gang talk everywhere.

Cultural criminologists have taken the lead in contesting the attempt to reduce the study of complex social movements into the denuded language of risk variables, and in opposition to the 'voodoo statistics' of Zombie criminology have asserted the necessity of engaging with the phenomenological reality of street organisation (Ferrell and Sanders 1995; Presdee 2000; Ferrell, Hayward et al. 2004; J. Young 2011; White 2013). Only through an appreciative ethnographic approach and one sensitive to the values and meanings actors give to their actions can the reality of the street world ever be fully disclosed – an approach exemplified in the work of critical ethnographers such as Hagedorn (Hagedorn and Macon 1988), Brotherton and Barrios (2004), Conquergood (1994) and Vigil (1988). And it is in the work of critical ethnographers such as these that we also find approaches to the study of informal street organisations suggesting that the organisation of informal organisations cannot be grasped through imposing upon them the bureaucratic properties of formal organisations such as corporations and armies.

All of which takes me logically to the question I want to pose and address in this chapter: How do we comprehend the structure of informal street based organisations if we accept that they are not corporate? Which is also to say, how do we move beyond gang talk and the deeply flawed representations of the street in which it trades? This is, at heart, a question of ontology as much as it is a question of epistemology and methodology. It is about the very conceptual lens by and through which we make sense of complex street worlds. A reality whose sui generis properties are, I contend, wholly different to that of the world of formal organisations such as those that most gang-talkers inhabit.

Evidently we need a different ontology but let me be very clear from the beginning about what this entails and what it does not. It cannot entail simply trying to fix and patch holes in orthodox gang-talking narratives because this not a narrative, I contend, that can be patched up and fixed. Like any other failed paradigm, we must consign it to the dustbin of history. We recognise, of course, that its death will no doubt be painful, extended and prolonged and, as George Romero's movies remind us, even the dead have a habit of returning to haunt the lives of the living. To understand the informal organisation of the street we need instead to begin anew. We need a different sociology of organisations. Ultimately, this requires a different paradigm.

In what follows, my aim will be to outline what such an alternative might look like and to do so I will draw upon the work of the philosophers Gilles Deleuze and Felix Guattari (Deleuze and Guattari 1977, 1988). What Deleuze's philosophy provides, I will argue, is an alternative way of comprehending the properties of informal street organisations, and in ways that mark an epistemic break with orthodox gang-talking traditions. This takes me then to Deleuze, nomadology, and the study of trees and grass.

Before I go any further, a brief note on Deleuze. Though one of the towering philosophers of the twentieth century, it could be observed that his work has not captured the interest of many criminologists. Indeed, even in the field of cultural criminology (which, one might imagine, would constitute that area of the discipline where his work would have most relevance), few appear interested in it or its possible applications. It appears, as such, relegated to the status of that obscurantist body of (continental) theory recently condemned by Jock Young as an unduly arcane, complex and irrelevant (J. Young 2011). Here I will attempt to demonstrate how wrong such an assumption would be. In so doing I will also suggest ways in which cultural criminology itself could be enriched through an engagement in Deleuzian thought and thinking.

To do so, however, requires some prior theoretical spadework. It entails, as a precursor, engaging in what might appear an extended digression, one well away from the study of informal organisations such as gangs, which, after all, is what we are supposed to be studying. But please bear with me and stay the course, because, like a medieval round, we will return to where we began – eventually. Before we return, though, we will need to examine the fundamental features of two very different kinds of society: that of the sedentary societies of the West and that of the nomads of the East. It will entail studying two opposed models of social organisation: the arborescent, tree-like systems that define Western societies and thinking, and, opposing this, systems which are rhizomatic and grass-like, the properties of which are exemplified in nomadic life.

Following this excursion into Deleuzian thought, I will develop an argument to suggest that the informal organisations of the street are fundamentally rhizomatic and their organisation needs to be interpreted as such. To grasp their nature we must leave behind traditional arborescent approaches to the study of street organisations (the stuff of which gang talk is constructed) and develop instead nomadic thought and thinking. I will also argue that the problems that gang-talkers typically experience in interpreting the world of the street stems from the fact that their ontic and epistemological horizons; the very lens through and by which they comprehend street realities, are ineluctably saturated with arborescent categories and assumptions.

The Sedentary and the Nomadic

For Deleuze and Guattari, Western societies are distinctive because they are sedentary and rooted by nature. Within them populations are settled and parcelled out in what is predominantly an urban civilisation defined by the logic of settlement (forts, villages, towns, cities, nation states) and enclosure (levees, gates, walls, channels, borders, fortifications). Citizens within this order are beholden to regulatory regimes presided over by a sovereign territorial state and its bureaucratic apparatus (the military-industrial complex). Within this social formation citizens live out their working lives moving in and between total institutions such as schools, factories, corporations, and sometimes prisons and hospitals. Within the sedentary society, power moves from the top downwards and this imperial pattern repeats itself in every institutional complex, including the state form itself.

In stark contrast to the patterned, ascribed, predicable logic of the sedentary order, Deleuze invites us to consider the world of the nomads who traverse the vast grasslands of the steppes and the deserts. If, within sedentary societies, people find themselves distributed into fixed spaces which they then occupy, hold and defend, in the nomads we confront a society 'without division into shares, in a space without borders and enclosures' (Deleuze and Guattari 1988). Unlike the rooted citizens of the sedentary society, nomads live life in movement. They occupy spaces that are then left behind as they move on to new spaces in a cyclical journey without end. Nothing is wholly fixed in nomadic life; no foundations around which life turns except the rituals of the seasons and those that are established around a society in perpetual movement. In Deleuzian terminology, if the logic of sedentary society is to territorialise life, that is to ascribe matter into fixed 'striated' space, nomads are by nature deterritorialised and deterritorialising. Far from inhabiting striated space, that of the nomads is smooth.

Sedentary societies and nomadic orders are not only fundamentally different; both pose real challenges to the other. Take the other great sedentary society of the East, the Imperial Chinese Empire. Despite having at its disposal a formidable bureaucracy, a great civilisation, and an army that greatly outnumbered it adversaries, it proved no match for the nomadic war machine of Genghis Khan and his sons and the nomads still returned to overrun China even after the Great Wall had been built to keep them at bay. In the face of the total liquidation of Kiev, Russia too would fall under the yoke of the Mongol hordes, and for 300 years, while the assembled Knights of Europe, composing the flower of the European warrior aristocracy, were slaughtered in their thousands when they confronted the Mongols in Poland in the fifteenth century. To an extent, the military success of the nomads could be credited to the tactical brilliance and uncompromising ruthlessness of their leaders; but it is also an issue of nomadic organisation itself and the superior advantages their speed and mobility would confer to them when they confronted the ponderous, immobile, centralised armies of the East and West.

All sedentary societies begin when their nomadic elements are suppressed, when the lands are farmed and when fixed settlements develop; when these, in turn, become consolidated under centralised systems of administration within territorially delimited borders. If the trajectory of sedentary societies is to forsake nomadic organisation, indeed, to aspire to its liquidation, nevertheless nomadic tendencies remain and are always experienced as a threat to sedentary society and on many levels.

As we have observed, sedentary societies function by allocating people to places that have ascribed borders; they are territorialising by nature, they striate space and people. Nomadic groups violate the terms of this order. They challenge the property rights around which sedentary regimes are organised, and pose as well an existential challenge to their grounding principles that demand that life be fixed, measurable and quantifiable. For centralised states in particular, which function by regulating flows of people, information and goods, nomadic life challenges their inherent tendency to ascribe and fix all matter in place.

This helps explains why Western societies allocate so much effort either to eliminating nomadic elements or to regulating them by ascribing to them particular places. Think here, for example, of the perennial problems posed to the state in the Middle Ages by the class of vagabonds who occupied the outlaw spaces between the cities; the ambient fears that gypsies, travellers and migrants continue to inspire today. Think back to the terrible solutions (the premodern genocides, as Mike Davis (2001) terms them) that nomadic tribes experienced in the age of empire by the colonial powers: the tragedy of the indigenous American tribes, the Aborigines, the Indian tribes of the North West Frontier. The fears that subcultural groups inspire among right thinking people today also stems in part from nomadic tendencies they possess and/or are ascribed. The same holds for informal organisations such as street gangs, but before we examine this further we need to look more closely at the key metaphors Deleuze mobilises to define the distinctive properties of centralised sedentary systems and the nomadic elements that oppose them. This then takes us into a consideration of two terms he borrows from the study of botany: arborealism and rhizomatics.

Arborealism

The tree, Deleuze observes, is a potent symbol in Western cosmology. Think here, for example, of the many images in which trees figure: the 'Tree of Life', the 'Tree of Knowledge', the 'branches of government'. Western people 'put down roots' to say they have arrived and will stay; others aspire to 'find their roots' in the sense of tracing family trees back to an ancestral point of origin; a fact displayed well in the popularity of TV programmes such as *Who Do You Think You Are?*, in which celebrities are invited to discover their ancestors. It could well be that the hold that trees exercise on Western thought derives from the fact that Western societies are home to great forests and they figure heavily in our imaginary; Western civilisation, in this sense, has always lived with trees in ways that nomads live with the grass of the steppes or Eskimos their snow and ice. But for Deleuze trees are not just part of Western life, they express in their structure fundamental truths about the way in which Western societies are organised; their structure expresses in this sense fundamental ontological truths about Western ways of thought and thinking (see Figure 5.1).

> It is odd how the tree has dominated Western reality and all of western thought, from botany to biology and anatomy but also gnosiology, theology, ontology and all of philosophy. (Deleuze and Guattari 1988: 20)

From branch tip to root, the tree, at least as Deleuze conceives it, is a command structure. It grows from a seed that constitutes a founding point of origin. It develops with a taproot that descends vertically beneath the surface of the ground, and paralleling this, vertically ascending, a trunk that rises towards the sky. Over time, radicals (the side roots) begin to develop, radiating symmetrically away from the main taproot; eventually these subdivide into smaller root systems which again subdivide, and the process reproduces itself. In complete symmetry with this subterranean development, branches radiate horizontally away from the central trunk. Like the root system, each branch also subdivides, and the process repeats itself into the formation of smaller branches. What is also unique to the tree is that it constitutes itself as a predicable structure whose nature can be comprehended. In

Figure 5.1   Tree structure: branches and roots

Source: Author.

Deleuzian terms, 'the tree plots a point'. There are common laws that define how the structure both develops and reproduces itself; symmetry and predictability are integral to this process.

This ideal typical description of the tree provides both a metaphor and template, Deleuze suggests, for understanding key aspects of Western life. As we have seen, the sedentary societies of the West are precisely of the rooted type. They are, by nature and type, arborescent societies. Like the tree, Western peoples invest heavily in their roots. They discover and affirm their racial heritage. Here the 'imagined community' of the nation does not wander; they inhabit homelands, or, like displaced diaspora communities, they aspire to reclaim them. Western states also invest significantly in ensuring that people remain rooted. To be 'documented' in this sense is to be a rooted citizen, just as to be undocumented, as many refugees are, is a potent symbol of the rootless outsider.

Western organisations are also inherently arborescent. The structure of the state is arborescent. So too are the political parties that constitute the polis. Think here, for example, about the branches of government. So too is the military-industrial complex. So too are the structure of corporations. In each, power moves relentlessly from the top down through centralised, hierarchical command structures. Such organisations comprise sites and spaces of domination and control. Within them, those at the top look down upon those beneath them; those beneath, in turn, are expected to look up to those above them. Within such systems status accrues to where you stand within the hierarchy. These tree-like structures, in turn, aspire to territorialise the lives of those they control, subjecting them to the logic of enclosure, and subjugating them as they do so. Through them, flows of information, money, power seep, but always vertically; everything here is organised, everything in its right place.

Western thought and science is also tree like. The modern idea of knowledge having an Archimedean founding point is a case in kind, as are various attempts to develop 'trees of knowledge'. Western science is paradigmatically arborescent and nowhere is this better exemplified than in the quest for certainty and Being expressed in Western philosophy. So too are the natural sciences such as chemistry and biology. So is social science, including, we might add, criminology (but to this we will also return).

Rhizomatics

Plant systems exist which are not arborescent, however, and the plant life they produce evolves in very different ways (and directions) to that of the tree. The alternative Deleuze presents us with is the rhizome. The grass that covers our lawns is a rhizome, ginger is a rhizome, and so too are many of the invasive plants we classify as weeds. Unlike the tree, which is essentially a vertical structure, the rhizome develops horizontally. The term derives from the ancient Greek, *rhizome*, meaning 'mass of roots'. These strike away from nodes in horizontal stems that also produce a profusion of offshoots which follow no predicable direction or pattern and constitute elaborate subterranean (and sometimes service) assemblages that may extend over large areas. Unlike trees, a rhizome may be cut into pieces and each piece will form a new plant (vegetative reproduction), and this is often how they are propagated. Like the tree, the rhizome constitutes both a sign and a signifier that can be deployed metaphorically to designate an array of human and non-human systems. Read as a metaphor, Deleuze uses the idea of rhizomatic structures as a vehicle to describe a set of organisational processes and practices that stand in opposition to and depart radically from those he associates with arborescent structures. Nomadic life in its entirety is rhizomatic, but so too are many other life-forms:

> Bulbs and tubors are rhizomes, plants with roots or radicals may be rhizomatic in other respects altogether: the question is whether plant life within its specificity is not entirely rhizomatic. Even some animals are in their pack form. Rats are rhizomes. Burrows are too, in all of their functions of shelter, supply, movement, evasion and breakout. The rhizome assumes very different forms, from ramified surface extension in all directions to concreation in bulbs and tubers. When rats swarm over each other. The rhizome includes the best and the worst: potato and couch grass, or the weed. (Deleuze and Guattari 1988: 6)

Unlike trees, rhizomes have no clearly defined symmetrical structure (see Figure 5.2):

> The rhizome is an acentered, nonhierarchical, nonsignifying system without a General and without an organizing memory or central automaton, defined solely by a circulation of states. (ibid.: 21)

Unlike trees, whose roots and branches evolve from and reach back to a common trunk (a classifying centre), in the rhizome each node can potentially connect to any other. Rhizomes, then, are not centred but decentred and distributed. If the tree represents a command structure that is vertically aligned and orchestrated from the top down, the rhizome epitomises a horizontally inclined, radically non-hierarchical system whose elements come together and intersect in different and unpredictable ways.

Whereas arborescent structures function by acts of territorialisation, the rhizome is characterised simultaneously by forces of deterritorialisation and re-territorialisation. Rather than conceive the rhizome as a body whose organs each perform a unique function in maintaining the whole (think here of functionalist sociology), rhizomes comprise bodies without organs, perpetually transforming themselves as they evolve and

Figure 5.2   Rhizome structure

Source: Author.

morphing into different states as they do. The metaphor Deleuze evokes is that of a map. But this is not the kind of map most of us are used to, which designates clearly and uncompromisingly where everything is in space. On the contrary, this is a map that

> must be produced, constructed, a map that is always detachable, connectable, reversible, modifiable, and has multiple entryways and exits and its own lines of flight. (ibid.: 42)

Nor is it accurate to say that in opposition to the tree the rhizome is simply disorganised, because that would be to misrepresent its nature. Rhizomes are structured, but their structure

> is composed not of units but of dimensions, or rather directions in motion. It has neither beginning nor end, but always a middle (*milieu*) from which it grows and which it overspills ... When a multiplicity of this kind changes dimension, it necessarily changes in nature as well, undergoes a metamorphosis. (ibid.: 21)

Rhizomes are composed of two elements: *domains* and the *linkages* that connect them. These domains Deleuze terms 'plateaus'. The defining characteristic of a plateau is that it is 'always in the middle, not at the beginning or the end'. It constitutes itself as 'a continuous self-vibrating region of intensities; a multiplicity'. These plateaus are in turn 'connected to other multiplicities by superficial underground stems in such a way as to form or extend the rhizome' (ibid. 43). A rhizome then is composed of one or more of these plateaus and these 'multiplicities' are themselves connected to others. What connects together, though, may by no means be read as like for like because what are linked 'are not necessarily linked to traits of the same nature'. Indeed, for Deleuze each connection may evoke very different regimes:

> What is at question in the rhizome is a relation to sexuality – but also to the animal, the vegetal, the world, politics, the book, things natural and artificial – that is totally different from the arborescent relation: all manner of 'becomings'. (ibid.: 42)

And it is in this term 'becomings' that we find another key distinction with arborescent ways of thinking. Whereas in arboreal thought things are held to have necessary states of being, fixed essences that define the whole, or a state of being to which they gravitate, there is no such determinate destiny to rhizomatic life. It develops, but not like a book with a beginning, middle and end, but as immanent arrivals in a world where there is no predictable pattern or destination, no fixed or final state to which there is a return, but simply to new becomings without end.

> It is a question of a model that is perpetually in construction or collapsing: and of a process that is perpetually prolonging itself, breaking off and starting up again'. (ibid.)

In attempting to delineate the two systems Deleuze is not attempting to suggest that we are looking at a stark binary. Western societies might well be defined by their arboreal tendencies but the composition of the social world is fundamentally rhizomatic, as indeed is the polity taken as a whole. Even in the most rooted system, rhizomatic tendencies can be found; offshoots break out and away, extending themselves in strange and unforeseen ways. And even if the arborescent state seeks to arrest, expel or repress rhizomatic elements, they nevertheless persist:

> the flow continues beneath the line, forever mutant. (ibid.: 242)

At the same time arboreal features may form in systems that are rhizomatic, or rhizomatic structures may begin to accumulate arboreal features; hierarchies may develop, despotic tendencies may evolve. A

General steps forward. But ... and this is the point, such tendencies do not define the rhizome or translate it into an arboreal formation.

Rhizomes cannot be grasped in thought from within arboreal thought systems even though, as Deleuze wryly observes,

> History is always written from the sedentary point of view and in the name of a unitary State apparatus, at least a possible one, even when the topic is nomads. (ibid.: 23)

This also explains why, even when the subject of history is the nomad, the nomad discovered or narrated invariably comes to appear arboreal (but more on this soon). Why is this? Ultimately, it's about the ontological categories at play in arborescent thought and the conceptual lens through which the world is comprehended which results from this way of seeing. Within the sedentary point of view, things are always seen from the top down (or from the bottom up); looking with arborescent eyes is always to gaze in a way that reduces the world to simple linear patterns (beginnings, middles and ends), closed narratives, bodies with organs (functional bureaucracies, cybernetic command structures).

To grasp the rhizome you have to engage instead with what Deleuze terms 'nomadic thought'. You need to think like grass. Deleuze has some suggestions:

> Never send down roots, or plant them, however difficult it may be to avoid reverting to the old procedures. 'Those things which occur to me, occur to me not from the root up but rather only from somewhere about their middle. Let someone then attempt to seize them, let someone attempt to seize a blade of grass and hold fast to it when it begins to grow only from the middle.' Why is this so difficult? The question is directly one of perceptual semiotics. It's not easy to see things in the middle, rather than looking down on them from above or up at them from below, or from left to right or right to left. (ibid.)

Back to the Street

Thinking from the middle, that is precisely what we need to do, but before we consider how we do so, we need to return to the object of this enquiry and that is the world of the street and the informal organisations that populate it. I have already put down enough signposts such that the following proposition can hardly come as a surprise: *Street life and street organisation, I contend, if not in its entirety, is predominantly of the rhizomatic form.* It is, as such, nomadic through and through. I will, of course, need to demonstrate why, but, for now, let's consider the wider implications of this proposition before I do so.

In arguing that the informal world of the street is rhizomatic, I mean to claim that it possesses nomadic traits that are wholly distinct from and which are irreducible to that of the formal properties of formal organisations that constitute and define the arboreal state and its constituent apparatus. I am claiming, in other words, that the world of formal bureaucracies and those that pertain to the world of the informal organisations of the street belong to two different modes of social organisation. Each, I contend has a sui generis logic, which means we need a different kind of sociology to interpret each.

Let me go further. To understand the sociology of formal institutions, we need a sociology capable of understanding the features of arboreal systems in a way that reflects their own distinctive mode of organisation. At the same time, however, we need to recognise that we need a very different sociology if we are to comprehend the world of organisations that are not arboreal but rhizomatic and nomadic. To grasp the reality of informal organisations as concrete in thought we need in other words a nomadology.

Given Western thought is in nature and substance shaped by arboreal categories and arboreal thought more generally, it is by no surprise that the sociology of formal organisations is already well developed. To find it we need look no further that Max Weber and his study of modern Bureaucracy (Weber and Gerth 2009). Unsurprisingly, perhaps, the Enlightenment underpinnings of this sociology of the sedentary society have also established the sociological foundations around which positivistic criminology is erected. Contemporary academic gang talk, I would contend, simply accepts these arboreal categories and unthinkingly applies them to the study of street organisations – and why not, because for arborealists everywhere tree-thinking is the only game in town. All of which is just fine, if only those pesky street organisations were arboreal. Only they are not and this is where it all goes so horribly wrong. From this comes 'gang talk' and the ludicrous categories in which it trades: the gang as a bureaucracy, the gang as rational actor, the gang as corporate, the gang as Being and Essence.

If the world of the street is rhizomatic then it must follow that we cannot or should not seek to interpret it from within this sedentary point of view. Why is this? Sanity demands it. Because, self-evidently, if the subject here is nomadic life, then we need a rhizomatic frame of reference with which to comprehend it. The trouble with gang-talkers, however, is that they cannot comprehend this. They cannot because they have trees growing inside their heads and this leads them to find trees everywhere even when the real subject of their gaze is grass. Sedentary thinking unfortunately possesses them like a devil. And this is why they do not see rhizomes even when they are staring at them. John Pitts, a tree-thinker par excellence, to his credit did his best – he at least tried to comprehend the rhizome but failed miserably and reverted to type (Pitts 2008). But then he has always worshipped at the church of latter-day arborealism, so why should we be surprised?

But let's be honest, such tendencies infect academia and all gang talk. But, what the hell, let's be magnanimous. I don't want to blame anyone. The Pittites are, after all, products of sedentary regimes. They come from sedentary orders; they inhabit sedentary organisations; they think sedentary thoughts and behave according to type. How can we ever be surprised when they do? And this is why they see the streets from a vertical perspective and corporatise them ruthlessly.

But this is also the gaze of power and this is why, in a very real sense, and despite their pretensions to be Progressive Thinkers and, for some, 'Left Realists', gang-talkers are in fact consummate idealists. And that is why, far from being on the side of the good people, they invariably occupy the space of the control imaginary.

So how then do we read the street rhizomatically? There are many ways to approach this question. But let's not be too obvious here, working, as they say, from the top down. Let's begin in the middle somewhere by demonstrating what the street is not. Whatever it is, the street cannot be grasped in a sedentary way despite the presence of arboreal features that sometimes appear within it. I will then consider, more closely, the conceptual categories by and through which we might begin to represent gang life and gangness. By drawing upon the work of critical ethnographers who, I will contend, are intuitively nomadic thinkers (whatever else they think they are), ways of comprehending gangs can be derived that stand wholly opposed to and distinct from the sad, dismal categories of arboreal gang talk. I conclude by suggesting ways in which nomadic thought and thinking can and have been applied to explain how gangs evolve and develop.

Reading the Street as Rhizome

Inherent to arboreal gang-talking traditions is the assumption that informal groups like gangs are organised, where the organisational form they aspire toward mirrors that of formal organisations. Given this, gang-talkers approach the gang with of the assumption that you can use the descriptive categories of formal organisations to make sense of them. This essentualising tendency is then reflected in the traits they subsequently 'discover' in the gangs they research. Gangs thus have the following:

- Clear determinate boundaries. These distinguish the inside of the gang from the outside and hence allow issues like membership to be clearly distinguished by positivist science and, not least, enforcement agencies.
- A division of labour. In this corporate vision of the gang, members are allocated into distinctive offices which perform clear functions for the reproduction of the whole.
- A vertical command structure. In this, power moves downward from the leader through various cadres of lieutenants, to street soldiers whose lives the gang leaders control.
- Bureaucratic procedures. They engage in 'grooming exercises' as part of their 'recruitment strategies'.
- They 'organise' and control crime.

However, as we shall now establish, the properties of formal organisations cannot unproblematically be applied to the street world of gangs even if some gangs want to appropriate them. But to get to this we need to return to Weber.

For Weber, modern bureaucracies, at least in their distinctively modern form, constitute hierarchical, centralised, command structures (Weber and Gerth 2009). Within bureaucracies power always moves from the top down through a system dominated by leaders who administer, through various subordinate levels beneath them. When people enter bureaucracies as employees they inhabit pre-established offices where their duties are carefully delineated by formal rules they are expected to abide by, where rules are made and applied impersonally. Positions within the organisation are obtained on the basis of technical merit such as qualifications; and promotion occurs by seniority. As Bauman, observes, the modern bureaucracy is a rational problem-solving machine (Bauman 1989). Whilst they often exhibit a range of perverse traits (not least their awesome capacity to grow and reproduce themselves), for Weber they are nevertheless the most effective tools humanity has developed for realising the various ends society establishes for itself, be this finding cures for a disease, or developing the means to destroy other humans. While not denying that gangs may aspire towards various bureaucratic features, as we shall now establish, whatever street organisations are, they are not corporate and nor can they ever be fully corporatised. They cannot, simply because, as we also establish, the street world is by nature a rhizome.

While it is evident that gangs have structures and large gangs have many arboreal features, it could be observed that in practice trying to create a rational bureaucracy out of an informal street organisation is rather difficult even if there is a will to create one. Let's begin at the beginning. By and large, people enter bureaucracies that pre-exist their employment in them. These are located in dedicated premises such as a factory or a set of offices. Cadres of administrators work to ensure that everything works; specialists are employed to realise the specific ends to which the organisation is geared (such as making things, or providing services), and these work to regimes presided over my managers who are specialists in management.

Much as functionalist-orientated gang-talkers like to fantasise that all of this holds true of gangs read as criminal corporations, in reality none of this holds true. Gangs, it is true, might well fall back on established rituals in order to reproduce themselves, but their structures are always emergent and have to be created and maintained in a habitus largely devoid of the supportive features corporations simply take for granted. More than this, they have to create their structures as an ongoing accomplishment and in the face of opposition posed not only by other gangs (many of whom will not even accept that they are a 'real gang') but also by enforcement agencies who conspire toward their destruction. Most gangs do not own property; they do not own extensive offices; they are literally urban nomads who inhabit the street and are often distributed across them, which creates its own set of problems.

While evidence suggests that the more successful criminals are those who are well networked and possess key criminal skills (Hallsworth and Silverstone 2009), it is also worth noting that the raw material out of which a gang is typically formed are not disciplined adults who eke out their 9–5 jobs with the comfortable expectation that they will receive regular wages in remuneration. Gangs are populated instead by young people, many immature, some with long-established histories of violent victimisation behind them – and that's only for starters. As Jankowski observes, they are often strung out on an unhealthy diet of fast food, not to say stronger, illegal intoxicants (Jankowski 1991). Nor, in the subterranean world of the street, do they live a regular 9–5 existence. In a world where boredom is a regular feature and where the threat of violence is never far away, simply trying to impose corporate structure on a gang, let alone persuading a group of 'defiant individuals' to accept such discipline, rules against the possibility of effecting a normal corporate structure. Given that most gang members typically drift into gang life and drift out after little more than two years (by which time most have had enough), we are not looking at organisations that can self-reproduce easily anyway – at least not by formal corporate means.

If a key characteristic of formal organisations is the subjugation of their employees to formal codes of conduct applied impersonally, this does not necessarily follow in informal street organisations beholden to the 'codes of the street' (Anderson 2000). Gangs are rarely, if ever, fully impersonal. They cannot be because gangs inhabit a habitus where personal and kinship relations matter and where clientelism is the primary method by and through which relations are organised. If we accept, as indeed we must, the fact that violence is a valued currency in the streets, then it also follows that a capacity to demonstrate and harness violence may well be the qualities that lead some to positions of dominance in gang structures. All well and good, only these are not necessarily the right qualifications you need if rational organisation is what you are after.

Indeed, far from being cold, impersonal organisations where objectives are formally established before resources are rationally distributed to realise them, gang structures are radically informal. In them the personal matters, which means personalities matter more than formal positions held by those employed on the basis of technical merit. Within most gangs, the organisational goals are less pre-planned and more situationally determined and driven. Within gangs, the world is not predicable but radically contingent. And whereas in formal organisations business imperatives are realised through the application of a cold, impersonal instrumental rationality, this does not hold for the street life of gangs where personal and business imperatives often overlap and blur, sometimes with tragic outcomes. The code of the street to which most gang members subscribe, it could be noted, is not a regime that is necessarily well geared to creating stable functional organisations (Anderson 2000).

It could be observed that this wholly self-destructive aspect of gang life lies at the heart of most fictional accounts of it. Indeed, it is precisely this feature of the criminal underworld that provides the dramatic tension around which the plot of the average gangster book or movie is organised. Pinky, in Graham Greene's novel *Brighton Rock* (1975), aspires to take the place of a recently deceased gang leader but his emotional instability negates this, as indeed does the opposition he faces from far more powerful gangsters around him. Alex, in Anthony Burgess' *A Clockwork Orange* (1962), feels he is an untouchable leader in the eyes of his gang of 'droogs'. After all, he provides them with a regular diet of ultra-violence, drugs and sex. What more do they need or desire? But they are experiencing relative deprivation and it's getting them down. They are unhappy at his bullying style, and not least the low rewards they feel they receive relative to the huge rewards they believe they deserve that other gangsters around them are getting. Eventually they topple their leader and Alex's time as a successful gangster terminates in prison.

Scorsese's film *Goodfellas* (based upon the 1986 book *Wiseguy* by Nicholas Pileggi) is again a wonderful parable on the inherent instability and banality of gangster life. Even as the group of men around whom it is set become more established and more successful criminals, irresolvable problems ensue from the endemic contradictions inscribed within the criminal habitus of which they are a part. From the very beginning the hero has to navigate through an environment saturated with the excesses perpetrated by men who are systematically violent and some, dangerously psychotic. By the time the movie ends, its hero has developed a drug habit, he is turning state's evidence against his erstwhile colleagues and his closest friend has tried to kill him.

Many real-life examples can also be cited that express how gangsters and their gangs become self-defeating. The career of the Kray Twins in London's East End ended effectively after Ronnie Kray walked into a pub and shot George Cornell dead in broad daylight. Coupled with his brother Reggie's instability, their inflated sense of omnipotence led them to perpetrate acts of excess that exceeded any business logic. And so the seeds were sown that created the preconditions for their self-destruction; in the words of the old maxim, 'Those who live by sword tend to die by the sword'. And this would certainly fit the context of a volatile street world of cities like London today where business and personal imperatives often intersect in troubled and messy ways (as we shall see in the next chapter); where strong emotions run riot and where young gang-affiliated men kill each other, often for the most pointless and stupid of reasons (Hallsworth and Silverstone 2009).

The point I am trying to make here is that gang life is inherently unstable, and even despite achieving a degree of formality in relation to organisation, instability remains integral to the grammar of street life and street organisations. Arboreal features, then, while a feature of gang worlds, do not define street organisations which are by nature inherently rhizomatic. Simply concentrating on the organisational features, creating various typologies distinguishing between groups in relation to the degree of organisation they possess, I suggest, is to miss the point. The street is an impossible space, a zone of radical indeterminacy.

To return to Deleuze, whilst gangs may aspire to territorialise, both in the sense of seizing space and creating structures, they confront, and from the beginning, powerful forces, externally and internally, that over-determine their capacity to do so. They are, I would suggest, as much, if not more, subject to radical processes of deterritorialisation, and this is a feature that leaves them better characterised as rhizomatic. Gangs, are, as such, permanently unfinished affairs, always social relations in movement, always overspilling, always intermezzo. They never simply assemble (as paranoiac gang task imagines the process), they disassemble and reassemble all the time, transforming themselves as they do, metamorphosing as they go.

To be Bataillean for a moment, it could be argued that in part the problem with arborescent thought is that it constitutes gangs in the same way that economists think about energy systems more generally, that is, as systems that consume energy which they then translate into surpluses valorised productively into system reproduction and growth. This, incidentally, is how most classical theories of economics function; functionalist sociology also begins with this premise, namely that the social system operates in a self-rectifying state of dynamic homeostasis (Parsons 1999). Drawing on Mauss' study of potlatch, read as a socially destructive mode of exchange (Mauss 1967), Bataille argues instead that social systems invariably produce surpluses that are not expanded functionally into system reproduction and growth and which, consequently, are squandered unproductively and often catastrophically in the form of deficit expenditure (Bataille 1988). This surplus, the 'accursed share' as he termed it, is never incidental to the life of the system that produces it. More to the point, the way this surplus is expended can and define the operation of the system as a whole far more so, in fact than its economic base.

Informal groups like gangs, I would suggest, can best be understood in Bataille's terms as assemblages that are rarely legible by reference to arboreal thought systems which want to construct them as if they were fully functional homeostatic entitles. They do not and never can be reduced back to systems that simply valorise surpluses into system growth; on the contrary, they exist and from the beginning in an *economy of excess*, and to get to this you need to think of them rhizomatically, as movements which invest in forms of glorious and sometimes terrifying and tragic deficit expenditure, much of which is anything but instrumental or rational. And this, it seems to me, is precisely the strength of Jack Katz in his observations on street life as radically anti-utilitarian (Katz 1988) and *excessive*. But there again, Katz is himself another intuitively rhizomatic thinker.

Rhizomatic Organisation

Consider the terms gang-talkers use to designate gangs. They have a division of labour, a pyramid structure, cybernetic control systems, they engage in 'recruitment' or 'branding' 'strategies', they 'organise' and 'control' crime. Isn't it simply so arboreal. If, however, as we have tried to argue here, the street simply cannot be corporate (even if it tried), it follows that we need to jettison the very terminology such gang talk trades in. What we need instead is a conceptual universe that better recognises the distinctiveness of informal organisations and which does so without committing the other cardinal error (again endemic to criminology) which, in opposition to corporate excess, reads the streets simply as 'disorganised'.

As we saw, when we studied the nature of the rhizome, it is not that they lack organisation, or indeed structure, it is only that the organisational features they display do not follow the predicable logic of arboreal systems. To grasp the world of the street as rhizomatic we need a language that recognises the characteristic features of street organisations in ways that respect their sui generis nature. To an extent, such an exercise does not entail trying to invent such a language from nothing. Ethnographers, true to their craft, have already begun the process. So let's start with them and work sideways from there.

We can begin with Thrasher (1927) and his description of gangs as a unit that spontaneously forms. What a wonderfully and refreshing rhizomatic image this poses to arboreal gang talking traditions who talk instead of recruitment and grooming. Aldridge, Medina and their colleagues also get close to rhizomatic thinking in their designation of gang life as 'messy networks' (Aldridge, Ralphs et al. 2011); far and away an infinitely more accurate designation than found, for example, in John Pitts (2008) arboreal fantasy of a 'super-articulated gang'. Other metaphors lend themselves as an alternative to the tired categories of corporate gang-speaking. Are they not instead better read, as Elke van Helemont (2013) suggests, as imperceptible, spectacular, spontaneous, impulsive and situational? And far from being characterised by firm boundaries that delineate where the gang inside begins and ends, as arboreal thought reads the gang, we find instead porous, fuzzy borders which, far from ever being clearly delineated, are always invariably *vague*.

Instead of possessing a clear corporate structure the gang read as rhizome instead presents itself as a fluid state that is intrinsically amorphous. It never 'develops', it always proceeds by way of 'flows' from one state of intensity to another. It does not congregate, it swarms; it does not march, it drifts, and in its drifting we discern its essential nature as a nomadic life-form. Arboreal thinking wants to confer on the gang a fixed immutable essence; the gang, however, read from within a rhizomatic frame of reference, is better understood as a perpetual, always deferred accomplishment.

Rather than read gangs as a command structure shaped in the image of a tree, let's capture them and their development instead rhizomatically as ramifications, lateral offshoots; in a sense, a glorious species of weed. And the metaphor fits. Like invasive weeds that survive in the most hostile of environments, gangs also flourish in the most hostile of terrains. And even if they are ripped up, as weeds often are, like weeds isn't it simply amazing how resilient they are; how they reproduce themselves despite all attempts to destroy them?

Some might find this all a little too abstract and obtuse? Is nomadic thought and thinking simply an inflated language without any meaningful use-value or; as Roger Matthews (2005) is fond of saying, 'policy relevance'? Let me now concretise some of these terms in order to show that they convey explanatory power.

Let's begin by taking issue with the issue of clear and determinate borders that arboreal gang-talk likes to impose around gangs. Think here, for example, of the many attempts that are made to quantify gang membership and typologise gangs by putting them into neat and tidy conceptual boxes. An entire industry has been established around this. Think too of those lovely corporate diagrams of the gang headed by generals presiding over various subordinate layers in what invariably is presented as a pyramid.

Contrast this instead with the world of the gang as it is described by the new generation of gang ethnographers such as Robert Garot (2010), Timothy Lauger (2012) and Rob White (2013). Here gang boundaries are never clear-cut, just as gang membership is never fully established or confirmed. In fact, in their narratives, nothing in the world of the gang is ever quite where it ought to be. What they present us with instead are vague and ambiguous identities in a world in which the inside and outside of the gang are never clearly defined; where gang reputations are contested both by outsiders and by gang members; where one's gang identity is sometimes elevated but also and at other times disavowed. Far from being fully accomplished entities as arboreal thinking constructs them, as Lauger's work shows, it is social accomplishment on the part of groups who have to struggle hard, and in the face of considerable scepticism, to demonstrate that they are, in fact, the real thing, a bone fide gang (ibid.).

And it is in the desperate attempt to demonstrate and reveal their true gangness that we find revealed another intrinsically rhizomatic feature of gang life, and that is the inherent propensity of gang members to myth-make. Far from being the calculating advocates of instrumental rationality, as functionalist models of gang development imply, gang members inhabit instead a life-world in which their fictional representations of themselves carry as much significance as, and sometimes even more than, their embodied material selves (whatever they are).

As van Hellemont's (2013) ethnography of gang life in Belgium attests, in gang life what you claim to be is often as much a product of fiction as it is a concrete record of things gang members have actually done. As her work and that of Lauger's (2012) also shows, you can be, and are, held to account for the reputation you claim; and should this be discovered as fictional you can be held to account for this as well, and one material consequence might well entail being shot for not being authentic enough. In gang worlds, facts and fictions interweave, and just how rhizomatic is that?

In corporations, of course, you know who is and who is not a member. Employment records tell you all you need to know. In the world of the gang, however, nothing is ever as clearly delineated and established in organisations where the borders between the inside and the outside are never exact.

This inherent vagueness is well conveyed by Hagedorn who presents us with a wonderful double take on the gangs of Illinois (Hagedorn and Macon 1988). He begins with the representation of the gang as fantasised by its enforcement agencies. He then provides an alternative representation derived from his ethnographic engagement with gang members (see Figure 5.3). The enforcement image reflects all the trademarks of gang-talking tree-thinking; the gang as a pyramid composed of various offices. In Hagedorn's representation we are faced instead with an entity composed of strange, amorphous shapes with blurred boundaries; where the linkages between levels appear anything but corporate.

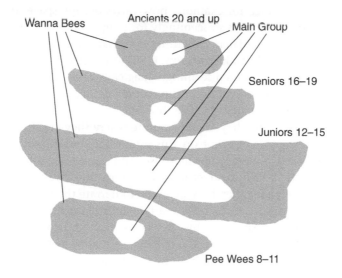

Wanna Bees   Ancients 20 and up   Main Group

Seniors 16–19

Juniors 12–15

Pee Wees 8–11

Figure 5.3   Hagedorn's alternative model of gang organisation

Source: Hagedorn (1988); reproduced by kind permission of J. Hagedorn.

Conquergood is another intuitively nomadic thinker. Like Hagedorn, he also recognises that there is no clear inside and outside to gang life which flows, he argues, through a multiplicity of borders. If you look closely at gangs, he says 'it becomes evident that borders are constructed on multiple and mobile fronts' He is nothing but emphatic: 'borders absolutely crisscross the entire domain of gang culture' (1991: 28). These include the border that separates the group as a bonded ensemble from the wider community they aspire to distinguish themselves from; borders between the groups and other gangs with whom they are in conflict; borders between gang members and their families, and the antagonistic border that separates the group from the enforcement agencies who conspire at their destruction. The culture of the group as such does not emanate from the top down or from a clear centre out to a periphery in the manner of arboreal organisation, it develops at these defining cleavages and processes in directions that are by no means linear and predictable.

In arboreal texts we find the gang represented as a functional agency with various post-holders performing an array of functional talks. But is it ever like this in reality? Is the gang ever a stable functional entity? Considered rhizomatically, they are simply multiplicities in movement. Consider, for example, how gangs occupy space. It hangs about over here and does so seemingly for long periods of time during which little happens. Then something does happen, its state changes dramatically; it might suddenly grow, it might disappear then reappear; split, disassemble, and then seemingly magically reassemble elsewhere. And so we are back to the idea of the ever changing, always modifiable map that Deleuze equates with the rhizome.

Wherever they are, they are never quite where they are supposed to be. They exist of course; not on this estate but that one over there, always displaced, always somewhere else. And this elusive subterranean quality reflects itself into street representations no more so brilliantly realised as when gang members are asked to narrate their gang realities which are never quite as clear-cut as arboreal thinking likes to imagine. This is captured beautifully by the Norwegian anthropologist Geir Moshmus who comments on the trouble he had in getting his street informants in Oslo to comment on their gang reality:

> I had several talks with Aki, Vat and others involved in gangs in Oslo's street worlds. These talks tended to reduce the gang phenomena to be about someone else. It was as if we talked about someone not present. When I tried to talk to my informants about their reality their reality became someone else's, even to them. Talking to me they did not use their own language to speak about themselves. They did not use the language they lived their reality in; the language they would use when they were living their gang reality. My informants were skilled in the language of the controllers ... but that was a language about them. It was not a language their experience lived in. (Moshmus 2005: 204)

The idea that gangs occupy and totally control life in the ghettos and estates where they are found plays a prominent role in arborescent gang talk. The truth of matter is that, like invasive weeds, gangs develop and take root in the interstitial spaces of the sedentary state and it's hard arboreal apparatus. It is not so much a process of seizing territory from the formal order, this is a gang-talking myth. In their subterranean world the everyday world of the wider society passes them by, literally. Their primary source of interest is in each other. Yes, they settle, but in the gaps and fissures. And once established, despite every attempt to uproot them, like invasive plants they persist and reproduce themselves. And even when the state aspires at their very extermination and removes them from their natural environment, they reproduce in the heart of the hard machine; exploiting as they do every crack and crevice in the administered order.

The recent history of American gang development and its expansion globally in the face of outright attempts on the part of the state to wholly exterminate it, exemplifies this, the American gang rhizome. We can trace the story from the 1980s when the postwar Fordist order began to fall apart, leaving in its wake a deindustrialised urban environment populated by a new urban underclass (Wacquant 2008). The emerging ghetto, provided, as ghettos always have, a fertile ground where urban street gangs could take route and thrive (Thrasher 1927). But whereas traditional gangs were traditionally short-lived, in a post-industrial, deindustrialising world no longer capable of providing secure employment for the new burgeoning precariat (Standing 2011), they started to persist for far longer (Hagedorn and Macon 1988). 'Multiple marginality', as Vigil (1988) observes, provides a hothouse environment for gang development. Nor was it simply a matter of established gangs simply continuing. In the manner of the rhizome they subdivided and subdivided again, throwing off new offshoots as they evolved, creating the basis for new cliques that would subsequently emerge in towns and cities that had never previously experienced themselves as having a 'gang problem'.

The response on the part of the state was simply to embark on a process of wholesale repression (Wacquant 2007). Far from destroying the gang, the American punitive turn created the preconditions for the gang rhizome to mutate again. As a direct consequence of the mass incarceration of thousands of gang members, like invasive weeds, the gangs took root and flourished in the prison system. Through the penal estate the gangs further extended themselves throwing out new offshoots as they did, again subdividing as they evolved.

In addition to the 'deadly symbiosis' the state was forcing between the penitentiary and the ghetto, the US state innovated further by embarking on a coercive programme that entailed the wholesale deportation of thousands of gang-affiliated young people back to their country of ethnic origin (including many who had been born in the US) (Parenti 1999; Brotherton and Kretsedemas 2008). Destination states would include the Dominican Republic and South American states such as Ecuador. Did this prevent gang formation? On the contrary, the gang rhizome simply threw out new offshoots that then took root in countries where previously they did not exist. Nowhere has this been more evident than in Ecuador where, in the wake of deportation, gangs that had their point of origin in the US penal gulag such as the Neta, and Almighty Latin King and Queen Nation, took root and flourished. Nor does the story stop here. Women from states such as Ecuador moved to European states such as Italy and Spain in the first decade of the twentieth century, to take low-paid work in the service sector. Eventually their children moved to join these economic migrants. Facing a hostile climate of racism, criminalisation and marginalisation, these young people brought their gangs with them. And so the Almighty Latin King and Queen Nation and groups like the Neta, founded in the US, began to establish themselves in European cities such as Barcelona, Milan and Genoa. And once again we are back to the rhizome, with its surface and subterranean ramifications – a rhizome that today is further extending itself and in the face of outright repression, and in what can be considered to be very hostile environments. 'The world of gangs' (Hagedorn 2008), it could be observed, is a world constructed by the gang rhizome.

Conclusion

While cultural criminology has accomplished much in its celebration of ethnographic research methods, and while the critical ethnographers they celebrate have provided key insights to our understanding of informal street organisations such as gangs, this tradition as yet has not clearly formulated the epistemological and ontological break their work necessarily implies with more orthodox gang-talking traditions. In this chapter, by drawing upon the work of Deleuze and Guattari, my aim has been to suggest that by reinterpreting the study of informal organisations within a rhizomatic frame of reference, not only can the *sui generis* properties of informal street worlds be captured in ways that better reflect their intrinsically nomadic status, but also such nomadic thought takes us decisively beyond the arboreal fixations of conventional gang talk.

At the same time, I have also tried to show precisely why conventional gang talk fails. Despite the fact that its subject is nomadic life, it invariably approaches it within an arboreal perspective. While such an approach might be relevant to the study of formal arboreal organisations, this desiccated sociology is not relevant to the study of street worlds that are ontologically very different.

Other policy prescriptions follow from this, and criminologists and sociologists of the street need to bear them in mind. Be aware of the trees that grow in our heads, for once they grow, all you will ever find are trees everywhere when really the object of your study is grass. To think like grass, avoid reverting to the old procedures. So don't study things from the top down, resist the General in you. Think from the middle and proceed sideways from there and see the world a better way.

6
Back to the Street

It was late in the evening of a winter's day in 2009 and I was travelling home on a bus that was winding its way along the Old Kent Road in south London. The bus stopped and four young men boarded. They were, I'd say, between 16 and 17 years of age, they were black and dressed in the de facto uniform of the urban street warrior: hoodies, baggy jeans and trainers. They were noticeably aggressive as they pushed their way through the bus. One, I recall, punching a fist into the cup of his other hand, muttering as he passed me: 'I've got a fucking rage.' As a calculated performance in what Jack Katz (1988) terms 'the seduction of evil', these young men were quite successful. Everyone, myself included, felt suitably intimidated.

At the rear of the bus sat a young woman of Asian appearance. She was slender and could have been no older, I guess, than 23. The young men settled noisily in the seats around her. One sat next to her. A couple of stops further along some people vacated the bus and the young Asian woman, evidently intimidated by these would-be gangsters, gingerly stood up and made her way forward and sat down on a seat next to one of the exit doors. At no point in time did she say anything to the young men or even look at them. I can say this with absolute certainty because I was watching them with intense criminological interest. A stop later, the young men left the bus. However, just before the door closed behind them, one boarded the bus and smashed his fist hard into the young women's face. Then he left. The violence was as shocking as it was unprecedented. She had, from the beginning made very clear she was intimidated by them and they, in turn, had gone out of their way to intimidate everyone else. Like everyone else, I found myself literally paralysed by what I had just witnessed. Hitting women was, by and large, precluded in the street culture I grew up in (at least publicly) – it was not the kind of thing men were supposed to do.

In this instance, at least, other weapons were not used. However, in cities like London today, street violence is weaponised with the result that a number of young men have lost their lives at each other's hands, pointless casualties of Britain's street wars. I came across one of the victims in the vicinity of my house in New Cross Gate in 2008. He was a young black man, no older than 17. He had been shot and was about to be placed in an ambulance by paramedics. One of his neighbours (whom I knew) asked him how he felt. His response was deeply philosophical: 'That's life, innit', he replied. Unfortunately, innocent victims have also been caught in the crossfire, as was a young Polish nurse who was walking home through a local park where I regularly walked my dog. On this occasion two men decided to have a gun fight and a stray round killed her in the crossfire. In the same park I often met and spoke with a 14-year-old boy. He was the proud owner of a Staffordshire bull terrier that liked to play with my pit bull terrier. The police subsequently raided his house and retrieved a haul of weapons including a semi-automatic pistol. He is currently in prison.

These cases have been blamed by many on what has been defined as Britain's 'gang wars', itself the outgrowth of a new ominous 'gang' and 'gun culture', now apparently rampant in Britain's inner cities. In this chapter, rather than contest the novelty of the violence, or the sensational ways in which it is reported, I will reflect on how best we might make sense of it.

While by no means losing sight of the fact that some of the violence and a number of the fatalities can indeed be laid at the door of the urban street gang, my aim in what follows will be to contest the reductive logic at play in this explanation by establishing that the violence we are looking at here cannot be reduced simply to a problem of gangs. Nor are many of the terms currently deployed to make sense of the violence, such as 'gang culture' and 'gun culture', helpful either. To make sense of the violence, we need to examine, I will suggest, the violent culture of the street world of which gangs are a part, and to do this we need to study street culture and the imperatives around which it is organised.

In terms of structure, I will begin by examining the problems attendant on blaming gangs for the kind of violence described above. I will also show why terms such as 'gun culture' or 'gang culture' are not really helpful either. I will then examine what I will term the culture of the street world studying the three imperatives around which social life within it is structured. These I identify respectively as the search for pleasure, the search for respect and the search for money. If these identify the ends to which social action in a street context is principally directed, what is unique about street culture is not so much these ends themselves (which are widely shared) but the particular way in which they are realised in a street context. Having outlined these imperatives I return to consider how and why the way in which they are realised creates an inherently violent and unstable world, one predicated quite literally on the self-destruction of its inhabitants.

In this attempt to move beyond the gang, I have two overarching aims. First, my aim is to suggest that the social meaning of gangs, in effect, what it is they are all about, cannot be understood by examining their internal dynamics or invoking that mythical alchemy 'gangness' to make sense of them. Gangs, it is my contention, are part of the street but do not envelope or determine street culture in its entirety. To suggest they are is, quite literally, to place the cart before the horse. To understand gangs, then, we have to examine the wider culture of the street of which they are a part. Gangs, in this sense, express and articulate in their actions imperatives that already structure street life more generally. All that gangs do, at least insofar as I understand them, is embody these principles in their self-actualisation. My second aim is to suggest that instead of reifying the gang as current fashion dictates, more can be gained by studying street culture in its entirety. Only when we grasp this can more sensible and proportionate responses be developed to confront the range of problems currently blamed on gangs. It could be observed that in adopting this orientation my aim is not only to take issue with current gang fixations but to suggest that commentators like Bourgois (2003) and Anderson (2000) exemplify better the direction of travel we need to take than the burgeoning academic gang-industry with its peculiar fixations. Both, in this sense, look at the wider cultural order of the street to make sense of the problematic situations that emanate from it. To change metaphors they look at the proverbial wood and do not get lost among the trees. Where they tread we need to follow.

Beyond the Gang

As we saw in Chapter 1, while many people like to situate the urban street gang at the heart of urban mayhem and blame it for the kind of weaponised violence that has left scores of young people dead, there is always a significant excess to the violence blamed on gangs which is simply not gang-related. As Chapter 1 also established, explanations for the violence attributed to gangs can be made without having to invoke the gang as a key explanatory variable. Let's complicate the situation further. Even if you are in a gang and carry a gun, the fateful situations that may lead you to use it might have nothing to do with your gang affiliation. Nor are gangs the only groups that carry weapons, as many peer groups do as well; so do a range non-gang-affiliated offenders, drug dealers and various lone operators in the criminal marketplace (Hallsworth and Silverstone 2009). If we consider some of the motivations for violence from honour slights, to violent territorialism, to the use of violence mediated as punishment, these motives are by no means monopolised by gangs. Given this, let's not overstate the significance of gangs as an explanatory variable or place the burden of explanation on 'gangness', as this approach, I am afraid to say, will not take us very far.

Similar problems accrue when evoking the term 'gang culture' to explain the aetiology of contemporary urban violence. What precisely a 'gang culture' is defies easy description. As with the term 'gun culture', we are dealing here with an undiscriminating blanket term with little explanatory value. Take, as an example, the way the term was deployed as an explanation for the English riots of 2011 where it was imagined as some form of criminal disease that had roots in Jamaica but had now crossed the Atlantic to infect poor kids everywhere. While evoking the term in this way clearly has a populist appeal, it remains devoid of any explanatory power.

While it is clear that some 'gangs' use guns, and whilst we recognise that, to understand the motives of gun users, we need to examine the culture of those that use them the most, blaming weaponised violence on what is often referred to as a new 'gun culture' is also theoretically weak, nevertheless. The problem here is that different guns are utilised by different populations for an array of different purposes (Povey 2004; Hales et al. 2006; Hallsworth and Silverstone 2009) Young people, for example, mostly use air pistols which are very different from the kind of artillery used by professional criminals. And even within criminal circles (as we shall see) there is not one gun culture but rather different players in a segmented criminal life-world. Trying to embrace all of these disparate acts into a reified term called 'gun culture' adds little to our understanding of why certain young men come to engage in lethal violence.

This criticism, however, does not mean that a concern to understand the visceral and violent social milieu of offenders is not important. The question is how best to study this world. Following the lead of cultural criminology (Presdee 2000; Ferrell et al. 2008), one potential way forward might be to invoke subcultural theory. The problem that arises here, however, is the extent to which street culture constitutes a distinctive subculture.

While it is the case that many young people tend to adopt a particular style, one typically influenced by American hip hop culture, to define this as the foundational aspect of a subculture would be to place far more emphasis on style than it deserves. Adopting the look and manner of the ghetto warrior undoubtedly remains a profoundly important reference point in some people's lives, but style and music do not define the relationship between the individual and the violence they do, or the weapons they carry. While the street world they inhabit certainly has its culture, it is not, as Bourgois observes, a coherent and unified space but rather 'a conflictual web of beliefs, symbols, modes of interaction of values and ideologies' (Bourgois 2003). Qualities, I would suggest, that defy being classified as a subculture read as some unitary if magical resolution to a structural crisis somewhere (Jefferson and Hall 1976). Nor is it easy to discern what it is that constitutes the 'sub' aspect of this subculture. While it is certainly the case that many of the young men most involved in the violence we are trying to make sense of here derive from poor areas, we are by no means looking at a population that is wholly excluded. On the contrary, it is shaped profoundly by the consumption logic of consumer capitalism, and to that extent the participants of violence are, as Jock Young observes, very much a culturally-included population (Nightingale 1993; Young 1999; Hall et al. 2008).

If we need to reject the label 'subculture' this does not mean we need to reject the object lessons of subcultural theory which conceives subcultures as a dynamic response to the social conditions in which people live (Hall and Jefferson 1976). As with the subcultures previously studied, the life-worlds of the street continue to be grounded in the terrain of lived experience as it unfolds in particular localities with particular histories, while also emerging as a (socially destructive) response to the wider social conditions in which people live – in this case, the forces of social exclusion these predominantly working-class men confront in mainstream society.

Street Imperatives

Instead of beginning with the gang and making this the focus of analysis, I propose that we need to foreground street culture and examine this instead. By 'street culture' I mean to evoke a subterranean world governed by distinctive norms, values, repertoires of action and practices that organise and define the patterns of social action that those who participate in this culture engage in. Those who participate in street culture are those who can be defined in the first instance as 'street orientated' in the sense that they find a home and meaning in the rituals of street culture and who become, over time, participants within it. The street world has both a core and a periphery. At the core, deeply immersed in it can be found those that quite literally live their life 'on-road'. This population includes many who eke our their living in the illegal marketplace. This section of the street world intersects seamlessly with what is often referred to as organised crime At the periphery we find younger people, predominantly but by no means exclusively male who typically coalesce in volatile peer groups and sometimes gangs.

One way to conceive this subterranean world would be to invoke the image of a whirlpool. Those at the periphery enter the edge of this maelstrom but most will not be pulled deep within it. They circle for a while in the outer eddies and are thrown out or leave. But then, for most, it was never their intension to seek full immersion anyway. Others become more heavily engaged (some willingly, some by accident) and are pulled more deeply into the maelstrom (pulled deeper and towards its centre). The more deeply involved they are (differentially associated), the more difficult they find it to exit.

In order to study street culture sociologically I propose to examine the various ends around which social action in a street context appears to be most directed. In suggesting we study the 'ends' as opposed to the 'end' I also mean to signify that there is not one 'end' but potentially many. We are thus looking then at more than one variable, even if, as we shall see, the ends around which street culture is organised intersect in various messy ways. These ends, in their various forms, constitute what I propose to term the governing imperatives of street life. To study these we need to identify both the ends themselves and, more specifically, study the particular means by and through which these imperatives are realised in a street setting.

Let us begin by studying the ends to which street life is directed. If we consider the wider literature then clearly, as Anderson's (2000) and Bourgeois' (2003) work testifies, and well, the search for respect and honour appears to be one imperative around which street life, particularly for young men, appears organised. Indeed, for Anderson and Bourgeois, it is precisely this feature of street life that they emphasise in their work. Bourgeois' study, however, is substantively about a group of men who make their money illegally through selling and dealing in crack cocaine. While it is clear that in pursuing their trade these men also seek to obtain respect, nevertheless we are also looking at a separate and distinct variable here, or, in my terminology, street imperative. This gives us two. Mindful of Jock Young's (2011) insistence that we do not make the mistake of making street life appear wholly miserable all of the time and construct its inhabitants in so doing as merely sad and miserable, let me add a third imperative to the mix, and that is the search for pleasure. Street life, after all, as the work of Katz (1988) and other cultural criminologists attests, constitutes a liminal space where risk and danger exists, but where all manner of intoxicating pleasures are to be found, quite literally 'there for the taking'.

Three core imperatives therefore govern street life and by extension the range of actions and situations groups like gangs find themselves engaging in. The first imperative involves the search for pleasure; the second, the search for respect; the third, the search for money. Social life in a street context is usually, if by no means absolutely, directed at realising the means necessary to achieve these desirable ends. In making this point, I am not suggesting that each imperative is pursued equally and at the same time insofar as one or more of these imperatives may be more important at a particular time in an individual or groups existence. Having fun, for example, is quite likely to define what younger people want most of the time, while making money might well become more important as they mature.

Before we explore further how these imperatives are realised in a street setting it must be observed that there is nothing extraordinary about any of them. Humans, as Freud (2011) observed long ago, are invariably beholden to the pleasure principle, or Eros, as he defined it (he also spoke of Thanatos (the death instinct), and I will return to this later). It is not in and of itself then anything extraordinary insofar as it is an imperative that governs the lives of those who are not part of street culture as well. It involves searching for, seeking out, or creating situations that will generate what we might colloquially refer to as 'a good time'; situations that, in various ways, will leave those engaging in the search feeling good or satisfied – sometimes happy, sometimes elated and sometimes as high as a kite. The search for pleasure, it could be observed, is, in part, stimulated for the highs it brings but is also motivated by the desire to minimise or transcend situations or events that involve un-pleasure, or which are pleasureless. This does not entail minimising pain or avoiding danger by any means, because pain itself can be intensely pleasurable just as danger can be exciting.

The search for respect is likewise by no means an abnormal behaviour insofar as it shapes the lives of many more people than inhabit the street world. It involves engaging in acts or creating situations where admiration may be accumulated on the part of those engaged in them. It involves engaging in pursuits designed explicitly or implicitly with aim of accumulating honour or status (White 2013). Becoming, in so doing, someone to whom respect is due. As we shall establish, this is also about cultivating a self that others will treat with due regard (respectfully). In part, this project is also about creating or manufacturing a persona that people will not disrespect. As an imperative, the search for respect is a process that has to be accomplished. It is something that cannot be presumed but which needs to be cultivated. Once achieved, it remains a quality that has to be retained, sometimes in the face of those who will deny it or contest it.

In a capitalist economy, making money is of course an overriding necessity. There are a variety of different ways of making it and these vary between the legitimate pursuit of wealth through the legal marketplace to less legitimate pursuit of it in the illegal economy. In a free market society organised around the logic of compulsory consumption, making money is not only about brute survival but about being able to live life as an active consumer, the *raison d'être* of neoliberalism and the culture of compulsory consumption around which it is articulated. Not having access to money or not having enough of it to sublimate socially induced consumption desires consigns those without it into the order of non-being (Young 1999; Hallsworth 2005; Winlow and Hall 2006). The implications of this for those who dwell in an 'on-road' existence are significant.

Three imperatives then, each of which is pursued more widely that the street world under investigation here, but which still constitute the key focus of the street world and those who populate it. Before we turn to consider the unique ways in which these imperatives are realised in a street context it pays to consider how each is interrelated to the others because, as we shall now establish, these are not wholly autonomous variables. We can begin this exercise by noting that the pursuit of each imperative also allows other imperatives to be pursued simultaneously. Making money, for example, can be pleasurable and obtaining vast amounts of it can allow those who engage in it to accumulate status as well through accumulating cultural capital. One can be proficient and skilled in a particular craft and gain pleasure from craftsmanship. One can be respected for this as well. In a society where status is also equated with the possession of the right branded goods, the search for respect is also intrinsically bound up with the search for money. Imagine these imperatives, then, like a Venn diagram.

It is not the ends to which street life and culture are directed that are unique because the pursuit of pleasure, respect and money is a desire widely distributed. What is unique and particular to street culture is how these imperatives are realised. In what follows we will consider how they are beginning with the pursuit of pleasure.

The search for pleasure

We might begin this task by engaging with the recent work of Jock Young (2011) who is scathing about a criminological tradition which he argues makes the serious error of failing to recognise that the lives of the young deviants, so often its focus of analysis, are rarely as dark and miserable as too much criminology suggests. This enterprise he terms 'liberal othering'. In line with this cultural criminological injunction let us therefore begin our analysis of these street imperatives by recognising that, in part, the lives of those who inhabit this world are orientated towards the pleasure principle. Like everyone else, having fun, seeking out pleasure, is what they are also about. Before we consider how they accomplish this it pays to reflect for a moment on the pleasures we are talking about, for there are many. We can begin by identifying what I propose to term the pleasures of everyday life; the everyday pleasures that can be found undertaking many seemingly innocuous things: enjoying a good meal, the company of friends, a sunny day – pleasures too often ignored by criminologists who are more attentive to what may be termed the pleasures of excess. Unlike the simple pleasures of everyday life, the pleasures of excess entail extreme affective states, a movement away from the natural attitude towards a state of transcendence that can in some cases be read as a state of ecstasy.

In the first instance we can note that the denizens of the street world seek out pleasures by doing many of the things that the wider population of non-gang, non-street-affiliated young men do. These certainly include playing computer games (often violent ones), watching DVDs (many about 'gangsta' life) and partying in various clubs and houses and, not least, playing the mating game. Much of the pleasure they find would fall into the category of everyday pleasures. However, they also search out pleasure in ways that are more peculiar to the street society of which they are a part, and in part they also seek out pleasures of the more excessive not to say transgressive kind. One way they produce it is through the time-honoured strategy of 'hanging around', often in 'street corner societies' in the vicinity of the estates where they are located, or in the playgrounds of the schools they attend (Whyte 1943). This is invariably read as indicative of anti-social behaviour on the part of the adult world.

While the street constitutes a place and space young men are decanted to, not least given poor living conditions, it must be remembered that the street is a place of wonder and enchantment as well. It is a place where little happens, often for a long time. It can certainly be a boring space, not least for young people who often complain that they have nothing to do. At the same time the urban street world is a place of adventure, a seductive environment that promises excitement and pleasure, tinged with the risk of danger that makes it that much more appealing (Hayward 2002, 2004). It constitutes a liminal space where the rule-bound conventions of everyday life can be magically circumvented, or, at least for a short period, suspended. The street world thus offers the individual with a space to achieve a sense of personal authentic sovereignty, a sense that everyday life, at least as it is lived by structurally powerless young men, is often bereft of (Bataille 1988). By escaping into the nocturnal order of the street the individual and the groups to which they are affiliated leave behind the rhythms of conformity that life lived within the straight, homogeneous world of the everyday proffers as its reward and enter instead into the wonderland of a heterogeneous order where normal rules do not necessarily apply. Against a world characterised by the usual space-time disciplines, 'on-road' you live by your wits in a world where risks and dangers abound. Integral to this shift away from the mundane and boring we find two intrinsic properties of pleasure production in street culture: first, the art of transgression and, second and by no means outside of it, rule-breaking (Katz 1988). In both activities not only is excitement generated, so too is the acquisition of power, an intoxicating medium for those who otherwise have little of it.

For the members of the peer groups and gangs who inhabit the street world, that is, groups populated by people not orientated towards living placid or pacific lives, pleasure is predominantly obtained, in Goffman's (1982) terms, by being 'where the action is'. This involves engaging in problematic situations that can have fateful consequences, where the events in question are by no means instrumentally driven and which, consequently, can have no end to them beyond themselves. Violent exertion and what Lyng (2005) terms 'edge work' are the media by and through which action is sought out. By 'edge work' we mean acts and activities that involve risk and danger to an individual where these dangers and the perils attendant on them are actively sought out. Fighting in an individual context or in a group is one way in which pleasure is generated; others include engaging in excursions into territory claimed by others; or, more recently, engaging in acts of online bravado where members boast about their daring exploits and disrespect others. Vandalism and joyriding are also pathways by and through which a good time may be had in a street context, as may drug-taking and graffiti (Fenwick and Hayward 2000); as indeed are a myriad of acts engaged in by those who, in Katz's terms, are not only attracted to the ways of the badass, but who, in their celebration of badness, take delight in offending the denizens of the straight world. While highs are certainly to be had through acts like violent exertion, the drug economy, invariably itself a key force in street life, also allows access to a range of chemically-induced highs. Pleasure, then, is a social good actively sought out but in ways that can be dangerous to the point of becoming self-destructive.

The search for respect

While bound up with the pleasure principle, the search for respect also constitutes an autonomous variable in its own right and it needs to be treated as such. Like the search for pleasure, the search for respect is not in and of itself an abnormal or deviant activity, it is a social good also sought by everyone else in mainstream society including the wealthy, powerful and privileged. What distinguishes the search for respect among more marginalised groups of street-orientated young men is the means by and through which it is achieved and the nature of the hyper-masculine norms around which it is structured.

One way to visualise how respect is established is to consider the task of obtaining it, a game that, like all games, is rule-bound and where the rules that govern it are implicitly understood by the players but never formally composed or articulated. There are two parts to this game. First, you have to establish yourself as a viable player in your own right. You have to establish that you are, in street parlance, 'on the level'. To evoke a footballing metaphor, to enter the game you have to demonstrate proficiency in your craft and be fit enough to be selected from the bench to play. Second, and this is particularly the case in urban street worlds, you play to win out over others around you who are also playing the same game. In a practical sense this means that 'to score' you have to accumulate and retain honour, and this is accomplished in an environment populated by rivals who are playing the same game and who, as part of this, are trying to prevent you from obtaining or retaining the honour you claim.

To be seen to be, as it were, 'fit to play' constitutes a social project in its own right. It involves cultivating and constructing a social presentation of self that is appropriate to the field. On one hand, it involves wearing the right clothes with the right brands in the right way. Street culture, it could be noted, is wholly incorporated (at least today) into mainstream consumer culture. Indeed, the young street-affiliated men I recently studied in Birmingham certainly ensured that they looked sharp (against them we, the university researchers, looked positively poor and shabby). It certainly means ensuring that you are not caught wearing low-brand goods. Integral to this project is ensuring that you are not seen as a person to whom respect cannot or ought not to be conceded, which is also about confronting head-on those that try to intimate that you are not what you claim and who as such challenge your honour.

In part the search for respect is a project that also involves embodying in word, presentation of self and deeds the standards that embody masculinity as it is dominantly constructed in Western societies (Connell 2005). Many of these qualities stem less from gangs or gang culture but are embedded in mainstream, not to say working-class, culture. Being tough and being able to handle yourself, confronting status challenges when they arise, and not least mobilising violence if required to settle them, embody these desirable traits. To an extent, playing the game also entails embodying other codes of the street, such as not talking or 'grassing' to police, and backing your brethren if they are threatened (Anderson 2000). For men in particular, it is also about being seen to be virile. Being a virgin and celibate are qualities that have no status in this world and will disqualify you from the ranks of the elect.

As in mainstream society, respect is also bound up with competence, being seen to be skilled at or in activities valued within the field. In the case of street life a competence for violence might well be one virtue that is recognized; many others are as well. Entrepreneurial ability, as we shall see, is itself a valued skill, as indeed is achieving a reputation for being trustworthy, which entails not just competence but not disclosing to outsiders inside business (Hobbs 1995, 1998).

The business of obtaining respect involves playing the game where the stakes being fought for are conducted in a social field that is ruthless, unforgiving and socially destructive. In this sense the struggle to affirm and retain reputation and accumulate respect is conducted in a highly competitive and, not least, sceptical street environment where men face disrespect and status challenges at every step along the way. In many respects the aim of those who enter a life 'on-road' is to successfully navigate their way through this environment; warding of status challenges as they arise while also challenging the authenticity of other participants in the street world. To win is to survive and to have accumulated along the way a reputation either for yourself or your group.

By being 'where the action is' a group and its members engage in the game through the medium of a dramatic performance where they put themselves and sometimes their lives, quite literally, on the line. As Goffman (1982) argues, they gamble with both their welfare and their reputation. In edge work, they take risks where the stakes can be very high with a consequential payoff that might well follow them into their future. They may run, for example, the risk of being caught by the police who exist to prevent the action – and prison might follow; or they may be violently assaulted by other men just like themselves. At the same time, by engaging in risky endeavours, they also have to demonstrate that as individuals they possess character; that they are capable of rising to the challenge, backing each other up, while also demonstrating in performance a range of other qualities valued in street-corner societies such as toughness, courage and integrity.

To an extent, the business of establishing respect cannot be separated away from the need to cultivate and affirm a viable masculine identity. Manliness in this world cannot simply be presumed but has to affirmed and demonstrated through action and in performance. To an extent the violent ways in which manliness is affirmed in this street world owes much to fact that in a society where masculinity continues to be equated with control and power over things and people (traditionally, women), for young men from predominantly poor communities violent assertion becomes for some the only power resource they can access and mobilise to produce an identity that corresponds with this patriarchal imperative (Messerschmidt 1993). To put this another way, middle-class men, by and large, do not have to assert and affirm masculinity through violence because they own and control things like people and resources. They can fall back on the power that status brings, exemplified, for example, in high office or a high-salaried job. No such presumption can be made by men who are consigned to precarious lives in a low-wage, low-status economy. Violence becomes part of the means by and through which viable male identities are constructed among subjugated groups because it is a resource that is available and ready to hand. It is also a currency that finds validation in their parent communities and, not least, in mainstream society through the medium of the culture industries that incessantly promote and celebrate it. This is a vision of purified masculinity where being 'hard' assumes a master status. This is a masculinity where backing down in the face of honour and status threat is difficult and where the onus to retaliate to provocation is an imperative (Hallsworth 2005).

What also makes the street search for respect significantly different from the ways it is established in mainstream society is that the task of establishing it has to be constructed in the context of a violent world where participants cannot take for granted that the respect they claim will necessarily be recognised by others. In his recent ethnographic account of the development of a street gang in a rustbelt city in the US, Timothy Lauger (2012) brings this aspect of the game into stark relief. He charts how a group of urban nomads try to constitute themselves as a gang by building a reputation for themselves, and he shows just how difficult realising this ambition is in practice. What made it difficult was less their capacity to be violent (they held all the right credentials as far as this was concerned) and more their difficulty in getting other people within the local street scene to take their gang claims seriously. In other words, who they claimed to be was not accepted by an audience that was inherently sceptical of such claims and saw instead 'wannabes' rather than the bone fide gang of their dreams.

In the street world, then, claims will be tested and if someone is discovered to be a fake (that is, a person whose myths do not accord with the claims they make) then brutal retribution can follow. Disqualification can also follow if public status challenges are made which are not effectively responded to. In some cases, not responding, or failing to rise to the challenge, will also be read as an indication that the person concerned falls short of the requirements necessary to be considered a viable player.

The task of warding off and confronting status challenges therefore has to be mastered as a key life-skill. As Anderson (2000) shows, it involves knowing and recognising the signs of disrespect when they manifest themselves. It involves cultivating a vigilant disposition, one that can discern disrespect in the way people look at you, let alone treat you. The ego structure that street culture encourages, it could be remarked, is hard but brittle. It looks out upon the world with suspicious eyes for signs of disrespect and responds violently when it is encountered. (To add a brief biographical note illustrating this, I found myself a few years ago in a situation that could have turned very violent very quickly. I was leaving a train at London Bridge when I tripped over and literally fell into a group of young men. Instead of behaving as most would by simply accepting my apologies, the young man I directly bumped into went into a state of war readiness and responded aggressively as if I had consciously elected to disrespect him. I had evidently violated far more than his personal space.)

Today, the game of respect moves well beyond the simple time-honoured medium of invective conducted in a street setting. In grime music and in the stream of videos produced and uploaded by men claiming street/gang authenticity, talented MCs 'spit bars' purposely designed to big up the reputation of a particular group (and the MC himself) while also throwing down status challenges to the other enemies. Given that video formats allow the producers to visually dramatise the status challenge as well as narrate it, such formats with their violent aesthetics function perfectly as media through and by which the game of respect is played out. The bulletin boards that accompany such videos also provide other formats that also work to exacerbate the challenges being made. The use of underground radio by the participants in this world to challenge and disrespect each other constitutes yet another medium in what remains a way of life predicated on the self-destruction of its inhabitants.

Though much is made of the threats that those who occupy this street world pose to the wider society, in many respects this paranoiac way of thinking ignores the fact that the search for respect occurs within the context of a subterranean street world where the overriding focus of attention on the part of the population who inhabit it is each other. They inhabit as such the interstitial spaces of society and though, at times, innocent bystanders, can become victims; the predominant enemy the participants of the street face derives from each other. The street, in other words, is the arena in which the game unfolds and is played out; the rest of the world is a distant sideshow.

The search for money

Street culture is found in its most developed form in areas characterised by high indices of deprivation where local labour markets provide little by way of secure employment where the jobs on offer are of the precarious form. In such a labour market, rates of youth as well as adult unemployment are high and for the young people destined to a life of labour within them, the possibility of securing secure, decent paying jobs cannot be guaranteed. For this, the new precariat, as Guy Standing terms them (Standing 2011), finding work will be difficult, while much of the work they will find will be low paid and temporary; where temporary work becomes a permanent feature of working life. Caught in a state of constant churn moving between low paying short term jobs and a welfare system that is set up to fail them, obtaining money, their 'P's', is by no means an easy talk for populations of young people destined to dwell in this precarious economy.

At the same time as they face manifest material exclusion, the denizens of the street are also culturally included to the extent that they have been successfully socialised into the consumption logic of free market capitalism (Young 1999). They as such are also seduced to believe that success in life is to be obtained by owning the right things. At the same time and as part of this lesson they will also come to recognise that failure lies in not owning the goods they have been taught to desire, goods that are invariably designed to become quickly obsolete, after which they will need to be replaced by the next model or style. Given that exclusive brand status is also bound up with the high prices needed to purchase them, the money needed to live a good life, or at least one that is consistent with the standards young people have been schooled to expect, is quite likely to exceed that which life in a precarious low-wage, low-status market will deliver. Adaption through innovation thus becomes, in a Mertonian sense (Merton and Nisbet 1963), the rational response for many street-orientated young people as they opt away from the diminishing returns of the formal labour market, to make their Ps (money) 'on-road' in the informal economy.

Within this economy, street-orientated young people seek to make money by mobilising whatever entrepreneurial talent they possess in whatever activity will deliver it. And opportunities always exist. For street-orientated young men who lack well-connected elder criminal contacts, some may engage in the time-honoured pursuit of street robbery to accumulate money where violence is the medium they mobilise for obtaining it (Hallsworth 2005); some might develop a capacity for breaking into houses or cars, while others will innovate in different ways, exploiting whatever opportunity comes their way. Dealing and selling drugs for more established dealers is another alternative, and in inner-city areas where drug markets are well established and saturated, this is a key net employer. For most young men who take this route, this will mean selling drugs in the lower echelons of the street retail sector, often in open marketplaces. Some entrepreneurs, using hydroponics, might be engaged in growing 'skunk'. Breeding illegal dogs might be another alternative; selling fake designer clothes and jewellery, another. More entrepreneurial participants may engage in fraud. As within the formal economy, success is largely contingent on the contacts street hustlers are able to establish with already established players and the entrepreneurial flair they may innately possess (Hobbs 1989). While some relatively young people may be very successful entrepreneurs and make considerable money, this will not be the case for most. The returns they make are generally low and certainly not likely to radically transform their lives even though a ghetto narrative suggests that vast riches will be accumulated beyond their wildest dreams.

In contemporary street culture, successful engagement in music might be for some the chosen way of making money, and there is no doubt that some certainly seek to do so in the street world. Talented MCs, looking to gain credibility and reputation by the authenticity of their street connections, work with street gangs producing well-crafted videos characterised by high production values, orchestrated around highly aggressive lyrics coupled with a violent street performance. Rapping your way to financial success is a potent ghetto narrative, though few performers are likely to make it big this way.

Illegal endeavour comes with noticeable risks attached. Just as the search for respect involves gambling with welfare, so too does the business of making money. Risk of arrest, and prosecution and imprisonment, is one likely outcome; becoming a victim of violence is another, and just how likely and probable the real risk of victimisation is can be adduced from the sample Hales and Silverstone studied in their research on gun crime: '40 had previously been threatened with guns, 29 shot at and eight had been shot; 28 had been stabbed, 17 injured with other weapons, 34 had been robbed and three had been kidnapped. Additionally, 26 reported friends or family members shot and injured and another 26 reported friends or family shot dead' (Hales et al. 2006). Accumulating enemies as a consequence of business endeavours such as robbing drug-sellers is also a risk (Jacobs 2000), as are rising levels of stress that living life on the line brings as its reward. For those exposed to high levels of violence there are psychological costs as well.

It is important to recognise that this level of criminal endeavour is not simply the prerogative of groups like gangs as these groups are themselves plugged into distributed networks populated by people who are not necessarily gang members. And even within gangs, individuals are quite likely to engage in scams as individual operatives working for themselves as much as they are part of a collective group enterprise. Many members of legitimate society are also involved in these hustling networks. The public might be the purchasers of stolen goods, or desirable goods such as drugs which state criminalisation ensures cannot be obtained legally. A number of 'legitimate' businessmen might also be involved in helping to fence and sell on illegal goods as well. This, then, is not a black market with clear boundaries that separate it from the licit, but a grey one given its intersection with the wider legal economy (Hobbs 1995).

Unless street-orientated young men are well networked into the wider criminal economy, that is, have close friends or relatives with significant criminal involvement, and successful criminal careers, it is unlikely that most will migrate from the order of small-time hustling to become players in the world of what might be termed more organised crime. Most individuals lead quite parochial lives; most will not have these contacts; most are not wholly committed to crime and will pursue the task of making money in the formal economy through legitimate means; and some might choose not to exploit such links even if they had them because they lack the requisite entrepreneurial talents. But some do, and this might well change the trajectory of their criminal careers.

A group that is relatively well integrated might begin to innovate in the development of its criminal involvement. If they are able readily to mobilise violence successfully and is populated by men willing to deploy it, this might lead them to identify arenas where they can do so. At this point weapons might be carried and used. Weaponisation, however, is contingent on two factors: the existing presence of weapons in the street culture, and the arrival into an area of men who routinely use weapons. In relation to the former, once one group uses or carries weapons then other groups will invariably tool up in response on the basis that not to do so would place them at a hopeless disadvantage to those that do. In the case of Birmingham, where we recently conducted research, guns became more commonplace because men trained in their use and who habitually used them began to arrive in the city. This population included Yardies who came from a parent society in Jamaica where weaponised violence is deeply embedded. Other groups such as Somalis also began to arrive from what was essentially a war zone.

From small-scale hustling, these street entrepreneurs become locked into wider criminal networks and gain criminal capital. They become educated in various scams, and learn how to become players in them. To begin with, this will take the form of undertaking junior and subordinate positions relative to more established criminals who, in effect, subcontract dirty work to them. From small-scale hustling and territorial conflict, these individuals and the groups to which they belong may begin to migrate into more organised crime and criminality. They may become more heavily enmeshed into the illegal drug trade, either as dealers or as groups who make a living robbing other dealers. In a world where business imperatives matter, the group and its members will learn, often from more established gangsters, to be more careful in relation to the way violence is exercised. It could be that they discover market opportunities that allow them to make significant money.

Although for some gang-talkers this transition is often spoken about in terms of the evolution of large corporate gangs with extensive divisions of labour and complex vertical command structures, we are looking here less at shadows corporations as Cressey (1969) once imagined the mafia, and more at distributed networks within which a range of actors; some individual, some in duos and some in larger collectives each play a particular role. Though much is made of large gangs sometimes imagined to possess hundreds of members, it could be noted that, were such groups to exist, this is not a functional way of organising to make money. The group is unwieldy, too difficult to organise, too leaky, and finally it is never entirely clear who is a committed member or simply a 'wannabe' (a street term of abuse).

Instability, Trauma and Street Life

One of the dominant themes that have accompanied the contemporary rediscovery of the urban street gang is the idea that the UK is confronting an organised counter-force that means it harm. Against this interpretation I would suggest instead that what we are dealing with is a street world populated by groups that certainly organise together to achieve common goals (having a good time, playing the game of respect and making money) but who do so in the context of a world that is neither corporate nor organised in the way in which bureaucracies are. The street world is a world that is radically contingent, where violence happens very quickly and where the violence in question often appears like the lightning that strikes at the door: unforeseen and unannounced. Here, business motives and more personal ones intersect in messy ways that make bureaucratic organisation near impossible.

What makes this street world so unstable is that the violence and edge work in which gangs and other occupants of this world engage penetrates into and profoundly structures the way in which each of the imperatives outlined above are realised. Having fun in the street world of gangs involves, as we have seen, violent endeavour, as this is where the action is to be found. Violence in this sense becomes a medium for transcending the routine, mundane and boring. It is through the medium of violence that street-orientated young people (in groups or as individuals) seek to play the game of respect. In so doing, they gamble reputation and welfare in a game of high stakes where the risk of violent repercussions is a risk that has to be faced and confronted head-on. Making money in the illegal economy, or at least in, those sections of it open to street-orientated young men, can also be an endeavour fraught with dangers. Leaving aside the very real danger they face of criminal conviction, the arenas in which money is made are themselves incredibly violent; none more so than in the street retail trade in drugs which is where a number aspire to carve out a living for themselves (Jacobs 1999). In an economy devoid of formal regulation by the rule of law, regulation through violence becomes the de facto mode of regulation.

The problem escalates because weapons like knives and guns have in some quarters supplemented fists and boots. The problem becomes even more problematic when guns are no longer simply the property and prerogative of more organised elder criminals and make their way down into the street world of young, unstable, adolescent men. This is certainly now the case in the UK. It becomes worse because once your enemy has weaponised you are left with little alternative but to engage in an arms race as well.

In a street world where these imperatives are not, as it were, vacuum sealed, seepage also occurs across and between them and this also makes this world unstable and unpredictable. A drug dealer might carry a weapon in order to protect himself (and his drugs) from the risk of victimisation from those members of the street world that might want to rob him. However, someone, somewhere may also look at him the wrong way, intimating an honour slight that has to be responded to. His weapon might well in this occasion be deployed, but not for the reason it was originally intended. Far from being predictable, the street world is inherently volatile and unstable precisely because business motives for carrying and using weapons can be overdetermined by far more personal motives. Whereas professional criminals like bank robbers mobilise violence instrumentally, in a street context violent events are often less pre-planned and more situationally determined. Here, bad stuff happens because someone, somewhere, looked at someone else the wrong way and someone somewhere else will have to be made to pay.

In a world where problematic situations proliferate, rarely resolved through legal channels in the civil courts and certainly not by a criminal justice system widely distrusted, formal means of conflict resolution are notable by their absence. Instead, they are resolved in 'fast time' (as opposed to slow, bureaucratic time) through violent extrajudicial means directed at those who cause offence or at proxies for them, such as friends or family members. The emotional intensity and enmity 'on-road' is all the more exaggerated because of the extreme parochialism of those who live the life. Within this world, small-scale disagreements, feuds and rivalries take on huge significance; a significance that would appear difficult to grasp for those who live outside of the claustrophobic world in which life 'on-road' unfolds.

Violence, then, is like the genie who refuses to enter the bottle once it has been released. It won't go back and it won't go away. More than that, it is contagious. In the street world, violence does not just provoke violent retaliation, violent acts leave in their wake brutalised, damaged individuals and a world of enemies with long memories who carry their 'beef' with them. These problematic situations in turn set in motion vendettas that continue which can be intra-generationally mediated. In fact, so lost in the midst of time can they become that the very reasons that set them in motion are often lost on those burdened with the necessity of taking them forward.

Though it would be fair to say that the logic of mutually-assured destruction that defines the grammar of this world can spill over into the world of innocent bystanders (nowhere more graphically demonstrated than in the drive-by shooting of the Charlene Ellis and Letisha Shakespeare in Birmingham), by and large the victims of violence in the street world are the young men and, sometimes, young women who populate it. Though the motives that legitimate violence might appear insane to the outside world looking in, in the hothouse world of the street seemingly small slights take on a significance and have an intensity that can provoke often disproportionate responses.

Living life in this violent milieu carries a range of psychological costs. Seeing a friend shot and killed or knowing a friend who has been murdered is a traumatic event. Living life on the edge carries with it high levels of stress. As one ex-gang member who had a heavy immersion into street life explained, this way of living often left him unable to sleep at night, staring at the ceiling. It left him feeling unable to use anything but public transport, so fearful was he that someone might just fire a gun into his car should he use it. It could be noted that research suggests that it is when a gang member eventually has enough of living with such risks that many elect to migrate out of gang life and seek a more benevolent alternative. Deeply internalised anger and rage are also endemic to the participants of this world, as is the absence of any clear sense of an alternative that might be different and perhaps better. Though trauma impacts at the individual level, it also impacts on the wider community itself. Self-maiming on this scale carries psychological costs that damage everyone.

One way to make sense of the horror that is being described here is to consider the fact that we are looking at a culture that violates the very meaning of the term 'culture' (let alone 'subculture') if 'culture' is meant in the simple anthropological sense of 'a way of life'. This is a way of life, certainly, but one predicated, to use Bourgeois' terms, precisely on the self-destruction of its inhabitants; a way of life in which psychological damage, trauma, violent injuries and sometimes death are ineluctable features. A way of life which, not least, accounts for the expression I have often heard the denizens of this street world use to describe their lot on more than one occasion: 'dead men standing'. For much the same reasons, the concept of subculture is difficult to apply to this street world. Subcultures 'magically' resolve the predicaments they face through the rituals they engage in and the narratives they weave to justify them. Does this realistically apply in a way of life in which Eros appears to have been evicted and only the spirit of Thanatos appears to figure? I suggest not.

While much is made today of large organised gangs it could be noted that, were they to exist, it is quite likely that the violence in which they engage would be more predictable because leaders would be able to control and regulate more effectively the violent inclinations of their subordinates. In the street world such a situation does not prevail, with the consequence that young men (some in gangs, some not) find themselves inhabiting a life-world where, in the words of one man, 'bad stuff' happens for often no reason and where you can, as one young man we interviewed found out, simply be shot by finding yourself in the wrong place at the wrong time. Rather than see street culture, then, as a game of chess played by rational villains confronting the forces of law and order (an image exemplified in films like *Speed*), street culture best resembles a game of snakes and ladders. The inhabitants of the street dream incessantly of the good times that will happen that will take them onwards and upwards (the final deal, the perfect heist, the successful rap), but the reality is that, too often, even when things go well, the snake is there to greet you: the policeman raiding your house, retribution for a past wrong that has never been forgotten, the murder of a close friend.

If we were to reach for a general explanation that might help explain and understand the social production of life 'on-road' then this might best be grasped through attending to what John Lea (2002), drawing upon the work of Mouzarios, terms the *destructive self-reproductive* logic of capitalist development. Underpinning this Marxist thesis is the idea that capitalism reproduces itself, but in ever more socially destructive ways. As Wacquant (2009) reminds us, we live in socially polarised cities where wealth inequalities proliferate and where spatial segregation has become ever more entrenched. These are cities whose poorest populations have become, under conditions of globalisation, increasingly surplus to production. Dwelling in de-racinated estates, trapped in areas characterised by permanent recession, bare life unfolds here for many in the context of structural long-term unemployment and underemployment.

The problem here is that just as capitalism destructively reproduces itself from above by marginalising and excluding its poorest citizens, it creates, as its concomitant effect, patterns of destructive self-reproduction from below, and this is what life 'on-road' ultimately represents. Here, the socially marginalised respond to their predicament destructively in what becomes, at times, close to what Thomas Hobbes described as 'a state of nature', what he termed a 'war of all against all' (Hobbes 1651). Life 'on-road' is not a world where the social contract has much salience or purchase. This is the zone of the outlaw. This is a zone where deeply internalised anger and rage among depoliticised and deeply alienated young men finds violent expression. The tragedy here is that the rage and anger they feel is not directed outwards and towards the world that marginalises them. Instead, it is directed inward and against each other.

Conclusion

In this chapter I have consciously sought to move beyond the gang, not only in order to understand it better but, in so doing, to focus on what I believe is a far more important phenomenon, street culture and the imperatives that define it. As we have seen, the imperatives I identify are by no means unknown to those who live beyond the world of the street. What is unique about the street world is the particular way these imperatives are realised in a street context and the structuring role that violence plays as an ordering process within them. As I have tried to establish here, to engage with the many problems currently blamed on gangs we need to forsake gang obsessions and study the street world of which gangs are a part. American researchers like Anderson and Bourgeois lead the way here, British criminology needs to catch up.

7
Continuities and Discontinuities in Urban Violence

Much has been made recently about the alleged novelty of urban violence today, and gangs, as we have seen, have found themselves singled out as 'the new face of youth crime'. Though, for reasons already discussed, I view this conjecture as one devoid of sense and meaning, this does not in and of itself mean that nothing has changed. After all, things do not remain the same. Given that society more generally has changed, and changed considerably, it would appear sensible to suppose that urban violence and street culture might be changing as well. With that in mind, in what follows I want to examine street violence in the postwar period using the UK as my case study. Are we looking today at an economy of violence that is distinctly new, and, if so, what is new or novel about it? Alternatively, are their far more continuities that shape contemporary violence than differences, continuities that we tend to overlook, caught up as we so often are in the 'infinite novelty' of the present (Pearson 2011)?

In relation to the question of establishing continuities, I begin by providing a brief overview of street-based violence in the post-Second World War era; a violence regime I will associate with the developing Keynesian welfare state. I then use this as the basis for comparing the violent street culture I described in Chapter 6. As we shall observe, if there are many dissimilarities between the two violence regimes, there are many continuities as well. In the final part of the chapter I return to consider the question of what might have changed or is changing. I conclude that, while continuities remain, neoliberal statecrafting is beginning to change the contemporary economy of violence, and the direction of travel is not for the better.

Street Violence in the Postwar Period

Mindful of Pearson's (2011) injunction that we ignore the lessons of the past at our peril, let us begin this enquiry by examining the forms of street-based violence that prevailed in the UK as Britain developed under the aegis of the Keynesian welfare state in the era of 'organised capitalism'.

So who were the violent young men of our immediate past and how best are we to understand the day-to-day violence in which they engaged? We can begin with social class as a precursor because class matters. By and large, the violence of the street then, as it is today, was an activity predominantly engaged in by young working-class men. Though this generalisation does not rule out the engagement in street violence of the middle classes or the scion of the ruling classes, the overwhelming evidence we have tells us that the gentle art of kicking someone's head in has overwhelmingly been a working-class pursuit. The enormous weight of evidence would also appear to suggest that this violence was overwhelmingly perpetrated by young men, even though young women were, then as today, also involved. To a large extent this disparity can be read as the direct consequence of dominant (patriarchal) gender codes that allowed males to dominate public spaces and which worked simultaneously to confine young women to the private realm of the home and household.

Before we consider more closely the violence these young men engaged in and their motives for engaging in it, it pays to situate their parent class within the wider social context of which it was a part. Though some young working-class men inhabited multiply deprived, perennially high-crime areas, most lived out the round of their lives in more stable, if by no means affluent, working-class areas. The population of young men, as such, contained the social residuum, the sub-proletariat that welfare capitalism had never included; as well as the male offspring of far more stable and affluent working-class communities. In what became at times close to a de facto ghettoisation policy, it could also be observed that the population of the residuum had a distinctive ethnic profile insofar as many migrants from Asia and the Caribbean were spatially located into already poor areas of British cities such as Handsworth in Birmingham, Tower Hamlets and Brixton in London, and Toxteth in Liverpool (Rex 1988; Pryce 1979).

Though there is a pronounced tendency on the part of the powerful to imagine that street violence is a the product of some strange and dysfunctional subculture, driven forward by deranged individuals, characterised by strange deficits; more can be gained by viewing the violence that most young men engaged in in the postwar period as simply an extension of values and norms already long established and deeply embedded in working-class culture. From this perspective, toughness and forms of violent machismo that accompany it were not exceptions to working-class norms and values but by and large an extension of them. Within working-class culture, as Walter Miller (1975) argued long ago, toughness coupled with an ability to handle yourself have always been valorised and, within limits, excused. Not only does a certain competence in physical violence find tacit endorsement and cultural acceptance ('It's what boys do') this culture has also traditionally stigmatised and censured forms of masculinity that depart from this mould. Being 'soft', a 'cissy' or a 'nancy boy', I recall, from my own experience growing up in a working-class school in the 1960s and 1970s, were terms of abuse applied to young men who fell short of this ideal.

If we consider why this validation of physical prowess finds such cultural endorsement then this follows directly through from the uncompromising tough, harsh and adverse conditions that the working class historically had to confront. In other words, toughness and being able to handle yourself are values that came to be valued because they were integral to physical survival. In a culture grounded on harsh uncompromising manual labour, physical hardness expressed resilience of the class itself.

If violence could be tacitly legitimated in working-class culture, it was also regulated by informal street-codes that placed determinate limits to the violence. In a patriarchal culture dominated by an aristocracy of labour (shop stewards, foreman, sergeants), the activities of the young were also policed internally by the working-class community itself (Lea 2002). In Lea and Stenson's terms, governance was regulated from below far more than it was achieved by formal policing agencies from above – despite their intermittently and by no means successful attempts to 'police the working-class city' (Lea and Stenson, 2007; Cohen 1979). By and large, this worked to keep violence by and large within bounded limits in a world where strong cohesive communities were able to exercise authority over young men who generally would grudgingly consent to it.

If the intergenerational cultural reproduction of norms that validated violence helped explain why some young men might mobilise it, this alone does not explain the contexts where they would predominantly deploy it. Violence then, as it is today, was a de facto response to interpersonal disputes, to honour-slights, to group rivalries, to the search for respect that acquiring a reputation as a hard man can accomplish. The means of violence, after all, are ready to hand, and violence exists as one plausible response to a range of problematic situations.

To this, we also need to factor in a range of non-instrumental motivations. Among these, we need in particular to factor in the quest for excitement and pleasure. The key characteristic of the violence that falls under this category is that it is predominantly non-instrumental, non-utilitarian and is often engaged in as a hedonistic leisure pursuit by men who, in Jack Katz's terms, get their kicks from walking the ways of the badass (Katz 1988). For young working-class men in particular, whose destiny in life was almost always going to be the factory, violence constituted the means by and through which they could seek to escape, at least temporarily, from the tedium of manual labour. Violence, in this sense, was an extension of leisure in a world otherwise organised around structured, repetitive work disciplines.

It could be observed that this is precisely the world that David Downes discovered in his seminal work *The Delinquent Solution* (1966). Based on an attempt to apply American Subcultural Theory to make sense of male street cultures in London's East End, he discovered less gangs adopting a 'delinquent solution' (Cohen 1955) but more 'street-corner societies' populated by young men who engaged in violence along with various other forms of wilding out (including hard drinking) as a leisure pursuit.

This hedonistic aspect of working-class culture is wonderfully exemplified in the gritty realism of Alan Sillitoe, nowhere more eloquently expressed than in the opening pages of his *Saturday Night and Sunday Morning* (1958), a novel set in an industrial mill town in the 1950s, and which follows the day-to-day exploits of its hero, Arthur Seaton, a machinist in a local factory. The opening page is a wonderful reminder to everybody that the hedonistic pleasure of life in the night-time economy is somehow entirely new. Like so much of our present, continuities as opposed to discontinuities figure:

> For it was Saturday night, the best and bingiest glad-time of the week, one of the fifty two holidays in the slow turning Big Wheel of the year, a violent preamble to a prostrate Sabbath. Piled up passions were exploded on Saturday night, and the effect of the week's monotonous graft in the factory were swilled out of your system in a burst of goodwill. You followed the motto of 'be drunk and be happy', kept your crafty arms around female waists, and felt the beer going down into the elastic capacity of your guts. (Sillitoe 1958: 1)

Nor is violence far away from Arthur's life either. Having been discovered sleeping with another man's wife, he finds himself violently assaulted. Interestingly, his assailants are squaddies.

Why, though, did some young men become more proficient in violence than others during this period? Paul Willis provides perhaps the most compelling explanation for this in his work *Learning to Labour* (1977), an account of why working-class men often tend to find themselves confined to low-status, manual working-class jobs. Based on ethnographic research conducted on a group of unruly working-class young men in a school in Wolverhampton in the 1960s, he shows how they effectively rebel against a middle-class school system whose value system they discover appears destined to fail them. Instead of engaging in what they came to view as effeminising intellectual endeavour, they reasserted instead more traditional working-class verities. They celebrated physical toughness and embraced misogynist, not to say racist, standpoints. In so doing they explicitly rejected the middle-class gateway to success through intellectual assertion and deferred gratification. The unintended consequence of their youthful rebellion, however, is that, far from rebelling successfully against the system, their adaptive response simply prepared them for work in the low-wage, low-status sector of the economy, which was always going to be their destiny anyway.

Was this violence predominantly group-based and were gangs present? If we return to the late 1950s and the appearance of the Teddy boys, it is clear that as far as the media and other right-thinking people of the time were concerned, gangs were certainly part of the problem. I would, however, suggest that most the violence that occurred in this period was group-related. In fact, going further, I would suggest that to Miller's core 'focal concerns' I would also like to add another: 'violent territorialism'. This is not new: it has always been a core and distinctive feature of male working-class culture in working-class communities, and a trait I have tried to describe in my own history of growing up in the postwar period.

For the most part, the violence I have sought to describe here was enacted not by people with psychological deficits and with proliferations of 'risk factors', but as an intrinsic property of the cultures of masculinity associated with particular strains in working-class culture. This gendered order produced men shaped by gender norms that valorised toughness as a virtue, where being able to handle yourself was in part what men (as opposed to women) were supposed to be. Given that the means of violence were always ready to hand (your fists or boots) violence could, as we have seen, be deployed for the purpose of leisure, as edge work, or for defensive and offensive purposes. In an adolescent world where the police have always been distrusted and the apparatus of the criminal justice system is rarely seen as a vehicle by and through which justice is achieved, violence has also been used as a regulating force in its own right.

As Matza (1990) rightly argues, for the most part, young people tend to drift into crime and violence. For the overwhelming majority it is not a life vocation or career. For most young people it is something they would have encountered at a stage of their lives. It will be first experienced in their neighbourhood, then in the schoolyard. Participation for some might become more prevalent as they enter adolescence. It is quite likely that more serious forms and prolonged exposure to it will take place in poorer areas but, by and large, for most it is something that will end as they mature. By navigating an orderly transition from childhood to adulthood, violence, at least for most, is something that will be left behind. Paid work and family life traditionally stabilised most adult-male personality structures in the direction of law-abiding behaviour. In a society where the wider violence rules are that adults should not engage in violence, engagement in it is actively discouraged and sanctions applied to those who fail to heed the injunction. While violence still remains valorised in the wider culture, where it appears is in the form of entertainment, by adulthood it is not something most adults are expected to engage in.

This account, I recognise, is very general, and before I conclude this section I want to reflect here for a moment on what we might colloquially refer to as the high-crime areas that persisted in the postwar period into which welfare capitalism had made but modest inroads. Many of these areas had always been poor and within them poverty and deprivation was always high, and crime in its various forms constituted an invidious feature of social life in them. While it is important that we do not lose sight of the accomplishments of the welfare state, not least in the expansion of affordable social housing coupled with welfare benefits, it could be argued that postwar planning also helped exacerbate as oppose to reduce the spaces for crime and violence. Soulless estates often appeared perfectly designed for encouraging crime and not least the fear of it. Though the council house movement was initially informed by the benevolent vision of providing decent housing for the working class, by the late 1960s many estates were being used as little more than social refuse sites into which various 'problem families' (as they were called) were being decanted. Unsurprisingly, in some of these areas, deeply entrenched subcultures of violence became embedded or simply reproduced themselves.

In the postwar period, the poorer areas of Britain's inner cities were also becoming ethnically reconfigured as new generations of migrants from both Asia and the African Caribbean began to settle in the UK, drawn here by the promise of work in what was becoming a dynamic postwar boom economy. The welcome many experienced, however, was by no means hospitable. Many ended up working in the low-status, low-pay jobs despite being qualified for better work. Though migrant groups often tend to migrate to areas fellow migrants also inhabit, Britain was also running its very own de facto ghettoisation policy (Rex 1988).

For the offspring of these migrants, life was shaped by the cruel intersection of harsh economic marginalisation coupled with overt racism deeply inscribed in the social fabric. Racism could also manifest itself in highly violent forms, and in response to it young migrants had no option but to organise to defend themselves. Though texts such as *Policing the Crisis* tend to paint a benevolent and rosy picture of life in these communities, where crime and criminality is explained away as little more than the acts perpetrated by well-meaning spivs (Hall, Critcher et al. 1976), as Ken Pryce's (1979) ethnographical account of a West Indian community brings home, there was an array of adaptive responses that were by no means benevolent or positive. He examined a world populated by some men who made their money as pimps living off women. He also examined the world of younger 'rude boys' who were not prepared to do 'shit work' for the white man in a low-wage economy and who drifted into a life of low-level crime and hustling. His work was also sensitive to the wider cultural and political currents that were also shaping social life in the ghetto he was studying. He examined the rise and political impact of reggae, which he read as both a subculture and political movement. He identified in the figure of the Dreadlock Warrior an oppositional culture locked into a pan-African vision predicated on a messianic return to a promised land and an escape from Babylon; a cultural current that was profoundly influential and which influenced far more than the Rastaman. I will return to this issue.

Continuities

So what has changed and what has not? Prior to looking at the latter, it pays to study the former because there are a lot of continuities. We can begin on a Durkheimian note by noting that the street level violence I have described here is a social fact that will reproduce itself at a certain level. It will do so because wider social arrangements will always produce the preconditions that will work to produce young working-class men who will draw upon violence as a social resource and mobilise it for an array of different ends. Which also means recognising the absurdity and impossibility of empty political slogans with grandiose titles such as 'ending gang and youth violence'; or which promise to deliver 'within the lifetime of this parliament', as one prominent Labour MP once stated 'an end to anti-social behaviour'. Durkheim was always right: crime is a social fact, and as Nils Christie (2004) reminds us, the question should be less about how much there is and more about how much people want and what constitutes a suitable amount.

With that in mind, until such time as we build a very different kind of society, street-level violence will recur because the preconditions that justify it persist then as they do today. Let us look at the continuities. We can begin with gender norms. Today, as in our immediate past, forms of masculinity are produced and receive validation which validate hardness and toughness as a social virtue and as a means by and through which status can be achieved. Despite living in a society whose key violence-rule is that there should be no violence, we also live in a contradictory space where violence is everywhere vicariously reinforced through a cultural industry that elevates and valorises it.

In deeply inequitable societies where hegemonic masculinity continues to be predominantly associated with the exercise of power and control over power resources (things as well as women) (Connell 2005), some young men, particularly from multiply-disadvantaged communities, will resolve the predicament of a power deficit by mobilising violence as a vehicle by and through which they can exercise power and become 'proper' men in so doing. As Willis (1977) and the British subcultural theorists also showed, and long ago, in a world whose institutions continue to be organised around middle-class goals, some young working-class men will adopt the longstanding subcultural solution of falling back on versions of a hard, purified masculinity, always already; an essence intrinsic to working-class culture, as we have seen. And the resilience we find ingrained in working-class culture and the culture of resistance simultaneously inscribed within some ethnic communities will also work to ensure that violence and violent assertion remains a potent currency.

In a street world populated by social beings as opposed to social isolates, it could also be observed that the violence will predominantly be group-based precisely because group-based delinquency is what young men do. They will, as they always have, 'hang around' street corners and they will always hang around them in peer groups. As I have tried to make clear, it is not that the gang today reflects the 'new face of youth violence', insofar as group-based delinquency has always been with us – as indeed has violent territorialism, as we saw in Chapter 2. What has changed is the way we now tend to focus on the group qua group (the gang has arrived) as opposed to particular categories of group offenders such as street muggers. More than that, in a society in a panic over gangs and, as such, addicted to gang talk, the idea that street crime can be explained any other way seems to have been lost to history, such is the power of social amnesia (Hallsworth 2011a).

While much is made of the sensational discovery of gang girls and 'she-male' gangsters, it could be noted that while it has always been the case that young women were capable of and have committed the same forms of crime and violence as their male counterparts, they have never done as much, and nor is their involvement as significant as that of males, as the work of Susan Batchelor and Tara Young tellingly shows (Batchelor 2001; Young 2011).

Prior, then, to accepting the populist mantra that everything today has changed along with versions of 'We have never seen anything like what we experience to day', it is worth bearing in mind that strong continuities with our immediate past remain.

But not everything is the same. I am by no means sanguine about current social arrangements and their trajectory of change. So, in addition to thinking through what remains perennial to the regime of violence I have described, it is also as important to consider discontinuities, and a few can be noted because they are beginning to make a difference. Life 'on-road' as I described the volatile habitus of our present, while profoundly shaped by many of the same forces that have always worked to mould street culture, is also being shaped by other forces.

Discontinuities: On Neoliberalism and its Consequences

We can begin by noting the stark changes that have occurred in British society in the last three decades, changes that have profoundly transformed the economic, cultural and political landscape. These have been summarised in different ways: as the shift from a Fordist to a post-Fordist society (Amin 1994), or as a shift from modernity to late modernity (Bauman 1997; J. Young 2007). I would, however, agree with Wacquant (2009) and suggest that the direction of change can best be read as the shift from welfare-state capitalism to that of free market neoliberalism. To put this in another way, until recently we lived within the aegis of a liberal welfare state and a managed capitalist economy. Today that state no longer exists, nor does the economic order it supported. What was a welfare state has been replaced by a neoliberal state, while what was once a managed capitalist economy has mutated into a harsh, deregulated free market.

What has this to do with the wider ecology of violence? As we shall now establish, the answer to this is, quite a lot. Let's begin with the issue of social class because the class structure has changed and is changing. Within the welfare state the social order resembled a diamond. At its apex could be found what Marxists would describe as the ruling class, those who owned and controlled the means of production. Beneath them, but still in the upper echelons of the diamond, could be found a more or less affluent middle class; beneath them, in the bottom segment of the diamond, the working class. In the postwar period the most successful sections of this class were becoming more affluent, many enjoying wages that paralleled those of the middle classes. This was both an accomplishment of welfare-state managed capitalism and, not least, political struggle on the part of an organised labour movement. This class had been born in the fulcrum of the industrial age, and had settled over the twentieth century into large, cohesive urban-based communities, patriarchal to an extent, by and large self-governing and self-policing. Beneath this section of the working class, occupying the areas of perennial poverty and deprivation, could be found the sub-proletariat, or the social residuum; a class which, despite the integrative programmes of welfare-state capitalism, had not been meaningfully integrated into the dream of prosperous material progress that the 'white heat of technology' was supposed to deliver. It could be noted that in the welfare state, material progress was supposed to compress the diamond, flattening it at the bottom as the poor became more affluent, merging eventually (or so it was hoped) with the middle class.

It is within this social formation that the ecology of violence I have attempted to map above can be located. Within it, violence occurred but, as we have seen, more as an extension of working-class norms into the world of leisure, in a world where the promise of factory labour would stabilise adult personalities and bring an end to the drift into crime and violence.

Only the class structure of the welfare state has changed, and the change has been such as to justify Guy Standing's (2011) argument that sociologically we need to recognise that traditional class typologies no longer map easily onto our present. Instead of a diamond-shaped society we move instead into a neoliberal present that can best be grasped through the metaphor of an hourglass. Not least, the image allows us to capture the realities of neoliberal policies and their impact, realities that have led to escalating inequalities coupled with declining social mobility for everyone but a nomadic, socially disconnected, feral over-class, the winners in a winner-takes-all economy (Harvey 2010). Also successful but a long way below the over-class can be found a qualified professional elite, the 'salariat' as Standing terms them. In the centre we find what is often referred to as the 'squeezed middle'. This is occupied by the middle classes. While the more successful elements of this class still lead prosperous and secure lives, their children are by no means likely to be as prosperous or secure. Nor will they be likely to enjoy the kinds of security taken for granted by their parents. This class, as a whole, is best defined by its sense of insecurity and by the fact that it is very security-conscious; nor does it feel connected to, or indeed inspired to support, the classes located beneath it (Garland 2001; Lea 2002).

In the bottom section of the hourglass we find a working class that is no longer upwardly mobile and which is fragmented and fragmenting. Decades of deindustrialisation; the rise of an increasingly atomised and individualistic society coupled with a ferocious class war waged against organised labour by successive neoliberal governments, have eroded its affluence, its cohesiveness and its consciousness. While sections of this class continue to live out the round of their lives in stable jobs and stable work, this is progressively becoming less the norm in what has become a deregulated, free market society. Instead of facing upwards migration into the diamond, under conditions of free market neoliberal accumulation, many sections of this fragmenting class are drifting down into the bottom section of the hourglass. This section is predominantly occupied by the precariat, so-called because precariousness now defines the social conditions in which it exists. This is not, as Standing argues, a class in itself, in the Marxist sense of the word: this is a class in the making. Nor is it the unfortunate by-product of neoliberal policy; on the contrary, it is a calculated product of neoliberal statecrafting. As the violent street culture described in the previous chapter is intimately connected with the growth of the contemporary precariat, it pays to reflect upon its constitution and the conditions of its existence.

We can begin by examining its membership. While it contains what would once have been considered the sub-precariat of the welfare state, the social residuum it never got around to including, its ranks have been supplemented by the downward mobility of many sections of the fragmenting working class. In a world where the ethnic composition of poor urban areas has been ethnically reconfigured following successive waves of inward migration, minority ethnic groups are also significantly represented. In what has become a post-full employment society and one where 'the spectre of uselessness', as Richard Sennett defines it (Sennett 2006), confronts many more people than the already poor, many other social groups are being decanted into the precariat and into precarious living. Aging members of the middle classes, working in companies that no longer feel compelled to invest in their staff, represent one constituency. Students now forced to hike up huge debts in order to get degrees for entry-level jobs which, until recently, did not require them, represent another. Young people are significantly overrepresented more generally in a world where the working-class jobs that would once have been available to them have noticeably declined. So what, then, is distinctive about precarious life? We shall return to Guy Standing.

The precariat has not yet come into focus. Many millions of people are experiencing a precarious existence, in temporary jobs, doing short-time labour, linked strangely to employment agencies, and so on; most without any assurance of state benefits or the perks being received by the salariat or core. Most lack any sense of career, for they have no secure social and economic identity in occupational terms. The precariat is not 'socially excluded', and that term is misleading. And the precariat is not adequately appreciated if we focus on income poverty alone. The precariat is socially and economically vulnerable, subject to anomic attitudes and without any social memory on which to draw to give them a sense of existential security. Those drifting into the precariat encompass what some see as urban nomads. (Standing 2009)

Surplus to production, or only allowed onto the lowest rungs of production in a flexible labour market comprising low-paid, low-status and insecure work; this population has been socially abandoned in an economic world where wealth has shifted upwards into the hands of already wealthy, while older social support systems such as welfare have been dismantled or reconstructed into coercive workfare (Wacquant 2009). This is a population that has been deliberately dispossessed and disenfranchised in equal measure. This is a population that no longer can expect the economic prosperity and stable work the welfare state promised; this population exists instead in an insecure world where the forms of security that the welfare state sought to provide have been abandoned or privatised. This is the world in which temporary jobs remain temporary and rarely become full time, not least for young people (Standing 2011).

If this population is materially excluded, they are also, as Standing observes, socially included as well. And this aspect of their contradictory standing in our society also needs to be recognised if we are to understand certain aspects of the violence under consideration here – for while evicted from meaningful work, the precariat is nevertheless included into the narcissistic culture of compulsory ornamental consumption around which free market society is organised (Hall et al. 2008; Young 1999). Shaped by ruthless marketing to desire branded goods – the possession of which is now worn as a necessary talisman of belonging – the precariat are remorselessly forged to become consumers and to define success in life through engaging in successful conspic-uous-consumption rituals (Hallsworth 2005). Jock Young (1999) uses the metaphor of bulimia to capture this feature of late modern life. Free market society, on one hand, materially excludes the precariat but culturally includes it as well. Unfortunately, these are consumers who cannot always consume legitimately given their material exclusion and the exploitation that is their lot. For Bauman (2000) they are, as such, the 'flawed consumers' of late modernity.

Social bulimia is a powerful metaphor with its intimations of a pathology organised around ingestion and vomiting. But let me offer a more overtly Marxist reading of the paradox we are describing here. What neoliberalism does is to colonise the individual while at the very same time it profoundly alienates them. It colonises them to the extent that it aspires to shape every appetite and every desire in the image of consumption and the market; but at the same time the political logic of neoliberalism is to alienate them from any and all vestiges of tradition and ritual beyond those demanded by the marketplace. Seabrook draws out well the implications of dwelling in this hyper-real world and in so doing captures a key attribute of a class which has 'no historical memory'. 'To grow up under the domination of consumer capitalism is', he argues,

> to see that part of us which used to belong to society to be colonised, torn away from traditional allegiances, and to be hurtled, alone and isolated into the prison of an individual's senses. The child tends to be stripped of all social influences but that of the market-place; all sense of place, function and class are weakened, the characteristics of region or clan, neighbourhood or kindred are attenuated. The

individual is denuded of everything but appetites, desires and tastes, wrenched from any context of human obligation or commitment. It is a process of mutilation; and once this has been achieved we are offered the consolation of reconstructing the abbreviated humanity out of the things and the goods around us, and the fantasies and vapours which they emit. (Seabrook 1978)

The process of 'stripping away' must itself be read as a productive strategy, a mechanism by and through which the new precariat is being produced. It functions through atomisation and individualisation where the individual self and its desires are now made a measure of all things. It functions through eliminating older social collectives and the organic ties that would once have bound them to place and community. To grow up in a neoliberal capitalist culture is to find yourself in an anomic space, where historical memories and any connection to a past history of struggle have been utterly attenuated. It is to inhabit a present wholly disconnected from the past that determined it. It is to dwell within the context of a depthless hyper-real culture that is fundamentally depoliticised.

Whereas the logic of welfare capitalism was predicated, in principle at least, on a class compromise based on the assumption that to negate class conflict it was necessary to deliver material benefits to the working class, neoliberalism no longer operates to a similar mantra. Instead, it functions by deliberately reversing and hollowing out the very gains that the working class had struggled to achieve. To grow up in the UK today is to grow up in a society in which welfare has mutated into a coercive form of workfare. It is to grow up in the context of a society where wages are relentlessly reduced and where work conditions for the burgeoning precariat only ever worsen. In the context of deindustrialised areas, it is to grow up in a world where regeneration no longer means investing in poor communities but rather subjecting them to forms of coercive management and control (Atkinson and Helms 2007).

The symptoms of this are described well by Mike Davis (1992) in his dissection of what he terms 'the ecology of fear'. Such 'regeneration' can be seen in the relentless target hardening of the urban environment; in the installation of now pervasive CCTV; in the development of an ever more extending police family, mobilising an ever more coercive battery of powers against young people. As Roy Coleman's (2004) and Lyn Hancock's (2003) works tellingly show, while regeneration in the developing entrepreneurial city supports the socially included, such inclusion is invariably exclusory insofar as it functions by coercively excluding the urban poor and not least its young from the citadels of regeneration, and not least from access to new housing developments that have been deliberately engineered to exclude them (Scraton 2004; Burney 2009).

Not only is the new precariat materially disadvantaged, it is also systematically demonised and stigmatised. In neoliberal society, poverty has the status of a disease that is self-authorised, and this version of underclass thinking saturates political and media discourse on deprivation and poverty. It can be seen graphically in the government's response to the urban disorder of 2011, blamed variously on criminal gangs, mindless criminality, dysfunctional families and dysfunctional culture. It is evident in the demonisation of the working class as a population of 'chavs', a term that now translates as 'stupid and ignorant people' (Hayward and Yar 2006).

Jock Young (2011) is right to remind us in his recent work that life for the urban poor is by no means as miserable as catastrophe criminology often intimates, just as life for the affluent is by no means a bed of roses. Beware, he argues, the dangers of liberal 'othering'. It is a fair point, but if we are to understand certain characteristics of the violence under consideration here, finding rays of sunshine in ghetto cosmopolitanism isn't really the answer. What we need to do instead is to reflect specifically upon the affective states that living life under the conditions described above actually induce, not least among the young men whose violence we are trying to make sense of.

My point is this: these processes, what we might generically define as the cultural logic of neoliberalism, are not abstract forces that bear down distantly on the precariat. Alienation is not an abstract quality of life but something phenomenologically experienced and confirmed on a day-to-day basis in the precarious lives people are forced to lead. Alienation is induced in the feelings that young people experience as a consequence of the stigmatisation they are subject to. 'We're seen as just lost' was one response given to us by a young man we interviewed in Hackney, who was talking about how he thought he and his friends were viewed. Alienation best describes what it is like to have job application after job application turned down, a regular experience for many of the young people we have interviewed. Anger and despondency coupled with a deep sense of lingering resentment are predictable and entirely rational responses to a world where the relations young people from multiply-deprived areas have to formal organisations, and their representatives are often relentlessly negative and hostile. Moreover, these affective states are actively confirmed in the direct relations young people and their families have with ever more distant and disinterested authorities – confirmed explicitly, for example, in the negative experience of being stopped and searched. Confirmed as well in the invariably negative experiences young people, and not least their families, have with benefit agencies that function to criminalise them (Rodger 2008).

Whereas the working class of the welfare state were bound to an economic order that aspired to secure their consent by embedding them into welfare state and welfare citizenship, the Achilles' heel of neoliberalism is that, in creating a precariat subject to deteriorating life-chances, it has not created a stable mode of regulation and one where generalised consent can easily be secured. While the logic of neoliberalism functions to maintain and produce a class that is internally divided and for the most part passive, there are good reasons to suggest that the adaptive response of some sections of the new precariat to its conditions of existence may adopt socially destructive forms. My conjecture is that the socially destructive way of life I categorised as 'on-road' constitutes one such adaptation. So, then, in what ways does precarity shape new patterns of urban violence?

Precarity, in the first instance, erodes the older patriarchal dividend that would once have worked to secure viable working-class male identifies. Violence and violent self-assertion under such conditions may become an alternative vehicle for securing a viable masculine identity among some sections of the precariat. This will particularly be the case for young males who are being produced as literally surplus to production in a post-full employment society (Messerschmidt 1993). While there is a sense in which violence as masculinity has always been an issue among males, in a world where more of them are consigned to structural powerlessness, this de facto fall-back position might become more as opposed to less likely.

As Bea Campbell's (1993) work in the deindustrialised estates of the North following the wave of 'white riots' in the 1980s demonstrated, when the local state is 'rolled back'; when its welfare structures become attenuated and 'hollowed out', in a world where the formal economy no longer offers the prospect of meaningful employment, violent men operating within an expanding illegal economy will fill the void. In such spaces it is also quite likely that socially-disconnected young men will assume positions in the lower rungs of the criminal economy, many operating in its most violent and lethal arenas; in particular, in the street retail sector of the drugs economy. This is certainly the situation now in the post-industrial, deindustrialised inner cities in England.

In a world where once stable and cohesive working-class communities are fragmenting, a case can be made for suggesting that the internal controls that such communities would once have been able to exercise over the activities of their young have themselves been eroded in what has become an ever more atomising society. The adult world fears its young, and sometimes such fears are justified. To an extent, this breakdown in informal social control also helps to explain the creation under New Labour of what would become its anti-social behaviour agenda (Burney 2009). While by no means suggesting here that the 'solutions' it pioneered, such as the much-derided Anti-Social Behaviour Order (ASBO), were justified, it was responding in its own way to the destructive consequences of neoliberal policies on the working-class communities it was also otherwise pursuing.

All of these factors combine in a mutually self-reinforcing way to create the preconditions for the socially self-destructive way of life I classified as 'on-road'. In its most developed form it constitutes a parallel subterranean society organised around norms and values which at time both overlap with those of the wider mainstream order and which also embrace norms and values that are peculiar to itself. While gang-talkers fantasise that at the heart of this culture stand corporate gangs ruthlessly plotting to take over the wider society, the truth is altogether different. This is a self-enclosed world populated by people who watch out for and deal principally with each other. The wider public can and do service this community in varies ways – as victims of street robbery, and as purchasers of the illegal goods in which it trades. Sometimes innocent people are also caught in the crossfire. But, by and large, this subterranean world proceeds according to its own sui generis logic. Gangs are certainly part of this world, as we have seen, but they do not control this world, and nor does the term accurately diagnose its inherently rhizomatic character.

This world becomes the destination for young men both as a consequence of the magnetic forces that make it superficially attractive and also a destination in which the losers in a winner-takes-all economy are themselves decanted. In opposition to the insecure uncertainties of life lived precariously, life 'on-road' proffers, in its own way, clear certainties. These are found in the collegiate fraternity of your group, your 'mandem' or 'brethren'. Certainty can be found as well in the space you claim, your 'ends'. Clarity is to be found in the 'beef' you have and which you carry. The legacy of past conflict and struggle constitutes for many the basis of the memories they carry (Winlow and Hall 2006). In a world where formal agencies are widely distrusted, this is a world where street justice is practised in fast time, and ruthlessly. This, too, provides its own certainty. Finally, in a world where work is insecure, mundane and low-status life and life 'on-road' hold out the illusory promise of fast cash and the possibility of access to riches beyond their wildest dreams. For the overwhelming majority this will never come true. But the fact that some get rich and display their wealth openly also works to confirm this ghetto rhapsody.

While rap culture with its violent aesthetics provides the vocabulary and establishes the choreography for the violent performances in which the participants of this street trade, by no means is it a determining factor in shaping the violence these men are capable of. It certainly becomes the means by and through which they dramatise their relations with each other, and not least the wider excluding society. And this culture is as contradictory as the street world it expresses. Within it, violent machismo is valorised; the excesses of ornamental materialistic brand-driven consumption are elevated, and women are reduced to sexual objects. If there is a wider politics or political message being dramatised and reproduced in the cultural productions of this subterranean world, not least by the MCs that produce it, then the message mediated is that of politics as violent nihilism.

If we return to Ken Pryce and his ethnography conducted in the 1970s, we can note that there has been a cultural shift of some magnitude here. Reggae was as much a political movement as a cultural one. It not least intersected with and cannot be disaggregated from the wider radical political currents of its time. Today, the dream of a mythical return to Africa no longer figures in the world of the street, while the oppositional culture that black radical politics once embraced appears attenuated in a street world where all that appears left is the neoliberal marketplace and your relation to it.

Most young men, it must be emphasised, exist on the edges of the subterranean street world I have tried to describe. Most will eventually drift out as they mature, age or become more productively entwined with the rituals of mainstream society. Having jobs and families will, for most, end their immersion in street existence. But whereas in the welfare state young men would drift into deviance and then drift out as they matured and obtained working-class jobs, in a neoliberal order that does not provide such work, or work of any meaningful status, this drift in is not necessarily matched by a corresponding process of drifting out. Instead of navigating an orderly transition to adulthood, neoliberalism instead makes available only the possibility of fractured transitions. My point is this: for many young men, their destiny will not be that of drifting out of this subterranean world; instead, they will become more embedded within it. As they do, they will become more brutalised by the violence that defines it, and the longer they remain the more likely they will experience differential association with other people also deeply immersed. While this world is adept at creating hard men adept at violence, it does not produce people who can easily intersect with mainstream society on its preferred terms.

For the most part, the deeply internalised anger and resentment these men carry with them will be expressed in the form of implosive inwardly-directed violence, and it is this violence that has and continues to produce the litany of fatal stabbings and shootings we witness in the UK's poorest and most deprived areas. However, as the riots of 2011 remind us, deeply internalised anger and resentment can also be externalised, and in the wave of destruction and looting and violence that accompanied the disorder, so this class dramatised in the form of violent performance their relationship to the wider excluding society. While the critical left appear to view such disorder as little better than the depoliticised acts of the deluded, 'flawed' consumers with the mindset of a 'rabble' (Bauman 2011; Žižek 2011), I think we need to be more charitable. In a riot, what is being dramatised is a fundamental repudiation of the very principles around which rule-based societies are constructed, namely that within them, people normally obey rules. This is mediated in the form of a dramatic, improvised performance in which the normal rules that govern everyday life are quite literally turned on their head. Riots, I hazard, are inherently carnivalesque occasions where rules governing normal life are turned upside down (Bahktin 1984). Instead of respecting property rights, property is burnt or destroyed; instead of respecting and obeying the forces of law and order, they are attacked. In a consumer-driven society you are expected to pay high prices for your designer goods; in a riot you loot them. In my reading, therefore, acts such as 'violent shopping' are intensely political. By and through its inversion of normal rules, so the rioters are dramatising their relationship to their objective conditions. Given that the precariat are a class in the making, I also fail to see why they would as yet have evolved a clear class-consciousness. They are not, as yet, a class in themselves. However, brutal tutelage under the conditions of neoliberalism might be changing this. Acts the left decry I find myself more ambivalent about. It wasn't pretty, but they were kicking back.

Conclusion

In conclusion then, there remain many continuities between the violence I described in the last chapter and the violent regime that characterised life in welfare state capitalism. In both regimes violence finds tacit endorsement; it is embedded within and reproduced in working-class culture; it is intrinsic to hegemonic versions of masculinity. But whereas in the welfare state era, young men typically drifted in and then out of deviance, where the violence they engaged in represented more a leisure pursuit than a criminal vocation, this is now beginning to change. The class structure of neoliberalism and the low-wage, flexible marketplace it has created have removed the material foundations out of which the drift out of crime would be accomplished. For the new precariat, the promise of stable and worthwhile jobs for many has been withdrawn. Meanwhile, the other gains that the working class had made in the welfare era are being attenuated and rolled back. Welfare transforms into workfare, while poverty itself becomes criminalised. While the new precariat are relentlessly colonised by the logic of the market, the attack on the very conditions of their existence create the preconditions in which deeply alienated men (and sometimes women) carrying deeply internalised anger and resentment, turn inwards upon each other. For the most part the violence will be internalised and will take the form of a slow, festering riot, but periodically it will be externalised, as it was in the urban disorder we witnessed in England in 2011.

Neoliberalism, then, is changing the ecology of street violence, and the direction of change is not for the better. While it would be amiss to suggest that the welfare state was a paragon of virtue, at least it provided, in its own contradictory way, a regime of regulation that worked to maintain the ecology of street violence within broad, regulated limits. The problem with neoliberalism, its Achilles' heel, is that it cannot sustain, nor is it capable of producing, a stable mode of social regulation. The problem here is that as neoliberalism destructively reproduces itself from above, lurching as it does from crisis to crisis, it has the unfortunate consequence of creating the preconditions for what we might read as destructive reproduction from below. And this is what life 'on-road' ultimately represents: a socially destructive world in which young men dramatise their alienation in displays of violence directed at other people who are no different from themselves.

Conclusion

Time to be serious now because, after all, we are talking about serious things. The genre demands it and, we must, as Roger Mathews is fond of reminding us, be 'policy relevant' ('whatever that means', as Prince Charles once famously replied when asked whether he was in love with Princess Diana). Here I take the injunction to mean one of two things. First, and with a view to supporting and helping practitioners everywhere, we need to establish how best to have and sustain a gang problem. This, it could be observed, is a pressing problem and one of considerable significance, given that the last thing a developing gang industry really needs is an end to the problems posed by gangs – especially, that is, when the government has been kind enough to make significant financial resources available to 'end gang violence'. Second, and I see no contradiction between the two, it is also necessary to have some sense of how to end or at least minimise your gang problem if, over time, the perception arises that you have too many.

How to Have a Gang Problem

There is, I will suggest, no need to be overtly academic about this task given that the lessons I am about to narrate here could be learnt by a child. So, with this in mind, let me begin by outlining a simple step-by-step guide, a Seven Point Plan if you will, which, if followed correctly, will enable you to have as big or as small a gang problem as you could ever possibly desire. I present this, needless to say, as an object lesson in 'what works' criminology, and in the spirit of good faith I will throw in some empirical examples to support the case I will develop.

Lesson 1: Turn a problem of groups to one of gangs

We have to begin somewhere, so let's begin by gang talking. As we have discovered, it's an easy discourse to master and you don't really need to have met any gang members to do it. Discover one or a set of incidents that involve groups of young men; street crime is a good one to focus on but various forms of public disorder will also fit the bill. This is not, as we have seen, difficult because crime in a street context is always likely to be group-based rather than perpetrated by lone individuals. In a society where most young working-class people are known by others by reference to the street or estate where they are based, it shouldn't be hard to find a number of ready-made groups to which the gang label can easily be applied. Obviously, it would help matters more if your group actually defined themselves by a name and committed crime systematically but, quite honestly, this is not too important. Ideally, it would also help matters if the kids in question come from minority ethnic groups – black, ideally (because the term 'gang' comes pre-packaged with a racist heritage from which it cannot easily be disconnected). If your audience are white and middle class, the discovery of black gangs will indeed pay dividends.

Having identified the raw material around which your gang problem will then be constructed, gang-talk-up the problem. Talk about new escalations and intensifications. Implicate that hoary old chestnut, 'new weapons of choice'. By now you should know the script: Once upon a time it was just fists but now they are innovating: dogs, weapons, sexual violence. Ensure you deploy the right discourse. Use terms like 'recruitment strategies', and 'grooming', and describe the strange 'initiation rituals' of the gang as you imagine them; sexual grooming is good' but having to randomly shoot somebody as a price for gang membership also works. Sound particularly concerned about the way that gangs are proliferating today relative to a past that was always better: 'We never used to have a problem round here like this, but today ...' And don't worry, you don't have to have any compelling evidence to make the case, just invoke the magic mantra 'according to anecdotal evidence' and you're safe because no one is likely to challenge you.

Evidence suggests that it helps to wildly overstate the number of gangs you have in order to ensure that you can demonstrate you have a problem worth worrying about. You can, of course, subsequently reduce the number to more proportionate and manageable figures. Take Glasgow as a case study. When their anti-gang task force began they identified over 300 gangs. Within a year the figure had diminished to 30. The Metropolitan Police Service (MPS), meanwhile, has now embraced such a permissive interpretation of the gang that the mantra 'gang-affiliated' can be stretched to include just about every crime known to man – which is useful precisely because it means they have as many gangs and gang members as they need in order to justify gang crackdowns in order to demonstrate their anti-gang credentials.

Lesson 2: Work closely with journalists

In a country undergoing a media driven moral panic around gangs, it pays to involve the fifth estate as closely as possible in the development of your gang problem. In a world where sensation sells and violence sells even more, you will have no lack of journalists interested in your gang problem and keen to report it. Nor will you have to field that many difficult questions if you involve them the right way. As a constituency to whom gang talk is second nature, they will be receptive to and very keen to report all talk about gangs developing, proliferating and expanding. As they do not operate around a refutation principle, nor will they be that concerned about contradictory assertions or the lack of compelling evidence. Just mention the term 'anecdotal' and that should be enough. And in the eventuality that you do find yourself confronted by a particularly impudent product of this species, such as an investigative journalist asking difficult questions, you can rest assured that their editors will not publish anything that does not conform to the gang-talking agenda. Stories of de-escalation simply do not exist in a world where everything connected with gangs simply must get worse.

On a practical note, invite film crews to film exciting dawn raids. They are particularly impressed by and most certainly like to attend the kind of dawn raids against gang members conducted with such panache by the MPS. Seeing doors blown off their hinges and paramilitary policemen piling into houses makes good copy, and that, realistically, is all they are after. If you don't manage to land your gang fish, never mind, that doesn't matter either. Simply embark on a fishing expedition and you will usually find something to charge your suspects with, then simply label it as 'gang-related', and the suspect, 'gang-affiliated'. If you want some personal glory it might be useful to actually attend these raids, but with the proviso that you must ensure that your quarry is at home. One newly installed head of the MPS notoriously began his public career leading his troops into a house where unfortunately the suspect was not at home.

Lesson 3: Create a dedicated 'gang-busting' unit

Within a relatively short period of time, you should have mustered enough local and ideally national support to justify establishing your very own dedicated gang-busting unit, or, at least a group of people with a dedicated gang-suppression remit. The issue of expertise we will return to below. At this point, all you need to note is that you don't actually have to have anyone in your team or squad with any meaningful grasp of gangs or the gang situation. Indeed, the last people you really want to employ would be real experts, because, as we shall establish below, they can be both difficult and counterproductive. With that in mind, apply the usual solutions. Rebadge an existing police squad as a gang-busting unit, or create a new one to hunt out your gang members. Employ bright graduates fresh from Oxbridge to become your policy advisers. Ok, they might never have encountered a gang member in their lives but it doesn't matter. Create committees or even think tanks with a dedicated gang remit and soon enough they will be able to gang talk with the best of them. Finally, ensure that all your walls are covered with pictograms of gangs. Ensure as well that they are suitably hierarchical and bureaucratic. The work of academics like John Pitts is worthy of consultation on this point, as are practitioners such as Jonathon Toy.

Ultimately, what you are really trying to achieve here is to constitute a body of people with a clear mission to suppress gangs and who consequently have a vested interest in sustaining them; a group that, when programmed to hunt down the gangs, will continue to do so and relentlessly, precisely as that is what their programme tells them they have to do. If constituted effectively, your group should have the capacity to discover gangs even when objectively there are not that many around. Peer groups, after all, look just like gangs and are often indistinguishable from them, so simply widen the net. Just make sure that your gang definition is broad enough so that when you run out of 'proper' gangs to suppress you can filter these in to take their place. On this note, if you set your staff clear targets to meet, you can guarantee they will meet them.

Lesson 4: Employ academic 'gang experts' to confirm your problem

It is an accepted truism in criminology that if you really want to have a serious gang problem, at some point in time you are probably going to want to invite a dedicated, administratively-inclined (ideally American) gang expert to provide the hard empirical evidence that you indeed have a bone a fide gang problem. We are, after all supposed to be living in a world where 'policy' is 'evidence-driven'. This might not be as easy as it might sound, so it pays to be aware of the many problems that will ensue if you do not get this right.

To begin with, remember that the academic community are not homogeneous, and just as there are certain kinds of expert you might want, there are also a range of them that you should seek to avoid at all costs. Avoid, in particular, gang sceptics – academics, that is, who don't appear predisposed from the outset to confirm a gang problem independently of researching the issue in depth. Be particularly wary of people who call themselves 'ethnographers' or 'critical criminologists'. The former almost invariably turn native and both sets, by and large, will raise problems where there should only be gang certainties. They are also quite likely to be unreconstructed lefties, to boot, which means they are likely to be hostile to all the good people you have employed to suppress your gangs. Avoid, therefore, people with names like Hallsworth and Young. And distrust as well those academics who, like Aldridge, Medina or Ralphs, make simple things like gangs sound a lot more complicated than they need to be. And bear in mind here the costs of getting things wrong. In the last decade there has been more than one local authority who has employed experts to confirm their gang problem but who have tangibly failed to deliver the goods. On at least one occasion, the council in question has been forced to employ other experts (of the right kind) in order to get the right result. The lesson here is that getting things wrong can be a costly affair.

With that caveat in mind, employ the right kind of expert, ideally one who has already demonstrated that they can gang talk like everyone else. If their previous work shows the gang to be large, corporate and serious then you can guarantee they will be the right kind of person for you. The UK has produced a few academics of this calibre, but the US excels and has produced a veritable army. More than this, it has exported its expertise with the consequence that it ought to be quite possible to employ one with relative ease near you – provided, of course, the usual financial inducements are applied. The good thing about most of the American 'gang experts' is that they normally privilege quantitative over qualitative research methods and as a consequence lack the uncertainties and doubts that ethnographers often display. Therefore they are often best placed to produce the kind of robust findings that researchers in places like the Home Office tend to like; that is, the problem of the gang reduced to numbers and risk factors with all that messy human stuff evicted.

At this point in time, you might want to employ them to do some gang surveys in your local schools. Pick poor areas where the usual suspects can be found because these are where you are likely to get the best results. Ok, they may not actually have a gang problem, and it is a fair bet that active gang members will be the last people who will complete a gang survey, but it doesn't matter; such surveys will, as a matter of course, deliver up a predictable percentage of people that will fit the criteria necessary to be classified as gang-affiliated, because what surveys do is produce gangs by definitional fiat. And remember this as well, the number of gangs identified will be directly related to the criteria used to define your gang. So if you want a lot, then keep your definition broad and inclusive. If you want fewer, add in more filters. And there you have it: the truth of the matter is that you can have as many or as few gangs as you need. At the end of the day it's not realistically about what is going down on the street. What exactly constitutes a suitable amount of gangs remains a political decision.

Ok, surveys often look complicated and scientific and thus beyond the comprehension of most practitioners. But do not worry. In truth they produce findings that tend to fall into one of two categories. On the whole, and with autistic precision, they tend to produce findings that are true but trivial and obvious. Alternatively they also produce findings that are simply absurd and ridiculous. Whatever they produce you can guarantee that the gang expert talking about them will present their findings as if they are narrating the Gospel. They may well be, as Jock Young (2011) notes, skating on thin evidential ice, but they will nevertheless skate on regardless. In the first category you will find findings that confirm what we know anyway: men are principally involved in gangs, they tend to be of a certain age and they tend to come from poor areas. Such findings also affirm in a wonderfully circular way the finding that groups of men whom you have already defined as more violent than non-gang members are indeed more likely to be more violent than non-gang members. For good measure you may also be told other pretty obvious truisms, such as they enjoy 'hanging around on the street' and are more likely to be distrustful of enforcement officers than others. All in all, staggering stuff, but when relayed with the requisite quantity of seriousness, it can sound as if they are narrating staggeringly new facts hitherto unknown to man.

Alternatively, such surveys will produce sensational findings you might find useful but which are clearly absurd. They might tell you, for example, that more girls than boys are now in gangs. This, apparently, is now the case in the UK, or at least it was for the American academic Jody Miller who relayed this staggering fact, at a recent international conference on gangs convened by that well known 'gang-afflicted' society, Sweden – which you can take either as confirmation that the UK has indeed become an equal opportunity society, or a society where feral female gangs are indeed taking over. Alternatively, you might just apply common sense and recognise that findings like this confirm that the methodology is totally suspect and should be disregarded. That said, if you are indeed hell-bent on having a worthy gang problem, findings like this can be quite useful because the idea of female gangsters on the loose makes for potent gang talk and should not be discarded lightly. Another finding this kind of research throws up is that gang life and membership is no different between societies which are culturally very different indeed. Again totally absurd, especially when the findings in question inform us, for example, that patterns of gang formation and membership in relatively non-violent societies (such as the Netherlands) are no different than quite violent societies such as the US ghetto. But do not worry or be off put by findings like this because they can be quite helpful insofar as you can use them to claim that your gang situation has, or is, assuming American proportions.

Lesson 5: Create a gang-intervention strategy

American gang experts are also useful in another way. After all, they come from a society that has invested huge sums of money and lots of resources into suppressing their gangs. In pursuit of this laudable goal, they have imprisoned tens of thousands of gang members, deported thousands more, and subjected those that still have some street life to a battery of incredibly punitive interventions. These range from banning them from hanging around, banning them from wearing particular cloths, banning gang members from seeing each other; and, if this is not enough, using gang affiliation as a justification for imposing even harsher punishment while stripping citizenship rights away from them. Ok, to be honest, none of this has worked to reduce the gang problem in the US which is arguably growing, despite (and in some cases because of) this repressive effort. But again, this should not occasion any concern to us in the UK. What the experts can do is provide you with lists of interventions you can nevertheless try anyway, even if they haven't worked that well in the US. It is what policy specialists like to term 'policy transfer' and is very popular in the UK. It is where, by and large, most current gang intervention strategies currently derive from.

This takes us logically to our next step and that is to produce your gang strategy now that you have your evidence and your gang-crackdown unit. You could of course commission someone to write one for you (ideally a paid-up gang-talker), or alternatively you might want to review the many that have been written. Having been involved in this process myself on several occasions, I have to admit that most are not that well thought-through, will rarely be read and will make little difference to what happens on the street. Nevertheless, they are par for the course.

If you want a gang problem you will of necessity have to create one of these documents even though, without question, it will be out of date and superfluous within a year.

As you develop your strategy, ensure you hit the right notes. Talk-up the necessity of partnership working, of exchanging information, and ensure as well you have in place not only response elements such as gang crackdowns, but also dedicated teams running dedicated wrap-around intervention programmes for the various gang members you identify. Talk-up in particular the importance of pre-emptive programmes because the government loves them; try and sell the state the line that you are seeking to intervene by developing systems that will enable you to identity would-be gang members at the age of three before they have even considered gang membership. Create, as part of this, risk profiles that can enable teachers, social workers, and so on, to recognise would-be gangbangers. And don't be worried here about listing innocuous everyday activities such as 'hanging around'. Once mediated through the medium of gang talk, it will invariably sound sinister.

As you develop your reactive response strategy, ensure you connect it to wider state programmes. As this book was being written, for example, problem families have been identified as the root of all evil and money has been made available to turn them around. Evidently it will also pay here to connect your gang problem to the 'problem families' agenda, and a number of agencies are waking up to this fact and are moving into this lucrative marketplace. Ok, the evidence linking the two is slight, but don't worry, because you will be knocking on an open door. Remember the golden truth: states never want to have their fantasies challenged but only ever reiterated and confirmed, and that is your job. Ultimately, you have to understand that it's about sex, not facts. You stroking the erogenous zones of the state and in the right way through the gang talking you do. Push the right buttons and money will come your way.

As you construct your intervention strategy, bear in mind the fact that what you write and what you subsequently do send out the right messages to the right constituencies. By and large the public want to have their worst prejudices addressed and the best way to do this is to sell them the idea that gang members are going to have their lives made very miserable indeed. Maybe as part of this you might want to use some anti-gang shock therapy mediated through the medium of a degradation ritual. The media like this kind of stuff as well. Go for big effect by, for example, packing a few would-be gangsters (twelve years old and onward will do) into a courtroom packed with coppers – then scare the living daylights out of them. Show them pictures of bodies with knives sticking out of them; tell them they will be hunted down like dogs if they don't turn their lives around, and then decant them back to the ghetto with vague promises of the great services they will receive if they agree to be Good Boys.

If you sound innovative enough you will get government money. But before that happens you will also have to demonstrate that your gang problem is significant and you will have to show that you have the mechanisms necessary to confront it. These, in turn, will be assessed through the mechanism of a visit composed of a deputation of self-styled 'gang experts' assembled by the Home Office. Though these visits often occasion considerable anxiety, don't worry, be happy. These are the right kind of gang experts and you can rest assured the only discourse they are interested in listening to is 'gang talk', so do it well. Most of these are police officers, and the rest, by and large, are composed of various self-styled gang experts, many of whom will fit well the practitioner profile developed below.

Lesson 6: Bring on the practitioners

Practitioners, like academics, are not a homogeneous community, so be careful when you involve them. A good proportion of this constituency are decent people wanting to do the right thing for their young people. Many work in poor conditions with limited resources in this age of austerity. Many will be running generic services which are not particularly gang-related but, like youth clubs, might have a positive impact. While these people are worthy and certainly worth supporting, it is unlikely that this is a constituency you want to engage from the outset. The reason for this is that in a neoliberal society the custodians of the money you need expect to see innovation and novelty in the programmes they fund and, as such, generic longstanding interventions are not usually well looked-upon. If they have been state-run they are even more unpopular.

With that in mind, engage instead with a more innovative section of the practitioner community. All right, they may well contain a fair share of fantasists and chancers, but these are the people you need to do business with because (a) they can be quite imaginative (which helps solve the problem of innovation); (b) they are often ferocious gang-talkers anyway (which means you share the same discursive space); and (c) they know that in a market economy, the product has to be right (which we also have understand has little to do with any traditional concept of 'working').

The UK at present is throwing up quite a number of people who meet these criteria and by and large they can be found at the centre of the emerging gang industry. In what follows, let me develop a risk profile that will enable you to identify them so you can engage with them:

- claims to have once been a 'badass' gangbanger in their immediate past;
- claims now to have seen the light after someone put their life back on track;
- claims to have arcane knowledge of the street which they alone have access to and can understand;
- is an excellent and proficient exponent of gang talk;
- talks with the passion of an evangelist (several may claim to be evangelical preachers);
- is wholly apolitical (will do business with anyone);
- is capable of dreaming up novel and interesting projects.

It could be observed that the black community in the UK is producing quite a number of practitioners who meet this risk profile. They tend to relate to you in the manner of a preacher, that is, as someone who has seen the light. To help show you the light they will then quite often show you a short film composed of violent gang imagery they would have constructed from YouTube. They will then gang-talk-up the issue, telling you, for example, that young people no older than three are now involved (the spectre of the 'tinies'); they will talk about the gangs 'new weapons of choice' ('the motherfuckers have arrived') and they will end their presentation on an apocalyptic note 'we have never seen anything like this before') before asking for your cash. If they are worth their salt they will touch every erogenous zone of the state. Typically, these depoliticised chancers and zealots will quite happily sell their community short in the pornography of violence in which they engage. But as none of what we are talking about here actually concerns morality, this need not concern us further. They are also quite happy to work with anyone and everything as long as they get their money. Finally, this constituency will also deliver unto you a raft of innovative projects, and cater in so doing to every market niche in the gangland marketplace. They will provide variously dedicated projects to work with gang girls and the survivors of gang sexual violence; they will offer bespoke boot camp experiences for young men designed to get them into work, while some, milking the 'radical fundamentalism' racket will offer models of intervention designed to prevent gangsters from mutating into armed terrorists.

Lesson 7: Cash-in and live well

If you have successfully followed these steps you should by now be in a position to have both constructed a gang problem of alarming proportions and levered-in government funds to suppress it, and be in a position to fund a raft of innovative headline-grabbing intervention projects. If your gang problem seems to be too big, don't worry – simply manipulate your definitional criteria and all of a sudden you will find you can have as many gangs as you need to show progress towards 'ending gang violence'. At this point you might want to start showcasing your success to the world. By now you might well have attended a few gang conferences and maybe even have considered presenting your work at some of them. And why not? Because if you have mastered this programme you are indeed a certified gang expert, eminently well qualified to gang talk with the best of them. Write a report with a suitably catchy title. 'Dying to Belong' has already been taken as a title, but you get the picture. Maybe even organise a conference, maybe even an international conference where you can showcase your success to the world. Yes, the world is your oyster if you gang talk well enough.

Koyaanisqutsi

Enough 'trivia and slapstick'. After all, we are dealing with serious subjects here. So let's be a little more serious now and consider what you need to do to ensure you don't have a gang problem. In the eyes of many, this question would appear pretty straightforward. Surely we are back to gang suppression, or at least a review of the various initiatives that have been and continue to be conducted against urban street gangs. But this was never going to be that kind of book, so stop reading now if a clampdown is what you are after.

What I propose to do instead is set out some fairly straightforward lessons in how to look at violent street worlds, but in ways that do not lead to the kind of exorbitant gang talking we are currently experiencing here in the UK, a country mired in strange gang fixations and in which strange and weird fantasies about gangs circulate like a clammy fog by a growing army of even weirder gang-talkers. Indeed, as I write these words a new gang-talking report is about to be published by that paragon of reactionary virtue, the Centre for Social Justice. Its findings have already made the headlines and representatives of this organisation have already appeared on TV to discuss them. I watched one with a sense of utter incredulity. Given that I am the last person in the world to ever presuppose that reason prevails within it, it could be observed, it takes quite a lot to shock me. So let me describe what I witnessed in order to situate the points that follow.

The spokesman was male and dressed in a dapper suit. The report he was discussing was a paragon of gang-talking stupidity. Its key message runs something like this: While the police appeared to be doing the right thing by arresting and imprisoning all those horrible gang members involved in the riots, they had not adequately thought-through the implications of their actions, because, out there, on the deracinated estates of broken Britain, a state of anarchy had broken out as a direct consequence. Why, you might ask was this? By arresting what the spokesman termed the 'pivotal' gang leaders, the consequence had been to create a terrible power vacuum on the streets among what were now headless and leaderless gangs. Feral gangsters everywhere, freed from the tyranny of their authoritarian leaders, were now apparently engaging in an orgy of violence as each fought with each other to fill the void. Solutions? Only the promise of more money thrown at the gang industry would work to solve the problem. This needed to be coupled with renewed vigour on the part of the government to crush the gang menace once and for all.

Compelling evidence substantiating these apocalyptic announce-ments, however, was noticeable by its absence. Apparently the researchers from the Centre had spoken to some practitioners somewhere and their anecdotal drivel ('the gangs are on the move, fighting as we speak …') was enough to persuade editors everywhere to take this nonsense seriously and report it.

The Hopi Indians have a lovely word that helps describe the insane situation that this book has tried to help diagnose: *koyaanisqutsi*. It means many things: 'crazy life', 'life in turmoil', 'life disintegrating', 'life out of balance'; but my favourite definition of all is 'a state of life that calls for another way of living'. So let me conclude here and try and think what kind of alternative we need if we to engage with violent street worlds in ways that avoid the gang-talking madness diagnosed above.

Bad is bad enough

A recurring problem with gang talk is that it relentlessly over-eggs its case by taking atypical cases and presenting them as if they are the norm. Some gang members somewhere abuse women, ergo all gang members everywhere are gangbanging motherfucking rapists. In part, the problem here is that gang-talkers appear to surrender any critical faculty they have, particularly when faced with evidence that is absurd and patently untrue. Rather than consider issues of refutation, they function, as we have seen, by iteration and confirmation. Lesson one, then, is retain a sense a critical distance. It is bad enough that some girls are abused by some gang members, but do not make the issue of sexual abuse an issue solely of gangs. It is bad enough that people abuse dogs, but do not make dangerous dogs a gang issue. And so we can continue ad infinitum. Be suspicious, therefore, of those who over-generalise, because they are not to be trusted.

Towards a principle of theoretical economy

When faced with claims that place the urban street gang at the centre of contemporary mayhem (the gangs caused the riots, arresting gang members has led to state of carnage on the streets), the first thing to do is be very suspicious of such claims and be very suspicious as well of the people who make them. Before reaching for the gang or 'gangness' as the key explanatory variable, consider instead the possibility that less sensational explanations possibly have more currency and explanatory power. This is, I must admit, not likely to generate you sensational coverage and it is quite likely to be the case that your work will not be heard or noticed by the gang-talking community. It will almost certainly infuriate practitioners, particularly if they have entrusted you with the job of discovering sensational gang truths. In the cold light of day, however, it is evident that if we do subject the many claims that have been and which continue to be made about urban street gangs to critical scrutiny then not only are most simply false, as we have seen, but you can develop explanations for the same phenomena that do not require foregrounding the gang as a key explanatory variable.

Put gangs into perspective

In part, the problem of gang talk is that it reifies its object. It highlights the gang, elevates it as an issue and then folds every social problem unproblematically into it. This is precisely what Katz (1988) notes in his description of the gang as a 'transcendental evil'. Reification, however, brings many problems in its wake. To begin with, it concedes to gangs a significance they often do not deserve. Second, by focusing so intently upon the gang, so we tend to lose sight of the wider complex ecology of which gangs are a apart. Third, by fixating on the gang as the primary harbinger of urban mayhem, or by attempting to blame all crime on gangs, so we lose sight of the fact that much of the violence and crime is not gang-related and requires responses that are not gang-related. By only focusing on the gang, we run the real risk of constituting it, in Girard's (1986) sense, as a sacrificial scapegoat for wider social anxieties and insecurities that are not gang-related. Such fixation also helps establish the gang as a suitable enemy, an enemy the construction of which no one disagrees with. This may fit well with neoliberal statecrafting and its criminalising agenda, but it is no way to build a humane society or indeed a proportionate one.

This is not to suggest that we lose sight of or ignore gangs and the harms they do, but it does mean putting them into perspective. Consider them, then, as part of the wider ecology of the street and recognise as well that this is a street world that is occupied by many groups who are not gangs and many individuals doing precisely the same kind of things as those perpetuated by gang members.

Make the street and street culture more generally your object of analysis. This, I should point out, is an injunction policy-makers also need to heed if they want to prevent yet more scarce resources being squandered on yet more pointless gang interventions.

Humanising the deviant

It has become commonplace now only to define gangs only by relation to the crime they commit and the violence they induce. For what I thought of as 'progressive' reasons I have also taken this path in the past but now regret my decision. But it is a dangerous path to tread and we should be very wary of taking it. This is because once you begin to define a group by reference to its delinquency and deviance then that is all you will see and we are back once again to the problem of reification, not to say criminalisation. Once you make crime and violence a master identity, then anything else progressive or otherwise a gang or gang member will do becomes invisible. Why? Because only the criminalising label remains.

To put this into perspective let us consider two case studies: the Catholic Church and the British political establishment. What we know about both of these establishments is that criminal elements and criminality are rife within both. Consider, for example, the culture of denial the Catholic Church has engaged in in its attempt to cover up the systematic sexual abuse its priests have perpetrated against generations of young, helpless children. Or consider the scandal that followed the exposure of the British political establishment when the public discovered what politicians claimed in the name of 'legitimate' expenses. My point is this: despite its criminality and despite its attempt to hide its criminality, we do not see the Catholic Church as a systematic criminal organization; nor do we consider the British political establishment systematically corrupt despite its systematic corruption. No such act of leniency, however, befalls the fate of the street gangs who are relentlessly criminalised.

Do not corporatise the street

Much as it is appealing to impose upon the informal organisations of the street the formal categories of formal organisations, this tendency must be resisted. The street is not corporate and nor can it ever be made corporate (even when attempts are made to do so). So resist, then, the seductive and beguiling tendency to find all those hierarchies and divisions of labour. Yes, we are well aware that this makes for administrative convenience, and not least for potent gang talk, but it does not allow us to comprehend the *sui generis* properties of street worlds that are not arboreal but rhizomatic.

To a point it means that we must be vigilant and suspicious of the categories we use; mindful as well of their provenance. Do they derive, for example, from a sedentary way of looking, because many do? What is needed is not just an alternative ontology but, as a prerequisite for this, a campaign of deforestation. It entails not least cutting criminology and social theory more generally free of the trees that infest it. It means cutting down the trees that grow in our heads as well. As the saying goes for charity, 'it should always begin at home'. Avoiding, then, a reversion to the old procedures. I accept that this is not an easy proposition. After all, the sociology of formal organisations has a long pedigree, and arboreal institutions like states tend to like it as well because it chimes perfectly well with their explanatory universe which is also relentlessly arboreal.

Think nomadically

If not trees, then what is left? We can begin simplistically. If the subject of our gaze is the street and nomadic life that ramifies across it, then evidently we need a nomadology. To think nomadically, however, requires that we think like grass itself; not from the top down, not from the vantage point of the arboreal state, but from the centre of things. This requires a frame of reference but its nature has to be rhizomatic.

One way to approach this is by trying to see things from the middle. Don't just see gangs, for example, but the whole ecology of which they are a part. In other words, do not reify. It means accepting all the lessons outlined here. It means being very sceptical of all tendencies to seek in groups like gangs clear determinate boundaries or essences of any kind. Why? Because if you begin here then the only thing you will find are forests. Reject, then, the striated and the territorialised, discover instead smooth spaces that deterritorialise as much and sometimes more than they territorialise.

Critical ethnographers lead the way here. Think fuzzy thoughts about fluid institutions that are only ever always interstitial and you are halfway there. Conquergood, as always, is right when he instructs us to reject the idea of simple cleavages, such as the one gang-talkers impose between the inside and the outside of the gang, as if that is all there is. Follow instead the cleavages that run through borders that permeate groups that are multifaceted and which are inherently rhizomatic. Ignore the roots and concentrate instead on lateral ramifications.

Making gang policy policy-relevant

As we have seen there is an industrial logic to the current fixation on gangs and, as such, a solution to the problem posed by them must include doing something about the developing gang industry that sustains the very gang it aspires to suppress. My suggestions for what they are worth entail the following. Place all Home Office certified gang 'experts' before a wall. Sack all gang advisers and disband every gang suppression unit along with the various gang 'think tanks' that have recently been formed to pontificate on gangland UK. Do this as you will save scarce resources that could more profitably be spent elsewhere, and young people a raft of programmes and initiatives that will almost certainly not work anyway. Shoot,as well, anyone who uses terms such as 'new weapon of choice' because they are invariably charlatans.

Avoid gang talk

Finally, avoid gang talk. Admittedly it has a potent currency, as we have seen, it carries cache, and in a society of gang-talkers it can get you money if you do it well enough. As we have also seen, it is an easy discourse to master, and to master it you don't actually have to have met any gangs because gang talk is a discourse that floats wholly free of gang realities as they play themselves out on the streets. As we have also seen, to become proficient as a gang-talker all you really need to know are the rules that govern the discourse as a whole.

A tempting way to go, certainly, but one that must be avoided if we are to see the street world aright. So avoid gang talk as much as you must avoid the tendency to tree-think. With this in mind, despite the usual array of temptations to do it (it is, after all, very addictive) deny yourself this drug of your own choosing.

I end here as I have ended before. Unless you have good reason,

Refrain from gang talking to yourself.
Refrain from gang talking to your friends.
Refrain from gang talking to your enemies.

Bibliography

Aldridge, J., and J. Medina (2005) *Youth Gangs in an English City*, ESRC.

Aldridge, J., R. Ralphs and J. Medina (2011) 'Collateral Damage', in B. Goldson, ed., *Youth in Crisis?: 'Gangs', Territoriality and Violence*, London: Routledge, pp. 72–88.

Alexander, C. E. (2008) *Rethinking 'Gangs': Gangs, Youth Violence and Public Policy*, Runnymede Trust.

Amin, A. (1994) *Post-Fordism: A Reader*, Oxford: Blackwell.

Anderson, E. (2000) *The Codes of the Street: Decency, Violence and the Moral Life of the Inner City*, New York: Norton.

Antrobus, S. (2009) *Dying to Belong: An In-Depth Study of Street Gangs in Britain*, Centre for Social Justice.

Atkinson, R., and G. Helms, eds (2007) *Securing an Urban Renaissance: Crime, Community and British Urban Policy*, Bristol: The Policy Press.

Bakhtin, M. M. (1984) *Rabelais and his World*, Bloomington: Indiana University Press.

Ball, R., and J. Drury (2012) 'Representing the Riots: The (Mis)use of Figures to Sustain Ideological Interpretation', *Radical Statistics* 106.

Bataille, G. (1988) *The Accursed Share: An Essay on General Economy. Vol. 1, Consumption*, New York: Zone Books.

Batchelor, S. (2001) 'The Myth of Girl Gangs', *Criminal Justice Matters* 43: 26–7.

Batchelor, S. (2009) 'Girls, Gangs and Violence: Assessing the Evidence', *Probation Journal* 56(4): 399–414.

Baudrillard, J. (1981) *Simulacra and Simulation*, trans. S. F. Glaser, Michigan: University of Michigan Press.

Bauman, Z. (1989) *Modernity and the Holocaust*, Cambridge: Polity.

Bauman, Z. (1997) *Postmodernity and its Discontents*, Oxford: Polity.

Bauman, Z. (2000) *Liquid Modernity*, Cambridge: Polity.

Bauman, Z. (2011) 'The London Riots – On Consumerism Coming Home to Roost', *Social Europe Journal*. Available at: www.social-europe.eu/2011/08/the-london-riots-on-consumerism-coming-home-to-roost/.

BBC News (2009) 'Increase in Number of Stray Dogs', *BBC News Online*, http://news.bbc.co.uk/1/hi/england/london/8245531.stm.

Bean, J. P. (1981) *The Sheffield Gang Wars*, Sheffield: D. D. Publications.

Becker (1964) *Outsiders: Studies in the Sociology of Deviance*, New York: The Free Press.

Beckford, M. (2012) 'Prisoners under Pressure to Convert to Muslim Gang', *Telegraph Online*. Available at: www.telegraph.co.uk/news/uknews/law-and-order/9298578/Prisoners-under-pressure-to-convert-to-Muslim-gang.html.

Bourdieu, P., and L. J. D. Wacquant (1992) *An Invitation to Reflexive Sociology*, Chicago: University of Chicago Press.

Bourgois, P. I. (2003) *In Search of Respect: Selling Crack in El Barrio*, Cambridge: Cambridge University Press.

Bracchi, P. (2008) 'The Feral Sex: The Terrifying Rise of Violent Girl Gangs', *Daily Mail Online*. Available at: www.dailymail.co.uk/news/article-566919/The-Feral-Sex-The-terrifying-rise-violent-girl-gangs.html.

Brotherton, D., and L. Barrios (2004) *The Almighty Latin King and Queen Nation: Street Politics and the Transformation of a New York City Gang*, New York: Columbia University Press.

Brotherton, D., and P. Kretsedemas (2008) *Keeping Out the Other: A Critical Introduction to Immigration Enforcement Today*, New York: Columbia University Press.

Burgess, A. (1962) *A Clockwork Orange*, London: Penguin.

Burney, E. (2009) *Making People Behave: Anti-Social Behaviour, Politics and Policy*, Cullompton: Willan Publishing.

Butler, D. (2009) *Fantasy Cinema: Impossible Worlds on Screen*, London and New York: Wallflower.

Calahan, P. (2008) 'Dog Gang Admit Terrifying School Attack', This is Local London, www.thisislocallondon.co.uk/news/topstories/3781805. WANDSWORTH__Dog_gang_admit_terrifying_school_attack/.

Cameron, D. (2011) 'Speech on the Fight-Back after the Riots'. Retrieved 15 August 2011 from: www.newstatesman.com/politics/2011/08/society-fight-work-rights.

Campbell, B. (1993) *Goliath*, London: Methuen.

Castells, M. (1996) *The Rise of the Network Society*, Oxford: Blackwell.

Christie, N. (2000) *Crime Control as Industry: Towards Gulags, Western Style*. London: Routledge.

Christie, N. (2001) 'Det idealiska offret' (The Ideal Victim), in M. Akerstrom and I. Sahlin, eds, *Det motspanstiga offret* (The Defiant Victim), Lund: Studentlitteratur, pp. 46–60.

Christie, N. (2004) *A Suitable Amount of Crime*, London: Routledge.

Clements, J., and B. Roberts (2007) 'Gun Culture UK: The Shocking Truth', *Mirror Online*. Available at: www.mirror.co.uk/news/uk-news/gun-culture-uk-the-shocking-truth-454434.

Cohen, A. K. (1955) *Delinquent Boys: The Culture of the Gang*, Glencoe, IL: Free Press.

Cohen, D. (2002) 'The rise of the Muslim Boysrk/*Evening Standard*, 3 February 2002, www.thisislondon.co.uk/til/jsp/modules/articles/print.jsp?itemId=16372042/ ass., accessed 2005.

Cohen, P. (1979) 'Policing the Working Class City', in B. Fine, ed., *Capitalism and the Rule of Law*, London: Hutchinson.

Cohen, S. (1972) *Folk Devils and Moral Panics: The Creation of the Mods and Rockers*, London: MacGibbon & Kee.

Cohen, S. (1984) *Visions of Social Control: Crime, Punishment and Classification*, Cambridge: Polity.

Coleman, R. (2004) *Reclaiming the Streets: Surveillance, Social Control and the City*, Cullompton: Willan Publishing.

Connell, R. W. (2005) *Masculinities*, Berkeley: University of California Press.

Conquergood, D. (1991) *Rethinking Ethnography*, Communications Monographs 53, pp. 179–94.

Conquergood, D. (1994) 'Homeboys and Hoods: Gang Communication and Cultural Space', in L. R. Frey, ed., *Group Communication in Context: Studies of Natural Groups*, Hillsdale, NJ: Lawrence Erlbaum.

Cressey, D. R. (1969) *Theft of the Nation: The Structure and Operations of Organized Crime in America*, New York and London: Harper & Row.

Critcher, C. (2003) *Moral Panics and the Media*, Buckingham: Open University Press.

Daily Mail (2004) 'Agencies slammed over Toni-Ann Murder'. Available at: www.dailymail.co.uk/pages/live/articles/news/news.html?in_article_id=260199&in_page_id=1770.

Davis, M. (1992) *City of Quartz: Excavating the Future in Los Angeles*, New York: Vintage Books.

Davis, M. (2001) *Late Victorian Holocausts: El Niño Famines and the Making of the Third World*, London and New York: Verso.

Davis, R. (2010) 'Are Dogs the New Weapon of Choice for Young People?', *Guardian*: www.guardian.co.uk/society/2010/feb/17/dangerous-dogs-as-weapons.

Debord, G. (1994) *The Society of the Spectacle*, New York: Zone Books.

Decker, S. H., and B. Van Winkle (1996) *Life in the Gang: Family, Friends and Violence*, Cambridge and New York: Cambridge University Press.

Deleuze, G., and F. Guattari (1977) *Anti-Oedipus: Capitalism and Schizophrenia*, New York: Viking Press.

Deleuze, G., and F. Guattari (1988) *A Thousand Plateaus: Capitalism and Schizophrenia*, London: Athlone Press.

Delingpole, J. (2011) 'If David Starkey is Racist then so is Everybody', *Telegraph Online*. Available at: http://blogs.telegraph.co.uk/news/jamesdelingpole/100100911/if-david-starkey-is-racist-then-so-is-everybody/.

Densley, J. (2013) *How Gangs Work*, Basingstoke: Palgrave Macmillan.

Downes, D. M. (1966) *The Delinquent Solution: A Study in Subcultural Theory*, New York: The Free Press.

Edwards, A., and P. Gill (2003) *Transnational Organised Crime: Perspectives on Global Security*, London: Routledge.

Eliade, M. (1955) *The Myth of Eternal Return*, London: Routledge & Kegan Paul.

Ellis, C. A., T. E. Adams and A. P. Bochner (2011) 'Autoethnography: An Overview', *Forum Qualitative Sozialforschung /Forum: Qualitative Social Research* 12(1) Art. 10. Available at: http://nbn-resolving.de/urn:nbn:de:0114-fqs1101108.

Ellis, C. B., and A. P. Bochner (2000) Autoethnography, Personal Narrative, Reflexivity', in N. K. Denzin and Y. S. Lincoln, eds, *Handbook of Qualitative Research* (2nd edn), Thousand Oaks, CA: Sage, pp. 733–68.

Fenwick, M., and K. J. Hayward (2000) 'Youth Crime, Excitement and Consumer Culture: The Reconstruction of Aetiology in Contemporary Theoretical Criminology', in J. Pickford, ed., *Youth Justice: Theory and Practice*, London: Cavendish.

Ferrell, J. (2004) *Cultural Criminology Unleashed*. London: GlassHouse.

Ferrell, J. (2012) 'Autoethnography', in D. Gadd, S. Karstedt and S. Messner, eds, *The Sage Handbook of Criminological Research Methods*, London: Sage.

Ferrell, J., K. Hayward, W. Morrison and M. Presdee, eds (2004) *Cultural Criminology Unleashed*, London: GlassHouse.

Ferrell, J., K. Hayward and Jock Young, eds (2008) *Cultural Criminology: An Invitation*, London: Sage.

Ferrell, J., and C. Sanders (1995) *Cultural Criminology*, Boston: Northeastern University Press.

Firmin, C. (2010) *Female Voice in Violence Project: A Study into the Impact of Serious Youth and Gang Violence on Women and Girls*, Race on the Agenda.

France, A., and G. O'Shea (2006) 'Pair of monsters aged 12', the *Sun*, 10 August 2006, www.thesun.co.uk/SOI/homepage/news/articles59102.ece/.

Freud, S. (2011) *Beyond the Pleasure Principle*, Peterborough, Ontario: Broadview Editions.

Garland, D. (1996) 'The Limits of the Sovereign State: Strategies of Crime Control in Contemporary Society', *British Journal of Criminology* 36(4): 445–71.

Garland, D. (2001) *The Culture of Control: Crime and Social Order in Contemporary Society*, Oxford: Clarendon Press.

Garot, R. (2010) *Who You Claim: Performing Gang Identity in School and on the Streets*, New York: New York University Press.

Geertz, C. (1973) *The interpretation of cultures*, New York, Basic Books.

Gilroy, P., ed. (1987) *The Myth of Black Criminality*. Law, Order, and the Authoritarian State: Readings in Critical Criminology, Milton Keynes and Philadelphia: Open University Press.

Girard, R. (1986) *The Scapegoat*, London: Athlone Press.

Goffman, E. (1963) *Stigma: Notes on the Management of Spoiled Identity*, Englewood Cliffs, NJ: Prentice Hall.

Goffman, E. (1982) *Interaction Ritual: Essays on Face to Face Behavior*, New York: Pantheon.

Goode, E., and N. Ben-Yehuda (1994) *Moral Panics: The Social Construction of Deviance*, Oxford and Cambridge, MA: Blackwell.

Greene, G. (1975) *Brighton Rock*, Harmondsworth: Penguin Books.

Gunter, A. (2008) 'Growing Up Bad: Black Youth, "Road" Culture and Badness in an East London Borough', *Crime and Media Culture* 4(3): 349–66.

Hagedorn, J. (2008) *A World of Gangs: Armed Young Men and Gangsta Culture*, Minnesota: University of Minnesota Press.

Hagedorn, J., and P. Macon (1988) *People and Folks: Gangs, Crime, and the Underclass in a Rustbelt City*, Chicago: Lake View Press.

Hales, G., with D. Silverstone (2005) *Gun Crime in Brent*, London Borough of Brent Crime and Disorder Reduction Partnership.

Hales, G., C. Lewis and D. Silverstone (2006) *Gun Crime: The Market in and Use of Illegal Firearms*, Home Office Research Study 298, London: Home Office.

Hall, S., C. Critcher, et al. (1978) *Policing the Crisis: Mugging, the State, and Law and Order*, London: Macmillan.

Hall, S., and T. Jefferson, eds (1976) *Resistance Through Rituals: Youth Subcultures in Post-War Britain*, London: Hutchinson, for the Centre for Contemporary Cultural Studies, University of Birmingham.

Hall, S., S. Winlow and C. Ancrum (2008) *Criminal Identities and Consumer Culture: Crime, Exclusion and the New Culture of Narcissism*, Cullompton: Willan Publishing.

Hallsworth, S. (2005) *Street Crime*, Cullompton: Willan Publishing.

Hallsworth, S. (2008) 'Street Crime: Interpretation and Legacy in Policing the Crisis', *Crime Media and Culture* 4(1): 137–43.

Hallsworth, S., ed. (2011a) 'Gangland Britain?: Realities, Fantasies and Industry', in B. Goldson, ed., *Youth in Crisis?: 'Gangs', Territoriality and Violence*, London: Routledge.

Hallsworth, S. (2011b) 'Then They Came for the Dogs!' *Crime Law and Social Change* 55(5): 391–403.

Hallsworth, S., and D. Brotherton (2011) *Reducing Riots to Gangs: A Critique and a Warning*, Runnymede Trust.

Hallsworth, S., and K. Duffy (2010) *Confronting London's Violent Street World: The Gang and Beyond*, London Councils.

Hallsworth, S., and D. Silverstone (2009) '"That's Life Innit": A British Perspective on Guns, Crime and Social Order', *Criminology and Criminal Justice* 9(3): 359–77.

Hallsworth, S., and T. Young (2005) *Group Related Violence and Disorder in Hackney*, Metropolitan Police Service.

Hallsworth, S., and T. Young (2005) *Interpreting the Gang and Other Criminal Groups*, Metropolitan Police Service.

Hallsworth, S., and T. Young (2008) 'Gang Talk and Gang Talkers: A Critique', *Crime, Media, Culture* 4(2): 175–95.

Hancock, L. (2003) 'Urban Regeneration and Crime Reduction: Contradictions and Dilemmas', in R. Matthews and J. Young, eds, *The New Politics of Crime and Punishment*, Cullompton: Willan Publishing.

Harding, S. (2012) 'Street Government: The Role of the Violent Street Gang in the London Riots', in D. Briggs, ed., *The English Riots of 2011: A Summer of Discontent*, Hook: Waterside Press.

Harding, S. (2012) *Unleashed: The Phenomena of Status Dogs and Weapon Dogs*, Bristol: Policy Press.

Harris, M. (1971) *1811 Dictionary of the Vulgar Tongue*, Northfield, IL: Digest Books,

Harvey, D. (1989) *The Condition of Postmodernity: An Enquiry into the Origins of Cultural Change*, Cambridge, MA: Blackwell.

Harvey, D. (2010) *The Enigma of Capital: And the Crisis of Capitalism*, London: Profile Books.

Hauffe, S., and L. Porter (2009) 'An Interpersonal Comparison of Lone and Group Rape Offences', *Psychology, Crime & Law* 15(5): 469–91.

Hayward, K. (2002) 'The Vilification and Pleasures of Youthful Transgression', in J. Muncie, G. Hughes and E. McLaughlin, eds, *Youth Justice: Critical Readings*, London: Sage.

Hayward, K. J. (2004) *City Limits: Crime, Consumer Culture and the Urban Experience*, London: GlassHouse.

Hayward, K., and M. Yar (2006) 'The "Chav" Phenomenon: Consumption, Media and the Construction of a New Underclass', *Crime, Media, Culture* 2(1): 9–28.

Hebdige, D. (1979) *Subculture: The Meaning of Style*, London: Methuen.

Hellemont, E. van (2013) 'Bewitched, Bothered and Bewildered: The Search for Seduction in Gang Studies', unpublished manuscript.

Hindley, D. (2005) Footballer's *Fight Club, Soccer and Society* 6(1): 16–33.

Hobbes, T. (1651) *Leviathan*.

Hobbs, D. (1989) *Doing the Business: Entrepreneurship, the Working Class and Detectives in the East End of London*, Oxford: Oxford University Press.

Hobbs, D. (1995) *Bad Business: Professional Crime in Modern Britain*, Oxford: Oxford University Press.

Hobbs, D. (1998) 'Going Down the Glocal: The Local Context of Organised Crime', *The Howard Journal* 37(4): 407–22.

Home Office (2008) *Tackling Gangs: A Practical Guide for Local Authorities*, London: Home Office.

Home Office (2010) Statutory Guidance: Injunctions to Prevent Gang Violence, London: Home Office.

Home Office (2011) *Ending Gang and Youth Violence: A Cross-Governmental Report Including Further Evidence and Good Practice Case Studies*, Violence and Youth Crime Prevention Unit, London: Home Office.

Horvath, J., and L. Kelly (2009) 'Multiple Perpetrator Rape: Naming an Offence and Initial Research Findings', *Journal of Sexual Aggression* 15(1): 83–96.

Jacobs, B. A. (1999) *Dealing Crack: The Social World of Streetcorner Selling*, Boston: Northeastern University Press.

Jacobs, B. A. (2000) *Robbing Drug Dealers: Violence Beyond the Law*, New York: Aldine de Gruyter.

Jameson, F. (1984) 'Postmodernism, or the Cultural Logic of Late Capitalism', *New Left Review* I/146.

Jankowski, M. S. (1991) *Islands in the Street: Gangs and American Urban Society*, Berkeley: University of California Press.

Kaspersson, M. (2009) 'When Deterrence Works – and When it Doesn't: A Comparison of Sweden's Prostitution Law and the UK's Dangerous Dogs Act', School of Humanities and Social Sciences Research Conference (unpublished), University of Greenwich.

Katz, J. (1988) *Seductions of Crime: Moral and Sensual Attractions in Doing Evil*, New York: Basic Books.

Katz, J., and J. Jackson (1997) 'The Criminologists' Gang', in C. Sumner, ed., *The Blackwell Companion to Criminology*, London: Blackwell.

Klein, M. W. (1995) *The American Street Gang: Its Nature, Prevalence, and Control*, New York: Oxford University Press.

Klein, M. W. (2001) *The Eurogang Paradox: Street Gangs and Youth Groups in the US and Europe*, Dordrecht and Boston: Kluwer Academic Publishers.

Klein, M., and C. L. Maxson (2006) *Street Gang Patterns and Policies*, Oxford: Oxford University Press.

Kuhn, T. (1962) *The Structure of Scientific Revolutions*, Chicago: University of Chicago Press.

Lauger, T. (2012) *Real Gangstas: Legitimacy, Reputation and Violence in the Intergang Environment*, New Brunswick, NJ: Rutgers University Press.

Laville, S. (2006) 'Brothers who terrorised streets since age 10 and 11', *Guardian*, 10 August 2006, p. 3.

Lea, J. (2002) *Crime and Modernity: Continuities in Left Realist Criminology*, London: Sage.

Lea, J. and K. Stenson (2007) 'Security, Sovereignty and Non-State Governance "From Below"', *Canadian Journal of Law and Society* 22(2): 9–28.

Lea, J., and J. Young (1984) *What is to be Done about Law and Order?*, Harmondsworth: Penguin Books in association with the Socialist Society.

Lee, A. (2008) 'Mob Violence: The Rise of Girl Gangs', *Express Online*. Retrieved from: www.express.co.uk/posts/view/45443.

Lefebvre, H. (1991) *The Production of Space*, Oxford: Blackwell.

Levi-Strauss, C. (1968) *Structural Anthropology*, Harmondsworth: Penguin Books.

Lodge, M. (2001) 'Barking Mad? Risk Regulation and the Control of Dangerous Dogs in Germany', *German Politics* 10(3): 65–82.

London Councils (2009) *Funding the Frontline: Tackling Youth Crime in London*, London Councils.

London Serious Youth Violence Board (2009) *Safeguarding Children Affected by Gang Activity and/or Serious Youth Violence*, Report for London Councils.

Lyng, S. (2005) *Edgework: The Sociology of Risk Taking*, New York and London: Routledge.

Madison, D. S. (2006) 'The Dialogic Performative in Critical Ethnography', *Text and Performance Quarterly* 26(4): 320–4.

Mahler, J., and H. Pearpoint (2010) 'The Use of Dogs by Gangs and Troublesome Youth Groups, Provisional Findings' (unpublished).

Malcolm X (1965) *The Autobiography of Malcolm X*, New York: Grove Press.

Mathiesen, T. (1990) 'General Prevention as Communication', in A. Duff and D. Garland, eds, *A Reader on Punishment*, Oxford: Oxford University Press.

Matthews, R. (2005) 'The Myth of Punitiveness', *Theoretical Criminology* 9(2): 175–201.

Matza, D. (1990) *Delinquency and Drift*, New York: Transaction Publishers.

Mauss, M. (1967) *The Gift*, London: Norton Library.

McGuire, M. (2011) 'Abnormal Law: Teratology as a Logic of Criminalisation', in R. Duff, ed., *The Structures of Criminal Law*, Oxford: Oxford University Press.

McLagan, G. (2005) 'Sin cities', *Sunday Times*, 25 September 2005. Available at: www.timesonline.co.uk/tol/life_and_style/article566875.ece?token=null&offset=0.

Merton, R. K. and R. A. Nisbet, eds (1963) *Contemporary Social Problems: An Introduction to the Sociology of Deviant Behavior and Social Disorganization*. London, Hart-Davis.

Messerschmidt, J. W. (1993) *Masculinities and Crime: Critique and Reconceptualization of Theory*, Lanham, MD: Rowman & Littlefield.

Metropolitan Police Authority (2009) *Multi Perpetrator Rapes and Youth Violence*. MPA: www.policeauthority.org/Metropolitan/committees/sop/2009/091105/07/index.html.

Metropolitan Police Federation (2010) oMants Best friend?e MPF: www.metfed.org.uk/metline?id=976.

Metropolitan Police Service (2010) 'Man Who Ordered Dog Attack on Boy is Found Guilty of Murder', MPS: http://cms.met.police.uk/news/convictions/man_who_ordered_dog_attack_on_boy_is_found_guilty_of_murder.

Miller, W. B. (1975) *Violence by Youth Gangs and Youth Groups as a Crime Problem in Major American Cities: Monograph*. Washington, DC: National Institute for Juvenile Justice and Delinquency Prevention, Office of Juvenile Justice and Delinquency Prevention, Law Enforcement Assistance Administration, US Department of Justice.

Monks, S. (2009) *Weapon Dogs: The Situation in London*, Greater London Authority.

Moshmus, G. (2005) *Migrant Users of Heroin*, Oslo: Oslo University Press.

Muir, H., and R. Ellinor (2003) 'Man Held over Double Murder: Seven-Year-Old thought to be Youngest Victim of Gang Violence', *Guardian Online*,

16 September. Available at: www.guardian.co.uk/uk/2003/sep/16/ukguns. hughmuir.

Myall, S. (2011) 'UK Riots: Gangs at Centre of Violence and Looting, Met Police Figures Reveal', *Daily Mirror Online*. Retrieved 17 August 2011 from: www. mirror.co.uk/news/top-stories/2011/08/17/riots-gangs-at-centre-of-violence-and-looting-met-police-figures-reveal-115875-23350035/- ixzz1ZL8DiQiX.

Naffine, N. (1997) *Feminism & Criminology*, Cambridge: Polity.

Nightingale, C. (1993) *On the Edge*, New York: Basic Books.

O'Brian, M. (2005) 'What is Cultural about Cultural Criminology', *British Journal of Criminology* 45(5): 599–612.

Ofsted (2005) *Annual Report on Schools in England and Wales*, Ofsted.

Parenti, C. (1999) *Lockdown America: Police and Prisons in the Age of Crisis*, London and New York: Verso.

Parker, H., J. Aldridge and F. Measham (1999) *Illegal Leisure: The Normalisation of Adolescent Recreational Drug Use*, London: Routledge.

Parsons, T. (1999) *The Social System*, London: Routledge.

Patrick, J. (1973) *A Glasgow Gang Observed*, London: Eyre Methuen.

Pearson, G. (1983) *Hooligan: A History of Respectable Fears*, London: Macmillan.

Pearson, G. (2011) 'Infinite Novelty', in B. Goldson, ed., *Gangland Britain: Realities, Fantasies and Industry*, London: Routledge.

Pileggi, N. (1986) *Wiseguy: Life in a Mafia Family*, Seattle, WA: Adamsfamiliesbooks.

Pitts, J. (2007) *Reluctant Gangsters: Youth Gangs in Waltham Forest*, London Borough of Waltham Forest Council.

Pitts, J. (2008) *Reluctant Gangsters: The Changing Shape of Youth Crime*, Cullompton: Willan Publishing.

Pitts, J. (2011) 'Mercenary Territoriality: Are Youth Gangs Really a Problem?', in B. Goldson, ed., *Youth in Crisis?: 'Gangs', Territoriality and Violence*, London: Routledge.

Pitts, J. (2012) 'Reluctant Criminologists: Criminology, Ideology and the Violent Youth Gang', *Youth and Policy*, www.youthandpolicy.org.

Podberscek, A. L. (1994) 'Tightrope: The Position of the Dog in British Society as Influenced by Press Reports on Dog Attacks (1988 to 1992)', *Anthrozoos: A Multidisciplinary Journal of the Interactions of People & Animals* 7(4): 232–41.

Povey, D. (2004) *Crime in England and Wales 2002/2003: Supplementary Volume 1: Homicide and Gun Crime*, Home Office Statistical Bulletin 01/04, London: Home Office.

Presdee, M. (2000) *Cultural Criminology and the Carnival of Crime*, London: Routledge.

Pryce, K. (1979) *Endless Pressure: A Study of West Indian Life-Styles in Bristol*, Harmondsworth: Penguin.

Rawlinson, S. (2010) 'Interdog and Interhuman Aggression', www.doglistener. co.uk/aggression/interdog.html.

Rex, J. (1973) *Race, Colonialism and the City*, London: Routledge and Kegan Paul.

Rex, J. (1988) *The Ghetto and the Underclass: Essays on Race and Social Policy*. Aldershot, Avebury.

Rodger, J. J. (2008) *Criminalising Social Policy: Anti-Social Behaviour and Welfare in a De-civilised Society*. Cullompton, Willan.

Ronai, C. R. (1992) 'The Reflexive Self Through Narrative: A Night in the Life of an Erotic Dancer/Researcher', in C. E. M. G. Flaherty, ed., *Investigating Subjectivity: Research on Lived Experience*, Newbury Park, CA: Sage, pp. 102–24.

Rorty, R. (1972) 'The World Well Lost', *Journal of Philosophy* 69(19): 649–65.

RSPCA (2010) *Briefing Note on Dangerous Dogs*. Retreived from: www. politicalanimal.org.uk/assets/files/NewDangerous dogs brief 04.03.10.pdf.

Said, E. W. (1978) *Orientalism*, London: Routledge and Kegan Paul.

Scraton, P. (2004) 'Streets of Terror: Marginalization, Criminalization & Authoritarian Renewal', *Social Justice* 31(1 & 2): 130–58.

Seabrook, J. (1978) *What Went Wrong? Working People and the Ideals of the Labour Movement*, London: Victor Gollancz.

Sennett, R. (2006) *The Culture of the New Capitalism*, New Haven, CT, and London: Yale University Press.

Sewell, T. (2011) 'Don't Howl Starkey Down. Gangsta Culture is a Poison Spreading Among Youths of All Races', *Daily Mail Online*, 15 August. Retrieved 29 September 2011, from: www.dailymail.co.uk/news/article-2026053/David-Starkey-Gangsta-culturepoison-spreading-youths-races.html.

Shultz, A., and A. Luckmann (1973) *Structures of the Lifeworld*, Evanston, IL: Northwestern University Press.

Sikes, G. (1997) *8 Ball Chicks: A Year in the Violent World of Girl Gangsters*, New York: Anchor Books.

Sillitoe, A. (1958) *Saturday Night and Sunday Morning*, London: W. H. Allan.

Standing, G. (2009) 'The Precariaty and Basic Income' . Available at: http://ec.europa.eu/italia/documents/news/ue_e_societa_civile/forum_poverta napoli_-_guy_standing.pdf.

Standing, G. (2011) *The Precariat: The New Dangerous Class*, London: Bloomsbury.

Starkey, D. (2011) Comments made in discussion, *Newsnight*, BBC2, 12 August.

Stephenson, S. (2011) 'The Kazan Leviathan: Russian Street Gangs as Agents of Social Order', *Sociological Review* 59(2): 324–47.

Thrasher, F. M. (1927) *The Gang: A Study of 1313 Gangs in Chicago*, Chicago: University of Chicago Press.

Tilly, N., and S. Bullock (2002) *Shootings, Gangs and Violent Incidents in Manchester*, London: Home Office.

Toy, J. (2008) *Die Another Day: A Practitioners Review with Recommendations for Preventing Gang and Weapon Violence in London in 2008*, Metropolitan Police Service.

Vigil, J. D. (1988) *Barrio Gangs: Street Life and Identity in Southern California*, Austin: University of Texas Press.

Wacquant, L. J. D. (2007) *Deadly Symbiosis: Race and the Rise of Neoliberal Penalty*, Cambridge: Polity.

Wacquant, L. J. D. (2008) *Urban Outcasts: A Comparative Sociology of Advanced Marginality*, Cambridge and Malden, MA: Polity.

Wacquant, L. J. D. (2009) *Punishing the Poor: The Neoliberal Government of Social Insecurity*, Durham, NC: Duke University Press.

Warner, K. (2004) 'Crime, the Media, Politics, Race and Sentencing', *Australian and New Zealand Journal of Criminology* 37(3): 344.

Weber, M., and H. H. Gerth (2009) *From Max Weber: Essays in Sociology*, Abingdon and New York: Routledge.

White, R. (2013) *Youth Gangs, Violence and Social Respect: Exploring the Nature of Provocations and Punch-Ups,* Basingstoke: Palgrave Macmillan.

Whyte, W. F. (1943) *Street Corner Society: The Social Structure of an Italian Slum,* Chicago, IL: University of Chicago Press.

Willis, P. E. (1977) *Learning to Labour: How Working Class Kids Get Working Class Jobs,* Farnborough: Saxon House.

Winlow, S., and S. Hall (2006) *Violent Night: Urban Leisure and Contemporary Culture,* Oxford and New York: Berg.

Wintour, P. (2011) 'Gang Culture Must be Stopped Early, Says Iain Duncan Smith', *Guardian Online,* 20 October. Available at: www.guardian.co.uk/society/2011/oct/20/gang-culture-stopped-early.

Wittgenstein, L. (1953) *Philosophical Investigations (PI),* 1953, ed. G. E. M. Anscombe and R. Rhees, trans. G. E. M. Anscombe, Oxford: Blackwell.

Wright, R., F. Brookman and T. Bennett (2006) 'The Foreground Dynamics of Street Robbery in Britain', *British Journal of Criminology* 46(1): 1–15.

Young, J. (1971) *Drug Takers: The Social Meaning of Drug Use,* London: MacGibbon & Kee.

Young, J. (1999) *The Exclusive Society: Social Exclusion, Crime and Difference in Late Modernity,* London: Sage.

Young, J. (2007) *The Vertigo of Late Modernity,* Los Angeles and London: Sage.

Young, J. (2011) *The Criminological Imagination,* London: Routledge.

Young, T. (2009) 'Girls and Gangs: "She-male" Gangsters in the UK?', *Youth Justice* 9(3): 224–38.

Young, T. (2011) 'In Search of the "Shemale" Gangster', in B. Goldson, ed., *Youth in Crisis?: 'Gangs', Territoriality and Violence,* London: Routledge.

Young, T., M. Fitzgerald, S. Hallsworth and I. Joseph (2007) *Groups, Gangs and Weapons: A Report for the Youth Justice Board of England and Wales,* Youth Justice Board.

Young, T., and S. Hallsworth (2009) *Assessing the Reality of Street Gangs in Brent,* London Borough of Brent Council.

Young, T., and S. Hallsworth, eds (2011) 'Young People, Gangs and Street-Based Violence', in C. Barter and D. Berridge, eds, *Children Behaving Badly? Exploring Peer Violence Between Children and Young People,* London: Wiley-Blackwell.

Žižek, S. (2011) 'Shoplifters of the World Unite', *London Review of Books Online.* Available at: www.lrb.co.uk/2011/08/19/slavoj-zizek/shoplifters-of-the-world-unite.

Index

Compiled by Sue Carlton